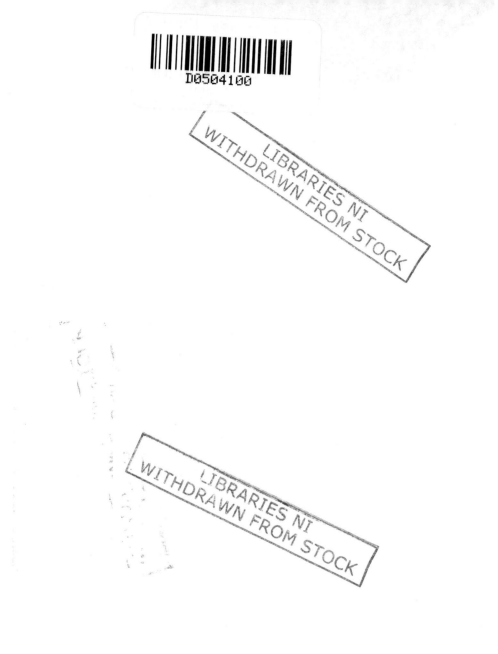

ANIMAL QC

My Preposterous Life

GARY BELL

MONDAY BOOKS

First Published by Monday Books

Festival House, Jessop Avenue, Cheltenham GL50 3SH

A CIP catalogue record for this title is available
from the British Library

ISBN: 978-1-906308-64-3

Typeset by Elaine Sharples
Printed and bound by CPI Group (UK) Ltd, Croydon, CR0 4YY

Web
www.mondaybooks.com

Blog
http://mondaybooks.wordpress.com/

Email
info@mondaybooks.com

Twitter
@mondaybooks

Dedication

To my wonderful mother, Maureen Bell,
who did not live to see much of this,
would not have thought the majority of it possible,
and still wouldn't believe it now.

The toad beneath the harrow knows
Exactly where each tooth point goes;
The butterfly upon the road
Preaches contentment to that toad.

– from *'Pagett, M.P.'* by Rudyard Kipling (1886)

CONTENTS

PROLOGUE

AS MY FACE was pressed into the mud for the umpteenth time by some meaty, grinning youth, I wondered what on earth I was doing here.

I was on the famous playing fields of Eton, taking part in a 'Field Game' fixture between an Old Boys' team and the current Eton School Field.

And we were being utterly trounced.

The Field Game, a sort of cross between rugby and soccer, has been played down the ages by boys who would go on to become prime ministers, captains of industry, financiers, generals, bishops and judges, by dukes and earls, by foreign princes, the future King of England and – on that wet November day in 1986 – by me.

Gary Terence Bell.

As the jeering, hooting schoolboy onlookers could clearly see, I was not very good at the Field Game.

This was not simply because I was fat and unfit, though that I certainly was – like most of us, I'd let myself go a tad since my schooldays, and was now a wheezing, sweating, twenty-seven-year-old wreck.

The rest of Ronnie Vickers' Old Boys' Scratch were in a similar state and, at half-time, Ronnie tried to rally the troops.

'We need to raise our game,' he said, as we sprawled on the ground, retching and groaning.

'I'm trying my best, Ronnie,' gurgled the Hon. James Percy – now the Duke of Northumberland. 'But I'm absolutely knackered.'

Pete Czernin, these days a respected film producer with box office hits like *In Bruges* and a couple of *Best Exotic Marigold Hotels* under his belt, could only manage a phlegmy cough.

'I've had it too, Ronnie,' said the Hon. Tom Henderson. 'Have we got a sub?'

'If there's a sub,' gasped Nick Wheeler, aka Charles Tyrwhitt, 'bags he replaces me!'

'Well, we haven't got a sub,' snapped Ronnie, 'so you're all going to have to play the second half. And at least *try* to stop sneaking, will you? Especially you, Gary! I know you're out of shape, but it's getting beyond a joke.'

I lay there, nodding and gulping oxygen, but I could have been as fit as an Olympic athlete and it would have made no difference.

I had no idea what 'sneaking' was, because I'd never played the Field Game before.

Truth be told, I'd never even been to Eton before.

In fact, that cold November afternoon marked my first visit to the place, which will surprise the many Old Etonians who are sure they remember me being at school with them.

These days, I look about as pukka as can be. I'm Gary Bell QC, no less, and married to Sophia FitzHugh, whose family is listed in *Burke's Landed Gentry* (and whose father, grandfather, stepfather, uncle, cousin and brother-in-law really *were* Old Etonians). I even have my own entry in *Who's Who*!

But appearances can be deceptive, and that entry gives away a little of my story:

Bell, Gary Terence (born 9 Nov. 1959) QC 2012
Born: Nottingham, 9 Nov. 1959; s of Terence Bell and Maureen Bell; m 1992, Sophia FitzHugh; two s one d
Education: Toot Hill Comprehensive School, Bingham, Notts; Univ. of Bristol (LLB Hons 1987)
Career: Coalminer, 1976; lawnmower mechanic, 1976; forklift truck driver, 1976–78; fireman, 1978; pork pie prodn line worker, 1978; homeless drifter, 1978–80. Called to the Bar, Inner Temple, 1989; in practice as a barrister, 1989–2015

PROLOGUE

An unusual CV – and that's without mentioning trainee fruit machine technician, door-to-door rag salesman, bricklayer (for one day), award-winning stand-up comic, convicted fraudster, or football hooligan.

But I'm getting ahead of myself.

CHAPTER ONE: BEGINNINGS

Fifty-two years to silk, and counting

I WAS BORN the first son of Terry Bell, a nineteen-year-old coalminer, and Maureen Corpe, a teenaged girl who worked at the John Player cigarette factory in Nottingham.

My mother's own short and rather sad life began in September 1940, at the height of the Battle of Britain, when she was born to Harold and Lilian Corpe. Unfortunately, in the period between conception and birth, Harold lost his legs to a German landmine, and Lilian was unable to cope with both a newborn baby and a disabled and traumatised husband. As a result, the infant Maureen was adopted by her uncle and aunt, Leslie and Gertrude Corpe. I don't believe that she ever saw her real parents again, despite the family connection and the fact that they lived only a few miles away across the city.

Like many working class people in those post-war years, she grew up in grinding poverty – in her case, in a cramped council house in Radford. She had an unremarkable childhood, with an adoptive brother and two sisters, and her academic record was also unspectacular – not one member of either the Bell or Corpe families had ever so much as taken, never mind passed, a single exam. At fifteen, she found a job on the John Player production line, and she had been working there for a couple of years when, one night in the autumn of 1958, she met young Terry Bell at a Teddy Boy dance.

Terry, too, had known little but the austerity and hardship endured by most ordinary Britons in the fifties, and lived in a prefabricated council house in Bilborough, sharing a bedroom with two of his four sisters.

Like the Corpes, the Bells were essentially decent, hard-working and respectable people, though two of my aunts did marry major local villains who were often in and out of prison and my father was something of a jack-the-lad who had his own brush with the law.

One night, so the story goes, he was out with some mates for a few pints. He missed the last bus home, and didn't fancy a three-mile walk in the rain. He decided instead to go to Nottingham station and 'borrow' a train – the railway line ran near to the bottom of his garden, after all. He climbed into the yard, found a locomotive parked on the right track, and managed to get it moving. His plan worked perfectly, for nearly a hundred yards. Then the engine was diverted by the points into a siding, crashed through a barrier, and was de-railed. Terry was put before the courts but, miners being a band of brothers, they kept his job open at Radford pit.

Unlike me, my father was whippet-thin and, at 5ft 2in in his stockinged feet, very short. But he still towered over the rest of his family, and my mum, and, with his piercing eyes, extravagant quiff and drainpipe jeans, he must have cut an imposing figure – relatively speaking. At any rate, the teenaged Maureen took an immediate fancy to him; within a very short time they were courting and not long afterwards she was pregnant with me.

Working class people were socially very conservative in those days, and pregnancy out of wedlock was shameful and scandalous. Family lore has it that her mother Gertie didn't notice until Maureen had taken on the proportions of a beach ball, but when she did notice she was furious. Terry's father Ernie was apoplectic with rage, and he delivered to his son a mighty thrashing which only ceased when he agreed to marry my mother.

My parents on their wedding day in mid-1959 – my mother's embarrassing bump hidden under a winter coat

Unable to rent a place of their own on Terry's meagre wages, the newlyweds moved in to an 8ft-by-6ft box room in the Corpe family home. It must have been quite a squeeze, particularly once I arrived, despite the diminutive stature of my parents. (My mother was only 4ft 10in tall; quite how I ended up at over six feet I am not sure.)

I was named Gary – not a very Etonian name, you may think, but then mine was not a very Etonian start in life.

The cramped conditions and lack of privacy *chez* Corpe did not dampen Terry and Maureen's ardour, now that it was all legal and above board. Six weeks after I was born, my mother was expecting again; when I was ten-and-a-half months old, my brother Kevin was born.

It was clearly impossible for a family of four to remain in the tiny box room, so my father scraped together the rent for a small, terraced house in St Ann's, a Nottingham slum crammed full of poor families and elderly folks, which would be our home for the next three years.

Like all the others, ours was a dilapidated, red-brick affair in a row of four. Set sideways onto the cobbled streets, the front door faced those of an identical row of four other houses, and the back door likewise faced the back doors of four more. To the rear of our house was a weed-strewn communal concrete yard, bisected by washing lines. An ancient mangle stood in one corner near the 'toilet block', which was a brick-built enclosure with a lavatory, and a tin bath hanging from a hook on the wall. These facilities were shared between our house and seven others.

We had one bath a week, on a Sunday, and all in the same water. (By 'we' I mean the children; our fathers mostly worked at the pit, where there were showers, and our mothers made do with a flannel.) No-one had running hot water, so we filled the bath by heating pots and pans on our stoves and carrying them out across the yard. It was a hazardous business; one Sunday my neighbour, a girl of about eight, was carrying an old pan out to the bath when the handle snapped off and the boiling water scalded her legs. She was taken away in an ambulance and was doubtless scarred for life, but I never saw; from then on, she always wore trousers. In all the commotion on that particular Sunday, the children's bath never happened – a lucky escape for me. As one of the younger children I was always among the last to bathe, by which time the water was like lukewarm gravy.

Inside, the houses were built to a pattern, with a small kitchen and a sitting room downstairs, and two small bedrooms upstairs. Kevin and I shared a room, with me sleeping in a hand-me-down bed from Granny Corpe's house, and Kevin in the cot in which my mother had lain as a baby.

The place was infested with ants and cockroaches, but my mother did her best to keep it clean, cosy and homely. This was no easy task. Times were very hard, particularly for the womenfolk, and she had none of today's labour-saving gadgets. In fact, we didn't own a single electrical appliance – though there was so much damp in the walls that none of the electric sockets worked, anyway. With a husband who believed firmly that a woman's place was in the home, she worked like a dog.

One weekend, the lady next door won fifty pounds on the football pools. She invested the money, wisely, in a washing machine: I still remember the permanent queue of housewives at her door, paying to use her machine rather than break their backs over a tub. My mother was one of her best customers, mainly because I was an inveterate bed-wetter. This problem has plagued me all of my life, and my father was infuriated by the expense of daily sheet-washing. He swore that it was merely that I was too cowardly to go outside to the single, unlit lavatory. I *was* scared of the dark, that much is true – even today, if I'm alone in the house I cannot sleep with the light off – but it turned out to be more complicated than that.

My earliest memories of my father are of a man beset by an eternal, simmering rage which lay – most of the time – just below the surface, flashing in his eyes. I suppose, to be fair to him, that he was working his fingers to the bone just to earn enough money to keep his family in abject poverty. Small as the house was, he struggled to keep it up. The cold, dank sitting room – which seemed enormous, but was probably 8ft by 8ft – had bare floorboards and ragged curtains that were always drawn. It was closed off in the early days as we couldn't afford to furnish or heat it; we only went in there to hide when the landlord came calling for his rent. We were not alone in employing that tactic. St Ann's was generally a noisy and lively place, but on rent day it was like the set of a Gary Cooper western, tumbleweed blowing along its deserted streets.

We lived mostly in the small kitchen, which had a sink, an ancient gas cooker, a tiny Formica table, and four rickety chairs. The table and chairs were purchased for five shillings from a rag-and-bone man who lived up the street, and they stayed in our family, like heirlooms, for twenty years.

The rag-and-bone man would roll out of his yard each morning in his horse-drawn cart and disappear to more affluent areas, returning in the evening with his cart overflowing with mountains of tat. As he trundled up our cobbled street, the mothers would rush out of their houses and besiege him for a bargain. One summer, my mum bought a dusty old rug and a threadbare, three-piece suite, and our sitting room was finally pressed into service.

The man's daughter always sat alongside him in his cart. A very beautiful girl a few years older than me, she did not go to school because she was deaf and dumb. I was a particular favourite of hers; she once gave me a battered Corgi toy car, a beige Dormobile with a tyre and a door missing. Toys were few and far between in St Ann's, and I treasured it for months until it was stolen by an older boy. I often wonder what became of that girl.

I'm not complaining, by the way. This was a very happy period in my life. Yes, we were poor, but so was everyone else, and there was a strong and tangible community spirit. There was very little movement in and out, though newcomers were welcomed, and we took care of our own. If a mother fell ill, everyone else rallied round her children. If you were short of food, and people often were, others would lend some bread or potatoes until pay day. I well recall children wandering past, carrying home to their mothers cups of sugar or half a loaf of bread which they had borrowed from neighbours.

But even as we were moving in, plans were afoot to clear the slums as a result of work by people like Pete Townsend – not that one, the famous sociologist who co-founded the Child Action Poverty Group, and whose landmark work *The Poor and the Poorest* had been partly informed by his study of St Ann's. The slum clearances duly happened later in the 1960s, when our house and hundreds like it were demolished and replaced with others dreamed up by the town planners. This new housing is undoubtedly better – there are indoor lavatories, and no-one washes in a communal tin bath any more. But the people were dispersed in the clearances, and the new homes were let to tenants who didn't know each other. Community spirit evolves over a long period of time, it can't be created overnight. So a place called 'St Ann's' still exists in Nottingham, but it is in all other ways unrecognisable from my time there. Now it is one of the city's two crime hotspots – the other being the Meadows Estate, whose old housing was demolished at roughly the same time. Instead of loaves of bread and cups of sugar, some of today's youngsters carry around guns and bags of cocaine.

* * *

RADFORD Colliery was an old pit, right in the centre of Nottingham, and it had once been among the most productive in England. But the coal was getting harder and more expensive to dig out and, in 1963, it was decided to close Radford down. At around the same time, the local council announced the demolition of St Ann's and we were served with an eviction notice.

10

CHAPTER ONE: BEGINNINGS

Out of a job and out of a home: I'm sure it all came as a veritable bombshell to my parents. But it actually turned out for the best, as life often seems to. My father was offered another job at the new Cotgrave mine, which had opened up in the countryside six miles outside Nottingham. Although it came with a (rented) house as part of the deal, he wasn't keen – he was a city boy, born and bred, and didn't much fancy the life of a country bumpkin. But since he didn't have much choice, the four of us took the rumbling, red-and-cream Barton's bus south to see what was on offer.

We were astonished by what we found. The pit was just a pit, but the National Coal Board had purpose-built a new housing estate on the outskirts of the chocolate box village of Cotgrave, which was surrounded by woods and meadows on the edge of the beautiful Vale of Belvoir. It must have been a terrible blow for the original villagers. From one window, a view of a thousand-year-old church, which had been used as a plague sanctuary during the fourteenth century; from the other, a new colliery and a huge carbuncle of a housing estate built for 1,500 miners and their families. But it was heaven on earth for us. The houses were all brand-new and semi-detached, and I gawped in awe as we were shown around one of them. It was like a mansion! The front door opened into a hall, which led to a large kitchen. There was an enormous sitting room off to the left, and stairs to the right which led up to *three* bedrooms – two of which were as large as the whole of the upstairs at our place in St Ann's. Most unbelievable of all, to our eyes, there was an indoor lavatory, and a bath with hot running water. Outside there were large gardens, front and rear, and two sheds.

It could be ours if my father took the job, said the man from the pit. The NCB would also pay a relocation allowance, and would assist with purchasing furniture. I remember my father standing there, contemplating the offer of a lifetime, as my mother, my brother and I anxiously held our breath.

After an age, he came to his decision. 'Go on, then,' he said, and the three of us ran to hug him as he took the contract of employment from the Coal Board man and signed it.

So it was that, in late 1963, I moved to the countryside.

Kevin and I had been leading up to a tremendous battle over who would get the biggest room, but my mother settled the question for us when my sister Dawn was born two months later. Kevin and I had to share a bedroom, but if I was disappointed at that then Cotgrave was heaven for a small boy. Many of the families around us had young children, and I was never short of playmates. My best friend at the time was a boy two months younger than I called Tony Ryland, whose family had lived next door to my paternal grandparents, and who had also moved to Cotgrave. It was nice to find a familiar face in all the newness.

Nowadays, parents keep their children close. Not then. We youngsters of four or five would wander off to play in the nearby fields and woods, city kids revelling in the open space and greenery. It was very foreign at first. One day, Kevin Booth and I climbed a tree, going as high as we could before the branches became too thin to support us. To our dismay, as we descended, we found a flock of sheep had collected under the tree and were now regarding us with curiosity. Afraid of being savaged, we stayed aloft for three hours until they wandered away.

My father always seemed to be around in those days, and had quickly settled into the country life. Kevin and I went with him on long walks to nearby lakes and canals, where we would catch snakes or frogs to take home to show my dismayed mother. He took up a hobby, collecting eggs from as many species of birds as possible. We often went with him as he set himself to climb to the top of impossibly tall and difficult trees to steal an egg from a nest. He would make a small hole in the top of the egg and a larger one in the bottom, and would then blow the contents of the egg through the larger one. This was – for some reason – very popular in Cotgrave at the time, though it now seems particularly disgusting.

When not out pinching eggs, he could usually be found in his shed, making us go-karts, stilts, and sledges. My mother rarely left the house, which she loved. In my mind's eye, she is always baking cakes, or knitting jumpers, or reading. I never saw my father with a book, but my mother devoured them, and I took my lead from her: Cotgrave had a new library, and we went there each week to choose our six titles. I raced through the children's section and foolishly moved on to reading everything about the occult – thus heightening my fear not only of the dark but of the monsters who inhabited it.

Slowly we acquired a few luxuries. A carpet for the sitting room; then linoleum for the kitchen. Some time in the mid-1960s we bought a fridge, and marvelled at the ice cubes which we could make in the small freezer compartment, and which we added to the fizzy pop which was delivered every Thursday by the Alpine man – Dandelion and Burdock for me, American Cream Soda for Kevin.

On my mother's twenty-fifth birthday, my father came home with a veneered Marconi radiogram, and music filled the house for the first time. Unfortunately, he bought only one record – *Frankie Laine's Greatest Hits* – and he played it so often that, nearly fifty years later, I still can't listen to *Jezebel, High Noon* or *I Believe* without wanting to take a hammer to whatever machine they are being played on.

Over Christmas 1966, he turned up with a black-and-white TV, our first. Kevin and I would watch anything – even the Test Card, which older readers will recall showed a little girl holding a balloon. Mum told us it was the girl's full-time job to sit there every day, and one day we stared at her for ages to see if she'd blink. Eventually, exasperated, we complained that three hours had gone by without any discernible movement.

'Ah,' said mum. 'That's probably because she's blinking at the same time as you.'

Our favourite programme was *Batman*. You can keep your Christian Bale; the only true Batman is Adam West, and it was in imitation of West that Kevin and I made ourselves a batcape out of old curtains and string. We took it out to the fields to test its aeronautical properties. I ran as quickly as I could to a small mound and launched myself into the air, and after I had landed my brother paced out the distance I had flown. It was amazing! I had covered about thirty feet! Of course, only about four feet of that had been airborne, and the other twenty-six feet had been my stumbling and stopping time, but Kevin and I were convinced.

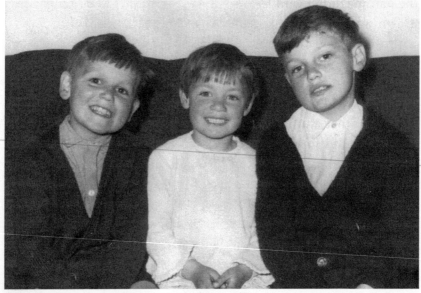

Kevin, Dawn and me, some time in the late 1960s

Nevertheless, we felt that a more rigorous test was required. We climbed onto the coalhouse roof, and I peered over the edge at the concrete path far below. I remember my toes curling into thin air, and my shame at finding myself too scared to make the leap. I offered the cape to Kevin, on the grounds that he was lighter than me, but he refused even to put it on. Our sister Dawn was then three years old, and, by dint of age, utterly fearless. It was quite tricky getting her onto the coalhouse roof, but she eagerly donned the batcape.

'You're going on a short flight,' I said, pointing to a pile of soft pillows gathered in the middle of the lawn about twenty feet away. 'You just need to land on those.'

Dawn looked unsure, so we gave her a little push to help her on her way.

She missed the pillows – by a mere twenty feet. Instead, she flew, like a stone, straight into the concrete.

Kevin and I were absolutely distraught at the sight of our young sister lying there, stunned and bleeding. All our efforts were in vain – the batcape didn't work!

Dawn was upset, too, but they were only milk teeth and, forty-eight years on, you can barely see the scar, as long as she brushes her hair forward.

Sadly, we were banned from watching *Batman* after that, though not because we'd nearly killed our sister; my father had read in *The Daily Mirror* that an American psychologist believed that watching the show might stimulate children to homosexual fantasies.

I never saw him happier than he was in those days. That eternal, angry flame never quite left his eyes, but, like the torch in between the Olympics, it was turned down so low that you could hardly tell it was burning. Once it had sunk in – that the grinding poverty of St Ann's really *was* behind us, and that the relative luxury of Cotgrave was how we lived now – he seemed to relax.

We had a comfortable home, material possessions, luxuries even. We were well-fed, happy, and healthy. I had no idea at the time that we only had such comforts because, five days a week, my father was travelling a mile underground to dig for coal in conditions which were close to hell on earth. It was dangerous, and a number of men died in accidents. Tony Ryland's father was one of them. Tunnels would collapse, poison gas would seep through the walls, men would be crushed by machinery. Even for those who survived outwardly unscathed, the dust was so thick in the air that miners spent most of their time above ground hacking up black catarrh. Their long-term health prospects were miserable. Miners' pensions were good: the NCB could afford them to be, for few would be around long enough to collect.

CHAPTER TWO: JUNIOR SCHOOL

Forty-seven years to silk

I DIDN'T LIKE Cotgrave Infants' School, and neither did anyone else.

The name of the headmistress, Miss Norman, is burned into my memory. We saw her as the epitome of evil, and would have swapped her for Roald Dahl's Miss Trunchbull in a heartbeat. But actually – apart from the odd whacked bottom for misbehaviour – my main gripe was her insistence that I eat salad and vegetables. Her tactic was simple. Dinner time (it was dinner back then, not 'lunch') started at twelve on the dot, and you were not allowed out to play until you had cleared your plate.

To look at my figure now, you might not think I would have struggled, but I did. I blame my mother. She tried her best to cook healthy meals, but tinned lettuce was hard to come by. Breakfast was cornflakes or Weetabix, covered with sugar, or white toast with margarine, or bread-and-dripping – a staple of the working classes in those days. Dripping was the semi-solid grease from a roasted chicken or lump of beef, or, if times were really tough, scooped straight out of the chip pan. (That pan sat on our kitchen stove throughout my childhood; I don't believe the fat was ever changed.) You spread it on a slice of bread and wolfed it down – and it had to be white bread, too. George Orwell wrote in *The Road to Wigan Pier* about his attempts to persuade working people to eat brown bread because it was healthier. In Cotgrave that was *never* going to happen. Not only had we never heard of George Orwell, we'd never heard of brown bread.

Dinner was beans on toast, or a sandwich made with pre-sliced, processed cheese. (If there was no cheese, we had four emergency fillings: brown sauce, tomato sauce, salad cream, or granulated sugar.) 'Tea' was our main meal, and might feature a tinned Fray

Bentos pie with tinned peas, tinned carrots, and tinned potatoes. After we acquired a fridge-freezer, we sometimes had fish fingers with beans and chips.

Me aged about ten – my hair has never been ruly

(Our meals were always eaten on our laps in front of the telly – we never ate together, around the kitchen table. And we employed 'knorks', a revolutionary new cutlery item which combined the blade of a knife with the prongs of a fork, and which my father purchased to save on washing up. To this day, to my wife's chagrin, I eat one-handed.)

If my mother cooked anything else I can't remember it. I *do* know that before Miss Norman intervened, I'd never tasted cabbage, or Brussels sprouts, or tomatoes, but this cut no ice with her; she stood guard over me, every mealtime, as I tried to force down that day's unpalatable sludge.

At least she made sure that I learned to read and write. I never really overcame my hatred of tomatoes but, at the age of eight, I left infants' school well-equipped for the challenges of Cotgrave Manvers Junior School.

My first teacher there was a formidable woman called Mrs Route, who swore by achievement and discipline. Not for her the non-competitive education of today: during the first term, the form seating plan was random, but thereafter it was dictated by the end-of-term exam results, and when the register was called she used not our names but our placings. I had come second, just behind Jack Fairlie, with Tony Ryland third, and we were 'One', 'Two' and 'Three'. Jack, Tony and I were happy with this, but I felt a little for 'Thirty'. The middle child in a family of fifteen, he never really stood a chance. His father's wages didn't stretch to luxuries such as clothes, or soap, and he stank, he was infested with head lice, and he wore an almost theatrically Dickensian collection of ragged hand-me-downs. If anyone in life needed a helping hand it was this poor, utterly friendless lad. But he didn't get it at school. He could barely write his own name and, shamefully, Mrs Route simply left him to rot.

One day it was announced that Cadbury had set up a national story-writing competition. You were guaranteed a bar of Dairy Milk merely for entering, and the winners would receive massive selection boxes. We were all chomping at the bit to get started as Mrs Route handed out pencils and paper, and left us to get on with it.

She had a clever, though slightly sinister, system of enforcing discipline. If she caught you talking or misbehaving, she would call out your number and you would approach her desk for a sharp whack across the palm of your hand with a ruler. The genius lay in what came next: you were then pressed into service as Mrs Route's eyes and ears, your task being to stand by her desk and act as an informer. If you saw or heard anyone else misbehaving, you called out that person's number and passed on the unwelcome baton, as it were.

There was one flaw. The noisiest and naughtiest boy in the class was a hulking great lout called Michael Pringle, and anyone who had the audacity to call out his number would be meeting up with him after school to discuss the matter further. It was simpler and safer – if you didn't want to spend the entire lesson standing in front of the class – to opt for the easy option: call out Number Thirty.

On story-writing competition day, an excited Jack Fairlie whispered to me, as he picked up his pencil, 'I'm going to win that massive box of chocolates!'

'Number One!' said Mrs Route, instantly. Her Stalinist purity permitted no favourites, and Jack was duly whacked and made to stand on guard. Sadly for him, everyone else was so busy with their stories that silence reined. Jack couldn't win his box of chocolates if he spent the next hour standing at the front like a lemon. Something had to give, and it was 'Thirty'.

There was a look of surprise and disappointment on the entirely innocent youngster's face as his number echoed through the room. He had been making a supreme effort – he might well never have tasted chocolate before, and I am quite confident that he would never have had a whole bar to himself. He trudged to the front of the class, in holey and oversized shoes, for a whacking and some guard duty, and there he remained for the rest of the lesson.

A few weeks later, the results were announced. Both Jack and I received huge boxes of chocolates, and everyone else earned a consolation Dairy Milk.

All, that is, but 'Thirty'. He hadn't had the opportunity to finish his story, so Mrs Route hadn't submitted it.

I'd like to be able to say that Jack and I took pity on him, as he sat tearfully in the corner watching the rest of the class filling their faces with chocolate, but we didn't; we ate it all ourselves. Children can be cruel.

At the end of the 1967-68 school year, the major exams were held, with whoever ended on top of the year being presented with a prize in front of the entire school. Jack was the favourite, having beaten me in both the Christmas and Easter exams. And, indeed, he did beat me – by a solitary mark – in the maths paper. But I upset the form book and took the honours in English by the same margin. We were each awarded a copy of *Aesop's Fables*. I still have mine.

The draw led to an argument between us as to who would be Number One in the register; we agreed to settle the matter like gentlemen, with a scrap in the playground. But school was out for the summer. It would have to wait until the autumn.

* * *

OUR SUMMER HOLIDAYS were very different to those that most children enjoy today. I'm sure modern kids feel the same sense of wonder at the free time stretching out ahead of them, and they, too, probably only remember the hot, sunny days, and not the wet, miserable ones. But things surely *were* different. Mum was usually at home, which lent a sense of familiar routine and a more relaxed pace to life; toys were fewer, so the imagination necessarily worked harder; and the paedophile bogeyman of modern parents' nightmares did not seem to lurk around every corner, or behind each bush.

So my Cotgrave summers were an endless and carefree stream of sunshine days, starting with a leisurely rise at elevenish, a hurried breakfast and then a speedy exit, not to be seen again until dusk. Most of our games involved a ball of some size or other, though I also joined the local boxing club. I didn't stick at it for long. I enjoyed the fighting, but the training was hard work and boring. Still, I learned enough rudimentary pugilism there to stand me in good stead in future life.

There were municipal tennis courts in Cotgrave, and I received a racket for my birthday one year. But as I was the only boy on the estate who owned one I could only play against a wall. This I was happy to do, for hours on end, until a particularly hard smash separated the head of the cheap racket from its handle. It was the same with cricket bats: one slog over cow corner, and the blade would split in two, or fly off from the handle.

Of course, football was overwhelmingly the most popular sport. All we needed were a couple of jumpers for posts and a ball. We played with leather 'caseys', lethally heavy when wet – heading was to be avoided at all costs, it was bad enough *kicking* one – or plastic 'ten-bob swervers.' A nightmare for the fat kid (otherwise known as the goalkeeper), these featherweight balls would swerve wildly in the air and could be burst by a single kick. That was no bad thing. A flat ten-bob swerver could be passed more accurately.

Like everyone else, I had only one pair of shoes – my school shoes. I had trendy Bata Wayfinders, which had a small compass secreted in the heel and boasted upon their soles a series of animal footprints – fox, otter, badger, red squirrel and so on, supposedly to help you to recognise and follow the spoor of the real thing. But mine had been liberated from a delivery lorry destined for Africa, and were a special 'Big Game' version. The prints on the soles were of hippo, wolf, rhino, tiger, zebra, and buffalo. I never found any of those near Cotgrave (and I defy anyone to find the footprints of a hippo, a tiger and a wolf in the same vicinity anywhere).

Unfortunately, the Wayfinder was next to useless for its primary purpose, playing football. On a wet day, you would slip and slide around like Torville or Dean, picking up so much mud that you resembled an astronaut wearing moonboots. You could play in the street, but you risked this only in desperate times i.e. during the Monsoon. With the miners on shift work, a third of the menfolk would be in bed at any given time. Any rowdiness in the street invariably resulted in a woken miner furiously throwing open his bedroom window and screaming at you. And if he recognised you and told your father, you were in for a whacking – plain and simple. I suppose it was part of the glue which held the place together.

I joined the cubs and learned to swim. I became rather a good swimmer and passed all of the available distance awards, up to a gruelling ten-miler. This got me into terrible trouble a year or two later, after I had started at Toot Hill Comprehensive School. At our Wednesday afternoon swimming lessons, accomplished swimmers

I was always a good swimmer. Here I am, aged eighteen months or so, after doing fifty lengths of the paddling pool in my grandmother's back garden.

were allowed in the deep end of the main pool, beginners were put in the shallow end, and non-swimmers in the children's pool. The main pool was as cold as the January Serpentine, while the children's pool was as the Caribbean in July; I declared myself a non-swimmer, and this strategy worked until one Saturday, when I spent the whole day ploughing up and down the pool with the scouts. I completed a pleasing 648 lengths, backstroke, but unfortunately my efforts were witnessed by Mr Hill, who had spent many weeks trying in vain to 'teach me to swim'. I was moved out of the children's pool the following week, and only allowed cold showers for the rest of the term.

* * *

THE LONG, HOT SUMMER of 1968 finally ended, and we all trudged gloomily back to school. Jack Fairlie and I had a score to settle, but we eschewed fighting in favour of a penalty shoot-out in the playground – one penalty each, against the school goalkeeper George McGregor. I took a long run-up and toe-poked the ball as hard as I could, but hit it straight at George and he saved it with ease. Being a bright boy, Jack learned from my mistake: he took a two-step run-up and side-footed the ball with precision. McGregor didn't fancy diving on the concrete, but, to my relief, it ran a few inches wide.

Our friends didn't have the patience for a second round, and ran off with the ball, leaving Jack and me arguing in their wake.

'I should be Number One,' I said. 'At least mine was on target!'

'The goal was too narrow,' said Jack. 'If it had been normal-sized I'd have scored.'

True, the goal – two metal struts and the cross-piece of the climbing frame – *was* narrower than the real thing, but a miss is as good as a mile. The argument was never resolved, but it didn't much matter because our second year teacher, Miss Marshall, didn't operate the same inhuman numeric register system as her predecessor.

(I lost touch with Jack when we went to different senior schools in 1971, but we recently met up in a pub in Cardiff. It was a joy to see my childhood friend after more than forty years; I bought a couple of pints, and we sat down, two middle-aged men with a lot to catch up on. 'How have you been then, Jack?' I said. He fixed me with a stare. 'If that goal had been normal-sized I'd have scored!' he said.)

I wasn't a bad footballer, and both Jack and I had high hopes of selection for the school team, but that September was one of the wettest on record and neither of us had boots. We slithered our way through the trial match in flimsy plimsolls, against boys who had cheated by getting their parents to fork out for a pair of white 'Alan Ball' boots, and wholly failed to impress the PE teacher, Mr Price. He put us both in the B team, and I was almost in tears as I poured my heart out to my mother that night. She persuaded my father to part with a shilling for our next-door neighbour Rob Grice's old pair. They were nice boots, in good condition, but Rob was twenty years old and they fitted me like canal boats. Still, I stuffed the toes with newspaper and wore them at the next football practice, determined to get out of the B team. I did, too – I was relegated to the C team.

When we weren't playing football we were fighting. Casual violence is endemic in many working class communities, in a way that middle class people perhaps don't understand, and the most important question in our lives was that of our fight rankings. Scraps after school were an almost daily occurrence, and they were generally fought only to establish which of the combatants was the hardest. In much the same way as the various governing bodies rank boxers, you could move up (or down) the order by beating (or losing to) other lads. There was an element of flux, but, on any given day, everyone knew exactly where he stood in the pecking order.

In my last year at junior school, a new boy joined. His name – David Heavyside – hinted at a certain fistic proficiency, but no-one knew how good he was. My own star was riding high at the time. Using a few tips gleaned from my time at the boxing club, I had beaten up the school bully, Andrew Whittaker, because he had been picking on a friend of mine. Some match-making idiot told Heavyside that I was a good fighter and, sensing his opportunity for an early elevation to the upper echelons, he challenged me to a scrap after school.

'I'll fight you,' I said. 'But to prove you're worthy you'll have to fight Michael Pringle first.'

What I knew, but the *ingénu* Heavyside did not, was that Michael Pringle was the undisputed heavyweight champ of Cotgrave Manvers Junior School. He was bigger, stronger and better at sport than anybody else, and by far the best fighter, so much so that nobody even *thought* to challenge him. The unsuspecting Heavyside duly approached Pringle and, like an eighteenth century dueller, demanded satisfaction of him that very afternoon. The challenge was accepted, and Heavyside turned to me.

'I'm going to beat the shit out of him tonight,' he said. 'And then it's your turn tomorrow.'

I don't think I've ever enjoyed watching a fight as much as I enjoyed seeing a startled David Heavyside being destroyed by Michael Pringle. As Hobbes might have put it, it was nasty, brutish, and short, and Heavyside was left in no fit state to make good his promise to beat the shit out of me the following day, or any other day. Once his bumps and bruises had healed, he contented himself with settling down amongst the lower-ranked men.

I didn't go looking for scraps, but they were sometimes unavoidable, triggered by the merest incident. During a football match for the school B team (I'd moved up again) against Tollerton School, I gently headed the ball back to my own goalkeeper, Tony Stephenson, and he let it trickle through his legs and into the net. We lost 1-0, and our teammates were divided as to who to blame. There was only one way to settle it. Tony challenged me to fights three days in a row. I beat him easily on the first two days, and before our third I asked him why he kept on at me when he was bound to lose.

'That's what you think,' he snarled. 'One of these days I'm going to beat you, and I'm going to fight you every single day until then.'

As usual, he came in flailing like a windmill and, as usual, I evaded his blows and knocked him down. But instead of leaving it at that, as I had done previously, I gave him as serious a beating as an eleven-year-old can deliver. I felt sick doing it, but it seemed the only way I could avoid fighting him every day for the rest of my life. It proved a successful strategy, in more ways than one. Poor Tony never challenged me again, and neither did anyone else.

* * *

IN SPITE OF THE all-pervading atmosphere of violence, and my never making it into the football team, I enjoyed my time at junior school immensely. But in 1971, when I was eleven, it was time for me to move on.

It was a memorable year, for a couple of reasons. In February, Britain went decimal – a terrific swindle, I thought. One new penny was the same as 2.4 old pence, but a penny chew still cost a penny, a scandalous price increase of nearly 150 per cent! A month or so later, one of my classmates, Malcolm Guthrie, suddenly died of a mystery illness, and then I fell ill with a mystery illness of my own. I spent two weeks in hospital. I can't remember now what was wrong with me; I just know that I felt incredibly nauseous, and spent my days listening to music on the radio whilst waiting to die. Two songs that were played very often were *No Matter What* by Badfinger and *Indiana Wants Me* by R. Dean Taylor. Even today, those records make me feel queasy.

But I made it to the summer, and thoughts turned to big school. All that needed resolving was which big school I would be going to.

Nearly everyone was going to Toot Hill Comprehensive in Bingham, but Jack Fairlie and I had been entered into the eleven-plus examination by our school. We both passed and were offered scholarships at the private Nottingham Boys' High School – *alma mater* of, among others, DH Lawrence, the MPs Ken Clarke and Ed Balls, the men behind Boot's Chemists and John Player cigarettes, and various directors of the BBC, academics and diplomats. It was a very long way from the little slum home I'd come from a few years before, and I don't know how I would have taken to it, or it to me, had I gone there. I do know that it is almost inconceivable that I would be writing this book, because I would surely have trodden a more conventional path. But I didn't go to the High School, thanks to a combination of political dogma, and my father's lack of interest in education.

The local education authority was fervently and ideologically against private and grammar schools and, while there was nothing it could do to stop me attending the High School, it had a trump card. My parents received a letter informing them that the LEA was not prepared to pay my bus fare, as there was a perfectly good comprehensive school in Bingham that I could attend with a free school bus laid on.

That settled it for my father: after all, school was only a necessary evil to be endured before you went down the pit.

So I was put down for Toot Hill Comprehensive with everybody else – except Jack. His father, also a coalminer, found the bus money, and he sailed through O Levels and A levels before going on to read German at the University of Dundee.

At the time, I was overwhelmingly relieved. Going to the High School would have meant leaving the house at seven-thirty in the morning, and also saying goodbye to all of my classmates – including the girls. I was desperately in love with a very pretty blonde called Kim Dixon. It was sadly unrequited – there was more chance of David Heavyside challenging Michael Pringle to a re-match than there was of Kim noticing me – but, given five more years with her at big school… I was confident I could wear her down.

Unfortunately, my plans to woo, win and then marry Kim were thwarted anyway. On our last day at junior school, a few of the girls got a little emotional about leaving, but Kim seemed to take it exceptionally hard. She was sitting in the playground, crying her eyes out, as friends consoled her.

'What's the matter with Kim?' I asked her best friend, Dawn McGovern, as casually as I could.

'Her dad's got a new job,' she said. 'They're moving to Manchester.'

They moved a few days later, and I never saw Kim again.

CHAPTER THREE: BIG SCHOOL

Forty-one years to silk

IT SEEMED TO RAIN that whole summer, and I spent a lot of it stuck in the house, kicking my heels and waiting to go to senior school.

My father was around a lot, too, and we didn't get along. The early headiness of Cotgrave had long worn off, and he seemed permanently to be in a bitter fury with the world in general, and me in particular. I still don't know why. My mother thought that it was because of my height: I was already several inches taller than he, and he didn't like it. I'm unconvinced. He was almost equally hateful to all of us. I remember a family drive through old Cotgrave in one of his bangers. It was cold and rainy, and a back door suddenly sprang open and sent Kevin sprawling onto the road. My father stopped, and mum jumped out and ran to Kevin. Fortunately, we had been travelling slowly, so Kevin wasn't badly hurt, but he was muddy and wet. When they walked back to the car, my father refused to allow him back inside, and left the two of them standing by the side of the road whilst he drove home to get some old towels to cover the car seats.

My prolific bedwetting didn't help. It had started during my early years in St Ann's, when I'd try to scare Kevin with stories of ghosts and monsters, but always ended up terrifying myself. As the lavatories were outside in the dark, I would never dare go, and the inevitable would happen. I carried on bedwetting into adulthood – indeed, it still happens, from time to time – and it was a terrible thing for me to bear. I could never go on school trips, or boy scout camps, or stay at friends' houses. But it was worse for my poor mother. She had to wash my sheets every day, and often my blankets, too. When he was in a good mood, my father simply left her to it; when the bitterness and anger rose up in him, the spite came with it, and I became an easy target.

One summer, a family friend loaned us his caravan in Skegness for a week. The excitement was palpable: we'd never been to the seaside before. It was long after nightfall when we arrived, and we went straight to bed. Of course, I wet the bed. In the morning, my father was furious. He made my mother pack everything up before driving us all straight home. On the way, he made it perfectly clear that it was my fault that we were leaving without even seeing the sea.

I was forever at the doctors, and was prescribed every quack cure known to man. Among them was an alarm which went off like an air raid siren if a drop of moisture touched the metallic cover under my sheets. But I'm a very deep sleeper: the alarm would wake half the street, particularly terrifying those residents who had lived through the Blitz, but it had no effect on me.

The GP finally settled on a new drug, Tofranil. Tofranil's primary application was for the treatment of depression and psychosis in adults, but one of the side-effects was urinary retention. It also prevented the patient from slipping into the deepest, 'delta wave' sleep, so I had no proper sleep for three years. I did have the odd dry night, but I also had the odd dry following day. Indeed, sometimes I would be unable to urinate for *two* days: when that happened, I would roll up into a ball, crying in agony. The doctor eventually discontinued my prescription – perhaps because of the discovery of further side-effects, including confusion, reduced concentration, nightmares, suicidal impulses and bizarre behaviour – and I went back to wetting the bed every night.

Dr Terry Bell then came up with his own solution. Surely I would learn not to wet the bed if I was forced to sleep on the same sodden mattress every night – a bit like rubbing a puppy's nose in its own mess? He ordered my mum not to change my sheets, so I had to get under the cold, damp bedding of the night before. It didn't work. After a few weeks, mum ignored his instructions and started washing my bedclothes again.

My father's rage was not limited to his family; he was angry with the world. The anger led him to obduracy, and he developed a catchphrase: 'Nobody tells *me* what to do.' I believed that this was true, until a small thing happened to drag the scales from my young eyes. We were out in his ramshackle Ford Thames van – registration 79 FYY, I remember it well – with my mother in the front seat holding my new baby sister, Samantha, and Kevin and me rattling around in the back with Dawn. Impatience pervaded my father's whole life: when we came up behind a line of slow-moving traffic he simply *had* to get to the front of them all, ignoring the no-overtaking line.

When he did arrive at the front, he realised why everyone else was driving so slowly: the lead vehicle was a police car. As we passed him, the police officer turned on his lights and siren, and my father, cursing, pulled over into a lay-by and sat there, absolutely simmering with fury.

The officer looked in at my father, and my father glared back. After several seconds, the officer broke the silence.

'I don't like the way you drive,' he said.

'So what?' my father spat back. '*I* don't like the way *you* drive.'

He looked over his shoulder at us and rolled his eyes, as if to emphasise the fact that no policeman was going to tell him what to do.

'Well,' said the policeman, taking out his notebook. 'Why don't we give each other a ticket?'

It would have taken a brave man to speak to my father during the rest of that day, but I'd seen a chink in his armour: he wasn't the most powerful force in the world, and people existed who *could* tell him what to do.

* * *

TOOT HILL IS in the village of Bingham, five miles away at the western end of the Vale of Belvoir. A big school, it then had 1,500 pupils, most of them from the surrounding villages: six coaches

31

collected the Cotgrave contingent from the Miners' Welfare car park every morning at eight-thirty.

Us apart, most of the children were what I thought of in those days as 'posh'. Our estate supplied the school's best fighters and also – if I'm honest – most of the less educable kids, and this was unfortunate for me. The school was ruthlessly egalitarian. The school houses were divided into two groups, 'A' and 'Alpha', 'A' and 'B' being unthinkable, and competitive exams were forbidden until mock CSEs and O levels in the fifth year. (In the days before GCSEs were introduced, you took either O levels or CSEs, the former being academically more taxing.) Setting was also prohibited – in theory. But I suppose the teachers had to find *some* way of separating the academic sheep from the goats, and they fell back on brute prejudice. If you were from Cotgrave, you were thick, and a troublemaker, and you were treated accordingly.

I arrived having just passed the eleven-plus, and having been an eager and successful student at Cotgrave Manvers. Over the next few years, all of the ambition was beaten out of me with the stick of apathy. I was taught not a word of Shakespeare, and learned not a jot of English history. Everything was thoroughly dumbed down; nothing was even remotely thought-provoking. The teachers hardly taught, and what they did teach was facile and trivial. I soon looked elsewhere for mental stimulation.

A bad bunch in the year above me flouted the uniform code by wearing *Clockwork Orange*-style white jeans and denim jackets, and hung around behind the sports centre smoking Consulate menthol cigarettes. I was desperate to join them, but I was a year younger and I always wore uniform. I needed an entrée, but it would take something very special and, for the life of me, I couldn't think of anything. Then, one day, I got my chance.

We were playing football with a ten-bob swerver and someone kicked the ball into a hedge. As I bent down to pick it up, something winked at me from the undergrowth. I pulled it out to investigate, and couldn't believe my eyes: it was a page torn from a pornographic magazine, and it featured a photograph of a completely naked woman. I quickly shoved it into my pocket and went back to the game. I kept it close by me all day, until I took it out for a closer examination at home. Frankly, I found it quite shocking: I'd had no idea that naked women looked like that.

The following lunchtime, I headed straight to the sports centre to join my new soon-to-be friends. Sure enough, all of the bad boys were there! They'd quickly cupped their menthol cigarettes as I rounded the corner, in case I was a teacher, and that brief interruption to their minty smoking had annoyed them. Now they were looking at me with open hostility.

'What the fuck do you want?' spat Fred Brown, the worst-behaved boy in the entire school (which was going some).

But I had a trump card.

I sauntered over, nonchalantly.

'Do you want to see a picture of a naked woman?' I said.

'Where is it?' he demanded.

'Here,' I said, patting my jacket pocket, smugly.

'Let's see it, then,' he said, impatiently.

They all gathered around as I carefully took the folded piece of paper from my pocket. Friendly hands rested upon my shoulders, all enmity gone from their eyes.

'You're not going to believe this,' I said, with a conspiratorial smile. 'You can see her cock!'

I could still hear their vicious, braying laughter as I fled, trying to hide my tears. In fact, I can *still* hear it.

Unsurprisingly, there came no invitation to join their gang.

* * *

THE SCHOOL WORK continued to be very easy for me – and anyone else who was at all literate – but then something happened which caused me to drop spectacularly off the pace. Like 'Number Thirty' in Mrs Route's class, no-one was there to catch me – metaphorically, or literally.

During the February half-term, I was climbing trees at a local beauty spot when a rotten branch gave way and I fell twenty feet to the floor.

Fortunately, I broke my fall.

Unfortunately, I broke it with my arms.

Both of them were fractured, my right one particularly badly. Complications set in, it needed re-breaking and re-setting more than once, and I ended up spending the rest of the academic year at home. By the time I went back, everyone else had moved on. The younger, keener Gary would have caught up easily, but I had enthusiastically embraced Toot Hill's non-competitive ethos, and any ambition had evaporated. I went properly off the rails.

My year had acquired its own crowd of rebels, and I joined them. My crowning moment came when I was caned in front of the whole school for smoking, never having smoked a cigarette in my life. The school was coming down hard on smokers, and one master in particular, Mr Hill, had made it a personal crusade. He was always popping up uninvited behind the sports centre, so we employed counter-surveillance, posting sentries from the year below at the corners. This worked for a while, and I like to think he spent long, evening hours at home coming up with his new plan, which was to climb out of a skylight onto the sports centre roof with a camera, creep to the edge of the building, and take a photograph of the entire crowd, catching the smokers red-handed with incontrovertible evidence.

Successful ambushes are a matter of timing, and he executed his plan a little too early. Five minutes later, and he would have caught half the school; as it was, only Deborah Tomlinson had had time to light up when he popped up with his new Polaroid. She had just taken a drag when the boy on sentry duty called out, 'Deborah, your shoelace is undone.'

34

She passed me her cigarette to hold whilst she knelt down to tie her laces; moments later, she took it back and carried on smoking.

Later that day I was summoned to see Miss Johnson, the deputy headmistress. When I protested my innocence, she brandished the photograph: there I was, bold as brass, undeniably holding a lit fag.

'How do you explain this?' she demanded. 'Empty your pockets!'

I couldn't grass Deborah up so, glumly, I did as instructed. Out came a few pence in loose change… and a packet of twenty Player's No 6.

'You don't smoke, eh?' snapped Miss Johnson.

There was an explanation for that, too. In those days, children could buy cigarettes simply by claiming they were for their parents. (My father sent Dawn out one day. 'Nip down to the Co-op and get me twenty Park Drive,' he said, 'and if they've run out of Park Drive just get me anything.' She returned twenty minutes later with a Mars Bar.) My downfall was due to simple capitalism. Monday's dinner money always went on cigarettes. I'd buy a packet of twenty for 21p, and sell them individually at school for 2p apiece, almost doubling my money. But while this explanation might persuade Miss Johnson that I wasn't a smoker, it appeared unlikely to save me from punishment.

I was caned in assembly – then and many other times.

I was caned by Mr Wheatley for being offensive on tape in the French language laboratory.

I was caned by Mr Froggat, the metalwork teacher, on a number of occasions. He liked to employ a three-foot-long blackboard ruler which he called Fred, and would write the name 'Fred' on it backwards in chalk, thus leaving its mark emblazoned on your bottom when he beat you.

Our geography teacher, Mr Allsop, was trying to leave the antediluvian world of corporal punishment behind, and preferred to apply a lunchtime detention during which one was supposed to write an essay detailing one's remorse. The first time he gave me detention – from memory, for making someone lick an electric cattle fence – I diligently scrawled down my sorrow, and handed my essay in. Without a glance, he tore it in half and threw it in the bin. My second detention came shortly thereafter, this time for selling beermats. (There was a massive craze for collecting beermats, and I could sell three for 10p; children would spend their lunch money on them and go hungry, which is why it was banned.) There were about half a dozen of us in that day's lunchtime detention, and, still angry about my recent wasted effort, I went to town. My essay contained no mention of regret, nor of beermats, but plenty on Mr Allsop.

He came in, collected the essays, and headed to the bin.

'Let's hope this has been a lesson to you all,' he said, beginning to tear them in half. Then something caught his eye and, with a startled look, he began to read the top sheet. His face darkened as he assimilated my opinions on a range of subjects, including his idiocy and incompetence.

Six of the best in front of the school again for Bell.

I didn't mind. It hurt like hell, but it earned me a great deal of kudos, particularly with those girls who liked bad boys. I was beginning to find favour with the ladies, not least because I had embraced the new glam rock craze with a passion. I had very long hair, and I had abandoned my school uniform for a denim jacket and ridiculous trousers. My favourite pair were turquoise-and-pink loon pants – the top half being turquoise and below the knee being shocking pink – with eighteen-inch flares and a seven-button waistband that came up to my chest. I teamed them with shoes so high I could barely walk and a shirt with a collar like aeroplane wings; my only concession to the rules was to wear a school tie, but I perfected tying a knot so large that nothing hung down from it.

I loved those fashions, and I loved the music even more. Kevin and I listened to the radio constantly and, in time, acquired a lot of records – though, since pocket money was sparse, there was only one way to build a collection. I'm sure there were honest burghers on the Cotgrave estate, but I never mixed with them. Shoplifting was just something you did, and it was not considered remotely immoral. We wanted sweets. We had no money. Woolworth's had lots of sweets. So we pinched them. Records were the same, with my favourite destination a famous Nottingham store, Selectadisc, where the second-hand singles were on a rack just inside the door. My record collection grew quickly.

Not to condone it for a moment, but it's amazing how easy shoplifting is. Only once was I caught red-handed – or would have been, if it hadn't been for Dean Daley and his coat of many pockets. Dean was a couple of years younger than me, and impressionable; one Saturday, Kevin and I had gone with him to Sisson and Parker's bookshop, where we had amassed a mighty haul which was concealed about our persons. But, as we left, a store detective pounced, frog-marched us to an empty room, locked it, and went to fetch the police. We had about half of Sisson's stock on us, and it looked bleak. But then I had an idea. Dean always wore his special shop-lifting coat, of which he was inordinately proud. It featured untold hidden pockets, and could hold an incredible amount of stuff.

'Why don't you hide everything in your secret pockets, Deano?' I said, shamelessly exploiting his pride and youthful naivety. 'The police'll never find it in there.'

Dean readily agreed, and eagerly packed all of our contraband into his famous coat.

Being young, he was let off with a caution, while Kevin and I were released to go on our way with nary a stain on our characters.

The next day, my father called us in for a talking-to.

'Ged Daley told me you two were arrested for shoplifting with Dean,' he said. 'Is that true?'

'Yes,' I said, shame-facedly.

'He said you put the blame on Dean, and he got done whilst you two got off scot free. Is *that* true?'

'Yes.'

'Well done,' he said. 'Remember, there's only one crime, and that's getting caught.'

* * *

JUST BEFORE WE broke up for Christmas in 1973, we had a school disco, and I made a beeline for the prettiest girl at school, Shirley Marshall. She had long blonde hair and was wearing shocking pink hot pants, and that night she became the first girl I ever kissed. I fondly imagined that we would be together forever.

Our love affair lasted for nearly a week, before she left me for an older boy, Manny Hesketh. To add insult to injury, he gave me a severe beating for having had the audacity to go out with her in the first place. Shirley is still my friend, though Manny Hesketh isn't; I confess that I would love to see her in those pink hotpants just one more time.

In other areas of school life I was doing well, in spite of myself. I was twice awarded prizes for fundraising and charity work, I was the school and county swimming champion for fifty metres' backstroke (I was only the third best backstroker in school, but the other two – who were among the best swimmers in the east midlands – did battle with each other over the front crawl), and I won the school chess championship two years running (although Tony Ryland insists to this day that he beat me in the final on both occasions). I even made the school rugby team. We played our fixtures on Saturday mornings, and when I saw my name on the team sheet posted on the wall on Friday I carried the news home with pride. My parents were in the kitchen when I arrived.

'I'm playing rugby for the school,' I said, proudly.

'That's good,' said my mother. 'When?'

'Tomorrow morning,' I said.

'How are you going to get there?' said my father, in his only contribution to the conversation.

I hitch-hiked, as I did every week – they never came to see me play.

Despite all of this, my end-of-year reports were still terrible. This line – and PE was one of my strengths – rather sums up my general approach:

Name G. BELL   Teaching Group 3 P   Tutor Set PG

PE
Has succeeded in making a thorough nuisance of himself this year and has made no progress whatever.

PHYSICAL EDUCATION

(Has succeeded in making a thorough nuisance of himself this year and has made <u>no</u> progress <u>whatever</u>.)

Most kids with bad reports were punished, but I was not – not least because my parents never saw any of them. At the back of each report booklet was a slip to be snipped off and returned, signed by a parent. I either forged my mother's signature, or didn't even bother returning them, but the school never chased them up and neither did my parents, who placed no value on education whatsoever.

My mother was always there for me in a maternal sort of way, but she gave me no encouragement or direction. My father's only interest in school was in what I could get out of it – literally. If we needed a new light bulb, or had run out of loo paper, I would be told to pinch some from Toot Hill (the loo paper had to come from the sports centre, as the children's lavatories were stocked with that sharp, tracing paper-type stuff). Even our kitchen clock was stolen from a classroom wall.

Neither of them ever attended a single parents' evening. I can only imagine that – given their own backgrounds – they thought that sort of thing was not for the likes of us.

My father did actually go to the school once, on an important point of principle raised by a concerned neighbour, Alf Thornham – a man unforgettable to me for what happened to him one day as he was having a pee in a darkened tunnel down the pit. He heard a cracking noise overhead, and, before he could react, a large piece of sharp coal fell from the roof of the tunnel, hit the hand that was holding his penis and sliced his thumb clean off. I remember asking him how he felt about it. 'It could have been worse, me duck!' he said, raising his eyebrows for emphasis.

One day, Alf rushed breathlessly round to our house with some disturbing news.

'I don't know how to say this, Terry,' he said, all sweat and bluster, 'so I'll spit it straight out. They're teaching our lads *cookery!*'

My father was speechless.

I knew his views on men and cooking from the time he caught my brother making a cake in the kitchen. There were many reasons why Kevin should not have made cakes, including his insistence on making icing with granulated sugar, but my father's objections were nothing to do with the quality of the finished article. 'I think our Kevin might be a poof,' he said to my mother that evening. I don't know if his strange philosophy originated in nature or nurture, but I gained some insight after the death in 1993 of his mother, and my grandmother, Emma Bell. My grandfather, Ernest, survived her for six months, and they were a miserable six months – mostly, as he confided to me when I visited him one afternoon, because he couldn't find where grandma had kept the tea bags. This was in a very small house, in which he had lived for fifty-five years.

Anyway, Alf Thornham and my dad led a posse down to Toot Hill, waving pitchforks and burning torches to demand that this sick practice be ended *tout suite*. The result was that a small group of us – those with the most reactionary, homophobic, and angry fathers – were exempted from domestic science. Whilst other boys learned how to make elaborate meals, like cheese on toast, or boiled eggs with soldiers, we sat outside the headmaster's office like a group of conscientious objectors, twiddling our thumbs and dreaming up mischief. Well done, Alf!

CHAPTER THREE: BIG SCHOOL

* * *

NOT THAT IT mattered much what my father thought about school, or anything. I kept out of his way as much as I could, and avoided catching his eye when I couldn't.

His wrath was occasionally justified. At Christmas 1974 he bought a bottle of brandy – the first bottle of spirits he had ever owned. He was immensely proud of it, and it was only opened on special occasions. Unfortunately, I got a taste for it myself, and he must have noticed. One day, after I had snuck the bottle down from its shelf and had a little nip, I noticed a pencil mark on the label – half an inch above the new level! Thinking fast, I took the bottle to the tap and topped it back up with a little water. That should have been that, but I enjoyed my occasional sharpener and over the next few months I 'stamped on it' quite heavily – as the heroin dealers say. It all came to a head the following Christmas. I was upstairs in bed and just dozing off when I heard my parents come back from the pub. They had friends with them, and I heard my father ask them what they wanted to drink.

'What have you got?' said one of them – and I was jolted wide awake by my father's reply.

'How about a nice glass of brandy?'

I leapt out of bed as my mother went to fetch the bottle from the pantry, and was just pulling on my second shoe when I heard the considered opinion of the first taster.

'Bloody hell, Terry!' he said. 'This is as weak as piss!'

I jumped out of my bedroom window just as I heard my father's footsteps thundering up the stairs, and it saved me a beating. He rarely hit me, but if he'd got to me that night he would have savaged me there and then. As it was, by the time he saw me again – although he was still extremely angry – he contented himself with shouting at me, his blazing eyes popping from his head as though on stalks.

I was happy to take it, because I knew I'd done wrong. Indeed, if he had confined himself to punishing me only for wrongdoing, I

41

would have been happy enough. It was his unjustness and unpredictability that I resented. It was like living on top of a volcano. One evening we were in the sitting room watching his favourite programme, *The Benny Hill Show*. My father lay on the sofa smoking cigarette after cigarette, flicking the ash onto the carpet for mum to clear up after he had gone to the pub and laughing uproariously at the various *double entendres*. There came a scene when Benny Hill was discussing horses with another man, who asked Benny where Bob was.

'He's gone around the back for a pony and trap,' said Benny.

My father clearly thought that this was unutterably hilarious, and laughed so hard that tears came to his eyes. I didn't understand it, but I was enjoying for once being in the same room as him when he was in a good mood, and I started to giggle along. He noticed me and, in an instant, he stopped and stared at me, goggle eyes ablaze with fury.

'What are you laughing at?' he demanded.

I swallowed my laughter and blinked back fearfully.

'The programme,' I muttered.

'Why?'

'Well,' I said, squirming. 'Because it was funny.'

'What was funny about it?'

His voice had risen an octave or two, and his eyes were protruding further with every question.

'You know,' I murmured. 'He said he was getting a pony and trap?'

'So what's funny about that?'

'I dunno,' I said, with a shrug.

'So why are you laughing?'

I could think of, and so gave, no answer; he stared at me in quivering rage for some time, and finally broke the silence.

'Get to bed,' he hissed.

'But I haven't had tea yet,' I said, by way of protest.

'Now!' he barked, and off I went.

After that night, I never passed more than a few words with my father for the rest of my childhood. If his car was parked by the house when I walked down our street after school, I would go to a friend's for tea – usually Steven Savage's, Mrs Savage was wonderful to me – until he left for the pub at about seven o'clock. I would make sure I was in bed before he returned, invariably drunk. He would come into my bedroom, all beery breath and silent anger, and Kevin and I would feign sleep as he prowled around, like a bear outside a camper's tent.

If anything, my father avoided home even more than I did. Often, he was working in other jobs to supplement his income from the pit. For a while, when I was aged around ten, he worked at weekends as a mechanic at a local garage-*cum*-petrol station, and I would go with him to operate the petrol pumps. One day another mechanic called George arrived with his shotgun, and a tin can which he placed on a fence – life being a bit different then.

'See if you can hit that,' said George casually to my father.

My father took aim, fired and missed.

'It's the recoil,' said George. 'You need to aim a bit lower. Does your lad want a go?'

The shotgun was handed to me.

'Don't fire at the can,' said my father. 'Try and shoot the tiger instead.'

It was an Esso petrol station, and Esso's TV ads at the time urged drivers to 'put a tiger in your tank'. A plastic tiger's head had been placed on the roof as an advertisement. My father had assumed that I would miss, and that he would then be able to mock me for it, but I had taken heed of George's words, and I aimed a foot or so below the target. There was a tremendous recoil as I fired, the gun lurched upwards, and the shot obliterated the tiger's head. That was the end of my father's job as a mechanic.

Around then, he also got a job as a bus driver. He didn't need me or a shotgun to help him lose that one. He was driving a group of schoolchildren in a double-decker when there loomed up ahead an extremely low bridge. Being an impatient man, he decided to risk it, and in doing so he peeled off half of the roof before the bus eventually ground to a halt. The top deck was full of small children; luckily, their heads were below seat level, and multiple decapitations were avoided. The bus company decided they could get by without my father's PSV skills after that incident.

Then, when I was sixteen, and in my final year at school, he suddenly left home.

He told my mother that he was going out to get some cigarettes, and just didn't come back. It later transpired that he had indeed gone to get his cigarettes from the pub, but that he had been invited to go to Blackpool for Frankie Leech's stag night, as someone had dropped out at the last minute. He agreed, and met another woman while he was up north. And that was it: he moved in with her.

My younger sister Samantha was only five at the time, Dawn was twelve, and Kevin was fifteen.

It was a shock to all of us, although a pleasant one for me. My mother took it badly. He was the only man she had ever loved, and she went to pieces, suffering a nervous breakdown and leaving the four of us children to fend for ourselves for a while.

My father paid my mother not a penny of maintenance and, since my education was going nowhere, the obvious thing for me to do was to leave school and get a job. I wasn't sure what I'd do. I'd certainly not been given many pointers by the school careers officer, who had made it clear that I would be following my father down the pit, not something that appealed to me at all.

'Ah, I see you're from Cotgrave,' he said, when I went to see him. 'What would you like to do when you leave school?'

'Er… I want to be a long-distance lorry driver,' I said.

'Splendid!' he beamed. 'You can get an HGV licence if you work at the pit.'

The lives of all male Cotgravers were mapped out in the same way.

'I want to work with animals,' said Michael Pringle.

'You can work with ponies and canaries if you go down the pit.'

'I want to be a footballer,' said Tony Ryland.

'They've got a very good football team at Cotgrave Colliery.'

'I want to be an astronaut,' said Steven Savage.

'You can get used to working on your own in the dark in a coalmine.'

It might sound amusing, but the sad truth is that this experience was shared – perhaps is *still* being shared – by thousands of children in poor schools. In its own way, it's a terrible scandal. How many other youngsters who could have gone on to become lawyers – or doctors, or entrepreneurs, or scientists – have instead ended up working in entirely unsuitable areas because no-one took them seriously, or thought to encourage them?

The national school leaving age had recently been increased to sixteen, and you couldn't now leave until the Easter of the year in which you reached that age, although there was no corresponding requirement to take any exams. Having no plans whatsoever, I told my tutor that I would be leaving at Easter, without sitting any O levels.

I'd just done surprisingly well in my mocks, but he didn't try to dissuade me. The school had set up a special class called ROSLA, for 'raising of the school leaving age', to cope with people like me, where we kicked our heels until we could leave. We were supposed to make models out of cardboard boxes and do basic sums, but the teacher offered us a deal: if we finished the maths, and got all the answers right, we could go and play football. In the four months before I joined the class, football there had been none. I'd got a grade B in my maths mock, and the ROSLA questions were elementary, to say the least. On my first morning, we started the test at nine-thirty, and we were out playing football fifteen minutes later. I was a popular addition to the group.

At least the ROSLA teacher helped us to apply for jobs. Mostly they were for labouring or factory work, but I was selected to sit a standard apprenticeship exam in Nottingham, which I passed easily. Armed with this piece of paper, I sent off a few applications. But when I received no reply, I applied – reluctantly – to the colliery.

My interview was conducted by a man called Tommy Morley.

'What's your dad's name?' said Tommy.

'Terry Bell,' I said.

'You start on Monday.'

And lo, the prophecy of the school careers officer came true and, like practically every other coalminer's son, I went down the pit.

CHAPTER FOUR: THE WORLD OF WORK

Thirty-six years to silk

I'D ACTUALLY HAD my first job at fourteen, as a paper boy. I didn't like it much. It made your hands filthy with newsprint – though you wouldn't get much change moaning about dirty hands in our neck of the woods – but my main complaint was the route. My patch was old Cotgrave, where the houses were higgledy-piggledy, unlike our neat rows, and you had to walk twice as far to deliver half as many papers. Worse, it took me past the churchyard. My fear of the dark had been honed by Hammer horror films and Stephen King novels and, early on winter mornings, with the sun still way below the horizon, I was honestly frightened of vampires, werewolves and zombies.

I loaded my bag with talismans, including a crucifix, holy water and an onion (Cotgrave Co-op didn't sell garlic), but I still couldn't work up the courage to walk past the cemetery in the dark. By early December, when the sun hadn't risen in time for me safely to deliver the morning papers before school, I started dropping them off with that afternoon's *Nottingham Evening Post*. Mr Mitchell, the newsagent, thought this an imperfect solution to a non-existent problem, and sacked me.

It was the first time I was sacked, but far from the last.

I next took employ at a fruit and vegetable stall on Bingham market. It was held on Thursdays, so I missed school, but I just made sure to keep my eyes peeled for teachers. On the first day, I worked for ten hours from eight in the morning, and finished tired but full of the pleasure of a job well done and money earned. The grocer had promised to 'see me right', but he must have meant 'see me coming', because he slipped me a fifty pence piece with a hearty clap on the shoulder.

'Well done, lad,' he said. 'See you next week?'

'Yeah,' I said, 'sure.'

The following week I indeed worked a further ten-hour shift for fifty pence, but I also devised a bonus system, paid directly to myself from the till, without involving the grocer, *per se*. A few weeks later he decided to let me go. I wasn't surprised; by then I was earning more than he was.

Then I left school, and I became a miner.

Briefly.

I felt extremely proud as I left home for my first proper day at big work, my beef paste sandwiches bundled up in a waxy Mother's Pride bread-wrapper. A bus was laid on to take us new lads to the training colliery at Moor Green, where it soon became apparent that mining wasn't the job for me, with all that crawling around through narrow apertures and down pitch-black tunnels.

It was a dangerous old job, as Tony Ryland's dad and Alf Thornham's thumb could have testified. Another Cotgrave miner sticks in my mind, too. Steve Wieczorek, a nice lad who'd been a couple of years ahead of me at school, was widely acknowledged to be highly intelligent – and not just because he liked Pink Floyd and wore an Afghan coat. Steve had had plans to stay on at school, take his exams, and break away from the village and the pit, and get an office job in the civil service. He had explained his design for life to the Toot Hill careers officer during his five-minute slot, and had received the same hearing at the rest of us.

'Well, that's *one* possible career path,' the careers officer had conceded doubtfully, 'though it might be best not to set your sights *too* high.'

Despite this 'advice', Steve *did* set his sights high. He stayed on at school, took his exams, and embarked on a promising career in the local Inland Revenue office. But Cotgrave pulled him back. A junior tax man's pay was miserable, compared to the starting wage for a young single miner, and all Steve's mates seemed to have more money than him. Not long after starting, he abandoned his office job and joined his mates underground.

It was a fateful decision. One day in April 1983, at the end of a gruelling, eight-hour shift, it was time for Steve to walk back to the shaft to take the lift to the surface. Steve was working on a very tight face, 360 yards long and about three feet high, and you could save yourself the back-breaking walk by taking a ride on the conveyor belt that carried the coal to the bottom of the shaft. This was against every safety regulation – the coal cutter, a giant machine which hacked the coal from the seam, was positioned somewhere along the belt, and you did not want to run into it – but, of course, everybody did it, just making sure they jumped off in time. On this particular day, the cutter had been left close to the shaft, hanging over the belt, leaving a gap of fourteen inches. Steve didn't see it, and he was crushed to death between the machine and the coal on the belt. It wasn't just a tragic waste of life, but a tragic waste of talent.

Incidents of that sort happened reasonably regularly in mines around the country, and quite a few people at my induction mentioned other hazards such as rock falls and poisonous gas. The instructors worked hard to allay their fears, but there wasn't much they could do to reassure me *vis à vis* the risk of encountering subterranean vampires. I wasn't going to crawl down those dark tunnels, even if my life depended on it.

I was saved from the ignominy of being sacked again by a reply to an earlier application, and departed mining in favour of a new career as an apprentice lawnmower mechanic with the prestigious Nottinghamshire firm of Henton and Chattell.

Initiation jokes are traditional at any new job of this type, and the wags at Henton and Chattel started early.

'Gary,' said one wit, 'pop down to the builders' merchants on Carrington Street and get me a packet of sky hooks.'

There was stifled sniggering, but I just went to the pub, had a few pints, and sauntered back an hour later.

'They didn't have any,' I said, 'so I tried the one up at the Victoria Centre, but they didn't have any, either.'

They all roared with laughter at my stupidity, but I wasn't as clever as I thought. The beer, drunk on an empty stomach, had affected my judgment. Shortly after my return, I was asked to move an open, fifty-gallon drum of oil with a sack barrow. I manoeuvred the lip of the barrow under the drum and pulled it back, but it tipped forwards and all fifty gallons spilled onto the shop floor. The manager was furious, but there was a strong union at Henton and Chattell and no-one – not even a drunken berk on his first day – could be sacked without three written warnings. So he had to content himself with giving me a bollocking and my first written warning.

I spent the rest of the day cleaning up the oil and made sure that I arrived early the next morning, stone cold sober and keen to show that I'd make an excellent mechanic. The manager handed me two piston valves covered in hard, black coke.

'Use that revolving wire brush to clean these up,' he said.

After ten minutes my arms were ready to drop off, but I'd hardly touched the coke. Turning the machine off for a breather, I noticed the grindstone opposite. Five minutes later, all of the coke had been ground away. Unfortunately, so had most of the piston valves.

'These are supposed to be accurate to a thousandth of an inch!' screamed the manager, handing me my second written warning.

On my third day I was put to work in the yard, sweeping and tidying up. Mid-morning, the manager came out carrying a tub of green paint and a spray gun. He pointed at a giant lawnmower adorned with the Nottingham City Council crest.

'Take this spray gun and paint that all over,' he said. 'But make sure you don't get any paint on the crest!'

'How do I do that?' I said, dumbfounded.

'Put a thin layer of grease over it before you start,' he said. 'Then just point the gun and pull the trigger.'

So I carefully greased the mower – bar the crest, over which I taped a protective piece of cardboard. Then I just pointed the gun and pulled the trigger. In less than half an hour, I was finished, and sought out my manager to tell him so.

'Well done, lad,' he said, with a smile and ruffle of my hair. 'We'll make a mechanic of you, yet. Just give it a couple of hours to dry.'

I went back to tidying the yard, stopping occasionally to admire the gleaming, bright green mower, and two hours later I skipped back to see my manager.

'What now?' I said.

'Just rub the paint off over where you put the grease,' he said, 'and that'll be job done. Let's go and have a look at it.'

A sense of dread came over me as we walked outside. What on earth did he mean: *Rub the paint off over where you put the grease*? I'd greased the whole thing – except the sign.

He ran a finger across the lawnmower, and his smile froze. Paint and grease came off together on his finger.

'I meant grease the *sign*,' he said, with a heavy sigh.

Then he removed my cardboard protector from the crest. Half of it was splattered in green paint. Bone-dry green paint.

Ten minutes later, my career as a lawnmower mechanic was over.

'Normally we assess an apprenticeship after the first year,' said the gaffer, 'but in your case three days is enough.'

My third written warning in hand, I went to sign on the dole, but, as a sackee, I had to wait six weeks to qualify. I was entitled to social security – a princely £7.70 a week – but I had to give my mother five pounds for board. I was poorer than when I'd had my paper round.

* * *

BUT JOBS WERE easy to come by then, and I soon got taken on as a fork-lift truck driver at the Pedigree Wholesale pet food warehouse.

I was paid seventeen pounds per week, and worked Monday to

Friday from 7.30am until 5.30pm, with half an hour for lunch. I only took the job as a stopgap until I could find another apprenticeship, but it was a very friendly place to work and I stayed for more than two years.

The manager, David Tuck, was a lovely chap, and clearly gay but firmly in the closet. Homophobia was rife in working class Britain at the time – though, as it happens, we younger Cotgravers didn't share the general preconception of homosexuals, that they were all big, soft pansies like Frankie Howerd and Kenneth Williams. We were much more enlightened, thanks to a boy called Paul Barker. He was massive for his age, both in height and girth, and, aged eleven, he had a hairy chest and a moustache. He was also very camp, and quite openly gay.

I mentioned Michael Pringle, the best fighter at junior school, and how – the unsuspecting David Heavyside apart – no-one had fancied taking him on. Well, one other lad did have a go. One day, Pringle made a homophobic remark to Paul Barker, and our gay classmate responded by slapping him across the face. A furious Pringle demanded they meet after school and so, at half-past three, we all trooped out to see the two gladiators in action.

'Scrap, scrap, scrap,' we chanted, crowding around and craning our necks for a better view. There wasn't much to see. Barker simply grabbed Pringle by the scruff of the neck, threw him to the floor, and pulverised him. A teacher arrived quickly and pulled Barker away, leaving the stricken former champion crying tears of pain and shame. And so we had a new best fighter in school. Paul Barker. A gay boy! I wish David Tuck had seen it – it might have made his life easier.

Most of the staff at Pedigree Wholesale were nice people, but one chap quickly took me under his wing. The exotically-named Crombie Thornton did as little as possible to get through each working day, and was anxious to pass on the craft. At lunchtime on my first day, with ten minutes of our break remaining, I picked up a copy of *The Sun* and stood up.

'Where are you going?' said Crombie.

'To the bog,' I said.

'Sit down, you idiot,' he said, snatching the paper from my hand. 'Never shit in your own time!'

Eventually, the one o'clock hooter sounded the return to work.

'Right, *now* you can go,' he said, with a grin.

Street-smart as Crombie was, Derek Slater – the owner – was miles ahead. A self-made man at home in the office and the warehouse, Derek had never forgotten his roots and, although he worked us hard and paid us next to nothing, everybody had the utmost respect for him. After I had been there a few months, he took me to one side.

'I've been keeping an eye on you, Gary,' he whispered, conspiratorially, 'and I'm very pleased with your work. I'm giving you an extra one pound a week. But don't tell anyone else, or they'll all want a rise!'

I was walking on air for the rest of the day.

Although I mostly drove the forklift, I was sometimes allowed to accompany a delivery driver as his mate. A few weeks after my rise, Crombie and I were sent with a load of Bonios and Pedigree Chum to Sheffield. On the way, he intimated that he had a secret, but that he could impart it to me only if I kept it strictly to myself.

'I won't tell a soul,' I said.

'Derek had a word with me a couple of weeks ago,' he said. 'He said he'd been keeping an eye on me, he was very pleased with my work, and he was giving me an extra two pounds a week!'

Thanks to such Machiavellian tactics, I was working a fifty-hour week for twenty-six pounds after nearly two years at the firm.

Two years! How easily time slipped by, how the horizon closed in! It was deadly dull, but I had stability and security, and the prospect of one day driving a pet foods lorry or, perhaps, becoming the warehouse manager. Staying there and growing into a middle-aged man like Crombie Thornton didn't fill me with dread. Pedigree

Wholesale was my career, and I had no ambition towards anything else.

* * *

BY NOW, MUM was back on her feet and working as a barmaid, but money was still tight – for her. I lived for the weekends, and spent my Friday, Saturday and Sunday nights pissing away my wage packet in a variety of pubs and working men's clubs.

The drinking culture was extremely important in Cotgrave, and a large measure of a man was in how much alcohol he could take. I had my first pint at the age of fourteen, in the Lime Kiln, a struggling country pub between us and Colston Bassett. The then licensees would serve anyone, and the children of Cotgrave kept them in business until they were finally closed down after Billy Campbell got hammered one night and ran full tilt into a road sign on the way home in the dark. He knocked himself out and fell into a ditch full of nettles. We woke him up by urinating on him, and he staggered home like Swamp Thing, with two black eyes, nettle rash everywhere, and covered in wee and mud. He'd told his mum he was only nipping out to get some chips.

Our underage drinking was temporarily curtailed, but it was actually a relief for me. Men drank bitter, so we drank bitter, but I hated the stuff. I couldn't admit this – it would have been like coming out – so I spent my evenings gagging on every mouthful in the Lime Kiln. Things improved once the 1970s lager revolution reached Nottingham and brought with it Samuel Smith's Alpine Ayingerbräu. It wasn't as nice as Coke, or lemonade, or even water, but at least it didn't make me vomit, and I took to it with alacrity, along with pretty much every grateful bitter 'enthusiast' of my generation.

From then on, my life revolved around drinking. I was paid on Friday (in cash, as everyone was – no-one had a bank account). After

I had given my mum my board, the rest of it was mine to do with as I wished. I saved some for a rainy day, put a little more aside for my work lunches and… Who am I kidding? My pay packet rarely lasted beyond Sunday, and many a weekday lunch consisted of cheese-flavoured Bonios and Good Boy Chocolate Drops.

My weekend routine was always the same.

Friday night, Nottingham with the lads, visiting at least ten pubs, drinking a pint in each, before staggering off to a nightclub to listen to terrible music and down a few horrifying Pernod-and-lemonades. At 2am, those who had picked up girls would disappear, and the rest would get a kebab and a taxi home.

Saturday was a rinse-and repeat, having first attended the Nottingham Forest match.

Sunday mornings, football for the Cotgrave Miners' Welfare with a blinding hangover, a couple of lunchtime pints, then home for mum's Sunday dinner.

Sunday evenings, the Miners' Welfare, a few more pints, then a late night visit to the village's Chinese takeaway to see off the last of our pay packets.

I don't want to come across all William Hague, but we really did go through around thirty pints each over a weekend – though I use the phrase 'go through' advisedly. I certainly didn't drink them all, because there were times when I physically couldn't. Another pint would appear, and you were honour-bound to empty it. You would surreptitiously pour it into a plant pot, or someone else's glass, or out of the window – anything but admit that you were not man enough to keep going. It was at this stage that my weight started to spiral out of control, unsurprisingly.

Fighting remained the other way of proving your manhood. Some of the lads who had been good fighters at school hadn't filled out much in their teens, whereas weedier contemporaries had blossomed into hulking great louts. Stevie Leech had been the best scrapper in Cotgrave, accorded almost reverential respect – on the strength of his fighting ability alone, he married the best-looking girl in the village, Helen Grice, sister of Rob. But he hadn't grown an inch since turning sixteen, and by twenty-one Stevie was trading on his reputation. One day, Helen left him and took up with a young lad called Chris McCann. A furious Stevie resolved to give McCann the beating he deserved – after all, the cheeky bastard had been a skinny young tyke three years below us at school last time he'd seen him. And that was the problem. In the interim, McCann had put on about two feet and five stone, and had joined the Parachute Regiment.

One night they bumped into each other in the Rose and Crown in the village. The eighteen-year-old McCann was a head taller and twice as wide as his adversary, but Stevie was as game as they come and quite undeterred by mere reality.

'You!' he said, in the time-honoured manner. 'Outside!'

'I don't want to fight you, Stevie,' said Chris, calmly.

'You should have thought about that before you started messing about with my missus,' spat Stevie.

'She isn't your missus,' said Chris. 'You've split up.'

'Are you coming outside,' Stevie ranted, prodding Chris in the chest, 'or are we having it in here?'

Sighing, Chris drained his pint and walked out to the car park. Stevie followed, tearing off his jacket as he went, and immediately punched Chris in the face as hard as he could. It was like a fly attacking a car windscreen: McCann didn't even blink.

'You can have that one for free,' he said. 'Let's leave it there.'

Instead, Stevie pulled back his arm and ran in again. McCann knocked him out with a single punch. Stevie was a broken man after that. He took to drink, and ended up being murdered when he picked a fight with a man armed with a knife. But it wasn't the loss of Helen that did for him; it was the loss of his status as Cotgrave's hardest man.

Around then, I decided to get myself a girlfriend. But I was going to struggle as a fork-lift truck driver in a petfood warehouse, and I didn't fancy fighting Chris McCann for Helen Grice. I needed something else in my life to make people respect me.

So I became a football hooligan.

CHAPTER FIVE: STREET FIGHTING MAN

Thirty-five years to silk

THE LATE SEVENTIES WAS the golden age of the hooligan. Every team had its firm, and Forest's was The Mad Squad. About a thousand strong, the core membership was the fifty-three of us who travelled to away matches on a coach organised by our leader, Mick Randall.

Randall's role within The Mad Squad was a bit like that of Butch Cassidy in The Hole in the Wall Gang: anyone was free to challenge him, but nobody did. Comprehensively tattooed, Mick stood 6ft 2in, weighed around nineteen stone, and took no shit from anyone. An ex-miner, he worked on building sites and had built up a fearsome resistance to Arctic temperatures. This was handy because, like most of the lads, he saw the wearing of a coat as an admission of homosexuality. Whatever the weather, Mick wore a white, cap-sleeve T-shirt – except on Saturday nights, when you needed a collar to get into the nightclubs. Then, bowing to convention, he would pull on a flimsy, short-sleeved polyester thing which was so thin that he rolled it into a ball and carried it around stuffed into his jeans pocket until the time came to join the queue for Annabel's (the one on Victoria Street in Nottingham, not the one in Berkeley Square frequented by John Aspinall and Aristotle Onassis). Surely no non-iron Ben Sherman shirt ever faced a sterner test?

Mind you, Nottingham's women were even hardier. It might be twenty below, but they'd still be staggering around in white stilettos, crop-tops and micro-skirts, revealing acres of mottled, corned beef flesh. It was after a Friday night encounter with one of these girls that Mick finally established himself as the indisputable king of the 'coats are for poofs' crowd.

Forest were away at Blackburn, which meant a crack-of-dawn start on Saturday. There were fifty-two of us already on the bus, and we were beginning to think that Mick wouldn't make it when he strolled into the Cotgrave Miners' Welfare Car Park, and thence into local legend. It was early January, the snow was a foot deep, and expectant undertakers were loitering outside the bingo halls. I was wearing two pairs of socks, my mum's tights, thermals, trousers, a shirt, a jumper, a trench coat, gloves, a hat and a scarf, and I was still absolutely freezing. Most of the other lads were shivering along in similar clothing, and one or two had brought hot water bottles and sleeping bags. Even the 'coats are for poofs' crowd were wearing jumpers over their T-shirts, although I remember Gary Duxbury had on nothing but a string vest.

Then Mick turned up. He was no Brad Pitt, and that and his obsessive love of football – he made Nick Hornby seem like a fair-weather fan – restricted his opportunities with the opposite sex. So Mick was on the horns of a dilemma. He'd spent the previous night with a girl, and he needed to tell the world. But he couldn't just start bragging about it. He had to be subtle.

And so it was that, utilising all the craft at his disposition, Mick strolled onto that Baltic car park, naked from the waist up. Several people gasped, and a couple of the 'coats are for poofs' crowd quickly muttered that they were a bit hot, and peeled off their jumpers; I'm sure Duxbury would have removed his string vest had he still had the use of his fingers.

But it was too late, anyway: Mick was king.

We got off the coach with admiring and incredulous cries of, 'Christ, Mick, aren't you cold?'

'You must be joking,' he said. 'I'm boiling!'

And then, stretching his arms high above his head into a gigantic yawn, he turned his back on us to reveal – accidentally, you understand – great claw marks in his flesh.

'Bloody hell, Mick,' I said. 'What's happened to your back?'

'What are you on about?' he said, innocently, and making as though to turn his 22in neck around to see for himself.

I fed him the line. 'It's covered in scratches.'

'Is it?' he said, a ham actor's best stab at an expression of puzzlement settling on his features. Then the moment of realisation. 'Oh, yeah,' he said, nonchalantly, with a raise of his eyebrows and a wry smile. 'That'll be that bird I picked up last night.'

Then we all piled back on to the bus and set off for Blackburn. I can't remember what went on that day, but it probably involved a fight. Hooliganism made perfect sense to us; I can tell you that there are few things in life more exciting than running, outnumbered – outnumbered is the important part – at a gang of rival youths, with fists bunched and wickedness in your heart.

We were looking for trouble, certainly, but – and this is the other important thing to remember – we only fought those who wanted it. At least, that was true of the principled and honourable lads. A minority were bullies and cowards, and they caused big problems for the rest of us. One such was a chap whom I'll call The Ferret. One of the oldest youths on our bus, he talked a good game but was mysteriously absent when anything happened. I only ever saw him hit one person, a young boy of about fourteen at Blackpool. We saw the lad standing at a bus stop near Bloomfield Road, an orange scarf tied around his wrist. He looked fearfully at us, but he was a civilian so we ignored him. All except for The Ferret.

'Give me your scarf,' he snarled.

The boy did as he was told, but it didn't save him; The Ferret grabbed it, and then punched him in the face, knocking him over. I was appalled, but The Ferret was much older than me and I was too scared to intervene. Fortunately, others were equally appalled, but not at all scared.

One was Paul Scarrott – Nottingham's most infamous hooligan, a man named by the tabloid press as 'England's Number One Yob', and who had proved his loyalty to our club by having 'FOREST' tattooed on the inside of his lower lip. Scarrott grabbed The Ferret roughly by the collar.

'What the fuck did you do that for?' he spat.

'He's one of their main crew,' said The Ferret, pleadingly. 'I've seen him before.'

'He's a little kid!' said Scarrott.

Mick Randall snatched the scarf back and handed it to the boy, whom he had picked up from the floor. The lad was sobbing quietly, blood running from his nose.

Scarrott turned The Ferret around, pinning the bully's arms up behind his back.

'Do you want to smack this twat in the face?' he said. 'I'll hold his arms.'

The boy shook his head fearfully.

'Do you want me to do it?' said Scarrott.

The boy nodded almost imperceptibly, and Scarrott immediately spun The Ferret around and punched him in the face. He fell to the floor, clutching his own bloodied nose.

'We're The Mad Squad,' said Scarrott, 'and we don't hit kids.'

The Ferret skulked off for the rest of the day, but he was shameless and he was back on the coach to the next match as if nothing had happened. His downfall came a year later, when fifteen of us caught a regular bus north to see Forest play Manchester United. We split into five groups of three to make ourselves less conspicuous, and I was with Jack Riley and 'Midnight' Joe Cyster. Our route took us past a pub which was teeming with United fans. We did our best to ignore them and just carried on walking, but one of them hurried over.

'Have you got the time, lads?' he asked.

This was the universal hooligan's question: no self-respecting hooligan wore his team's colours, but your accent told the questioner where you were from. The only accent we had between us was pure Notts. What were we to do?

Luckily Jack had a plan.

'It's Forest time!' he said, and put the questioner on his arse with a straight right.

The bloke's friends immediately started over to get stuck into us, but the rest of our crew had run to back us up and the United lot disappeared back into the pub. We swaggered off, happy with the outcome of our first meeting with the opposition…

…for about thirty seconds.

Then the doors to the pub flew back open, and a horde of vengeful United supporters streamed out. We legged it, and piled inside a Brentford Nylons store, locking the door behind us. Unfortunately, Man U fans are nylon aficionados and they knew the store like the backs of their hands; even as we celebrated our narrow escape, the rear doors burst open and hundreds of Mancs poured in. Like Vikings who had burned their own boat, we formed a tight circle and awaited our fate. The battle raged for several minutes before the police arrived; we ended up bloodied and bruised but unbowed, our circle unbroken, and having given at least as good as we got.

All except The Ferret. He was nowhere to be seen.

The police first cleared the United fans from the store, and then decided to escort us to the ground.

'Right, are you all ready?' said a sergeant.

'One of them ran downstairs when the fight started,' said a member of the Brentford Nylons staff.

The sergeant went to have a look and we all followed him. There was a furniture department down the stairs, full of beds and chests, but there was no sign of The Ferret. Then, just as we were about to give up looking for him, we heard a faint sobbing noise. The sergeant opened the door of a wardrobe. The Ferret was hiding in the bottom of it, snivelling.

'Alright, lads?' he said, wiping his eyes and getting up to step out of the wardrobe. 'I was just looking for some tools to sort them United bastards out.'

He was thick-skinned enough to try to get on the bus for the next away match, but Mick Randall was having none of it.

'Sorry,' he said. 'No wankers.'

CHAPTER FIVE: STREET FIGHTING MAN

* * *

CONVERSELY, AND I CONFESS not wholly deservedly, my own reputation was very high indeed. Thanks to thirty pints a weekend and a diet of kebabs and Chinese, I now weighed fifteen stone. (At the time I thought this was fat, but it's a weight which, regrettably, I haven't seen for some years.) This excess of *avoirdupois* meant that, whenever our fans ran away from a scrap, I was somewhat handicapped, and odds-on to be caught by the opposition.

As a result, I was forever to be seen exhorting our firm to 'Stand and fight!' and I developed, somewhat accidentally, a reputation as a man without fear, whereas the truth was I was in a permanent state of abject terror.

I also acquired a nickname, one of which any self-respecting hooligan would be proud: 'Animal.'

Young up-and-comers were anxious to address me as such in the street.

'Alright, Animal?' they would say, nervously.

'Alright, lads,' I would nod back, gravely.

In fact, people from those days still address me as Animal when I see them, and I'm happy to answer to it: it was a name which seemed to speak to my courage and ferocity, and it brought me respect and notoriety in Nottingham and beyond.

It's a good thing that most people didn't know how I'd come by it.

Whenever Forest were playing in the North West, our coach would go through Derby, and we would stop there to stock up on free drink at a Lipton's supermarket on the ring road, in a sort of cross between *Supermarket Sweep* and *Crimewatch*. We'd arrive mid-morning, the bus would empty, and nearly everybody would converge on the drinks aisle, like a plague of thieving locusts. The skeleton staff would try in vain to stop us, but within five minutes the entire section would have been stripped bare, and we'd be on our way.

I say 'we', but I was never actually involved in pinching booze. No: while my colleagues were grabbing all the alcohol they could carry, I could be found elsewhere in the shop – loading up with gastronomic necessities. When I returned to the bus I would be laden with biscuits, cakes and sweets and, as the rest of the lads cracked open cans of lager and bottles of whisky, I would be tucking into a family-sized Mr Kipling Bakewell tart, or chomping on a giant Swiss roll.

On one warm, early-season morning, I came back to the bus with a huge block of Walls ice cream and a packet of wafers. I had no way of cutting it up, so I simply put a wafer at each end of the block and ate it like that.

The rest of the lads broke off from their drinking and stared at me, aghast.

'I don't believe you, Gary,' said one of them, the improbably-named Herman Lyking. 'You're a fucking animal!'

Thereafter, I was known as 'Animal'.

* * *

IN SPITE OF MY NATURAL cowardice, I did do my share of fighting – when it was absolutely unavoidable. There was one occasion in Liverpool where we were being chased all over Stanley Park and I hid behind a coach. I soon heard a horde of what I assumed were ferocious Scousers running down the street towards me. Having no choice but to make a stand, I jumped out and smashed the first lad in the face as he drew near. He didn't so much walk onto the punch, he ran onto it like Wile E Coyote; his head stayed stationary on the end of my fist but the rest of him carried on running until he was horizontal in the air, before he fell to the ground with a thud, spark out.

I turned to front out his mates; there were about ten of them, so I tensed myself for an almighty kicking. It's hard to explain how frightening this sort of experience is, and how the adrenalin surges, to the point where you can scarcely see straight, never mind think clearly. Luckily, the other gang were similarly affected and, to my relief and amazement, they turned and fled as one.

This was an interesting example of the strange behaviour of crowds in violent situations. Very often, small groups can see off far larger ones, and I've been on both sides of that. I was once one of a group of four Forest fans, along with 'Boo' Buxton, Colin Henderson and Mick Randall, which was being followed by a group of several hundred Sheffield United fans. The Sheffield lads made a lot of threatening noises, but it was like Grandmother's Footsteps; every time one of us turned round to front them, they all scattered. Finally we could take it no more. We turned and charged at them, and they all legged it.

Anyway, back in Liverpool, I made my way to our bus and took my seat. I was feeling pretty pleased with myself for having chased off ten Scousers, and I was still boasting of my exploits when one of our own chaps climbed aboard with a busted face and a sorrowful expression. My heart sank. I'd clearly dished out some friendly fire.

'Christ,' said Mick Randall, to my bloodied victim. 'What happened to you?'

'There was ten of them,' he replied, wincing. 'I dropped the first two, but then they got me.'

Over time, I became one of the best-known hooligans in Nottingham, though fortunately I never achieved national infamy. Only one Forest fan did so, the aforementioned Paul Scarrott. Scarrott wasn't the toughest member of The Mad Squad, and there were others much stronger than him, but he had the heart of a lion and he was also a man of fierce integrity. He *always* wanted trouble, but he was only interested in fighting men bigger than himself, or groups of opposition hooligans who outnumbered us greatly. He never used a weapon and, although I saw him take some fearful kickings, I never saw him take a backwards step.

His finest moment came at Derby, our deadliest rivals. Home and away fans were strictly segregated, but attempts were often made to insinuate yourselves onto the opposing terraces, and I had reluctantly joined a small raiding party which managed to sneak in to the Derby end. We installed ourselves next to their unsuspecting main crew, who were all chanting abuse at our fans; on the agreed signal, we launched ourselves at them. They scattered in surprise and terror, but regrouped and launched a fearsome counter-attack when they saw how few we were. We fought a furious rearguard action until – eventually – the police battled their own way into the stand, dragged us clear and expelled us from the ground.

These were naïve times, and we simply paid again to re-enter our own end, confident that we had done our bit for the honour of Forest. All save Scarrott, who wanted to get back in amongst it. A few of us had suffered quite nasty injuries, and there was little appetite for a rematch, so we left him to go alone into the seats above the Derby lot. A few minutes later, we watched in awe as he stood above them, whipping them into an hysterical frenzy with abuse and gestures, before diving over the balcony into the fray. For some time, until the police arrived to save Derby from further punishment, it was Scarrott against several thousand.

He attended every England away match, and was arrested for fighting opposing fans in all four corners of the globe. He was convicted of football-related violence forty times, was sent to prison on thirteen occasions, and became a national anti-hero. I remember one of those occasions which ended in him being jailed. We had invaded the pitch at Oldham, charged the whole length of the field, and attacked the opposition in their own stand. After a brief but bloody battle, the police winkled us out and twelve of us, including Scarrott and me, were marched out of the ground and locked in the back of a police van. We were kept there for the rest of the match, which gave Scarrott the chance to come up with a plan.

'Listen,' he said, 'we're all going to end up being charged. Let's jump them when they open the van. They might catch a couple of us, but that's better than us all getting done, int it?'

We all murmured our assent, although privately I had no intention of attacking any coppers. Currently, I faced a fine. If I assaulted a police officer, it was prison for sure.

A few minutes later the doors were opened. Scarrott leapt into action with a bloodcurdling oath, and attacked the surprised policeman on the other side – as the rest of us sat tight and watched. Scarrott was soon overpowered, forced to the floor and cuffed. The officer who had originally opened the back of our van, his nose now streaming blood, turned to us.

'Right, lads,' he said. 'Off you go. You've missed the game, let that be a lesson to you.'

With that, they threw the cursing Scarrott into the van and drove off. He received three months in jail for his pains.

I last saw him in France in 1995 – long after I had undergone a series of dramatic life changes, and was now a rising barrister. Forest were playing Auxerre in the UEFA Cup 4th round, and I had driven over to see the game. I was sitting outside a wine bar in the afternoon sunshine, enjoying a decent glass of Côte-Rôtie, when he walked past with a group of younger lads. They were all clearly looking for trouble.

'Alright, Animal,' he said, spotting me loafing there.

'Alright, Paul,' I replied.

Two months later he collapsed and died in Spain. The cause of death remains a mystery, but the news was greeted with glee by some – Tony Parsons in *The Daily Mirror*, for instance, described his condition as 'satisfactory'.

I recall an incident which serves as a better epitaph than Parsons' gratuitous attack.

After a game at Anfield, we had gone in search of Liverpool's main firm. That was rash. You'd be safer picking a fight with Al-Qaeda in the Bora Bora caves, and thousands of them ambushed our twenty-strong group, pelting us with rocks, bricks and milk bottles. When the police arrived, ambulances were called for several seriously injured lads, and the eight of us who were unhurt, myself included, were loaded into the back of a police Transit and told we'd been nicked for violent disorder.

There were four officers already inside, and they told us to sit on the benches running along either side of the van. We did as we were told, but one officer then piped up: 'Not the nigger, he can sit on the floor.'

Jack Riley, the one black guy among the eight, was clearly no stranger to this sort of thing. He sat on the floor with a weary sigh.

One of the other officers turned to the chap nearest to Jack.

'Is he your mate?' he said.

'Yes,' said the Forest fan.

The officer punched him in the face.

'I'll ask you again,' snarled the custodian of law and order. 'Is he your fucking mate?'

The man, his nose streaming blood, looked down at the floor.

'No,' he said, quietly.

They continued along the line, asking the same question, and each man they asked shamefacedly denied that Jack was his friend. I was at the end of the line, wrestling with mounting fear. Jack *was* my friend, and I was determined to say so. But did I have the courage?

I was saved by Paul Scarrott.

'Yes, he's my mate,' said Paul, looking the copper in the eye.

Smash!

Paul ignored the blood flowing over his mouth, and stared at the officer with contempt.

'Is he your mate?'

'Yes.'

Smash!

'I said, is he your fucking mate?'

'Yes!'

This time, all four coppers set upon him, beating him savagely.

'Is he your fucking mate?' screamed one of them, grabbing Paul by the throat. By that time he was in a pretty bad way, but, through puffed and bloodied lips, he spat back, defiantly, 'Yes, he fucking is!'

At that, the police officers realised that they'd gone too far. After a brief conference outside the van, they opened the doors.

'Fuck off,' they said, 'and don't come back!'

I hope I'd have been as brave as Paul Scarrott. I'm glad I was never put to the test. I wonder what Tony Parsons would have done?

From certain points of view, of course, Parsons was right. Perhaps there is no place for men like Paul Scarrott in modern Britain. But then, if it hadn't been Derby fans he'd dived into, but Napoleon's men at Waterloo, and if it hadn't been a police officer he'd attacked at Oldham, but an SS storm trooper at Arnhem, he would have been a national hero. Football hooliganism is the legacy of lies told by the ruling classes to the working classes. We were force-fed patriotism and jingoism for centuries: without it, who would fight and die for so little reward during all those years of Empire? And what was the method of maximising the working class's desire to commit acts of violence? Make sure they love Queen and country, and make sure they hate Johnny Foreigner.

But the xenophobic beast is an unruly one. We grew up on a diet of *Commando* comics, full of 'Krauts' and 'Japs' yelling 'Achtung!' and 'Banzai!' before dying in a hail of good old British lead. We were born to fight Germans – and if there were no Germans to fight then we'd make do with lads in the next street, the next village, or supporters of Derby County. Scarrott had no time for terrorising innocent people; he just liked fighting other men who liked fighting, and he lived and died by the maxim, '*Dulce et Decorum est pro* Forest *mori*.'

* * *

BY GREAT GOOD fortune, I was only ever charged with one football hooliganism offence. On our way back from Manchester, we had stopped in Chesterfield for a drink at The Painted Wagon, then the home pub of the Chesterfield Town hooligan element. A vicious battle soon broke out, which only ended when two vanloads of riot officers arrived. By then, the pub was wrecked, and we were all arrested. The landlord, identifying the perpetrators, alleged that I had thrown a bar stool at the optics.

It was absolute rubbish – I'd been fighting off two Chesterfield fans on the pool table at the time – but I was charged with violent disorder and remanded to appear at Chesterfield Magistrates. Luckily, I secured the services of a brilliant young solicitor from Nottingham who was the discerning football thug's lawyer of choice; he tied the prosecution up in knots and got the case against me laughed out of court.

It was the first time I had met this solicitor; it wouldn't be the last.

This run-in with the law helped to persuade me to pack in the hooliganism. I still bump into a lot of the old Mad Squad hooligans at Forest matches to this day, and the majority of us look back on our youthful indiscretions with a measure of embarrassment. A small hard core are still at it, into their fifties. I don't condone that – I think it's rather pathetic – but in some ways I can understand it. Like many of us, I moved on to achieve other things in life, which brought me a little of the respect I suppose we all crave. But there are those for whom those doors never open, and their fighting reputation is all they have.

And, if I'm honest, there was another reason I retired. One night after a game in Derby, I nipped into an alleyway for a pee. When I came back, The Mad Squad had vanished, to be replaced by several hundred local savages.

'Where you from, mate?' said one huge lout (since the Derby accent is very close to Nottingham's, the old 'what's the time?' trick wouldn't work).

'Spondon,' I said, naming the first Derby suburb that came to mind.

'What street?' he said.

Football legend had it that if you hit the biggest member of a rival gang, and hit him hard enough, the rest would run away.

'Forest Street!' I snarled, and punched him in the nose. It was a fantastic punch, if I say so myself, and the effect on his mates was instantaneous.

They pounced on me and kicked the living shit out of me for what seemed like weeks.

Eventually, The Mad Squad turned up and made it more even, but I was *hors de combat*. After it was over, I was taken to hospital. The damage was only superficial – a couple of black eyes, a missing tooth, a cauliflower ear, two broken ribs and a broken arm – but it was time for Animal to hand in his cards.

Surely there were better things to do of a Saturday?

CHAPTER SIX: MOVING ON

Thirty-four years to silk

I WAS A WAGE-EARNER, I had a steady girlfriend, Sally Robinson, from nearby Keyworth, and I was a widely-respected man who retained a blood-curdling and awe-inspiring nickname.

Life was good.

But one Sunday evening I came home from the pub to find my father sitting on the sofa with my mother, watching television, like he'd never been away.

I stood there, dumbstruck with horror and swaying drunkenly.

'Where have you been?' he said, his eyes blazing. 'You're pissed.'

'I've had a couple.'

'You reckon you're the big man now, do you, going down the pub, coming in when you like?'

'No,' I said, weakly, looking away.

'Get to bed,' he said, with a contemptuous laugh.

Off I went: my reign as man of the house was over.

Next morning, I crept out to work. I'd bought myself a moped on hire purchase, and I pushed it half a mile before I dared start it up, so scared was I of disturbing his sleep.

Later, my mum told me that he had returned from Blackpool but had shacked up with another woman in Ollerton, and had transferred to Ollerton Colliery. But he'd felt so guilty about leaving his family, she said, that he'd decided to come home. I had my doubts, but I soon fell back into going round to Steven Savage's house until the pubs were open. I remember saying wistfully to Steve that he was lucky his family were so much wealthier than mine. They had a better car, a colour television, a phone, and took summer holidays together. Steve pointed out that our dads did the same job, for the same wage; mine just spent his money on beer and fags, whereas Tony Savage put his wife and kids first. He was right. Ours had long been one of the poorest and worst-dressed families in Cotgrave. I'd often had no trousers or shoes for school – or, rather, I had some, but my trousers had no knees or arse left in them, and my shoes were lined with cardboard wrapped in plastic carrier bags to plug the holes in the soles.

You may be wondering why I didn't deal with my father. After all, I was Animal – the infamous hooligan. I was over six feet tall and I weighed fifteen stone – possibly sixteen, by now. Surely I could have handled a spindly, 5ft 2in midget? Maybe, but I'd never have dared try. I couldn't even meet his eye. In fairness, he was a fearsome fighter. On one occasion he beat a much larger man literally senseless in the Welfare when the man persisted in swearing in front of my mother. My father grabbed the swearer by his throat, bludgeoned him to the ground, and rained blows into his bloodied face, screaming, 'Swear in front of a lady would you!'

I found it astonishing, and still do, that he thought that his own behaviour towards my mother was acceptable – or that women might be upset by swearing, but not by witnessing a man being smashed unconscious. But in so thinking I was in the minority in Cotgrave. As a result of my father's one-sided 'fight', the Welfare consulted him about codes of conduct regarding swearing. I still remember them.

> Ladies are allowed in the lounge at all times, and there is no swearing allowed.
> Ladies are not allowed in the snooker room, and swearing is freely allowed.
> Ladies are encouraged not to go into the bar, but allowed to go in if they wish. However, if they do so, they must accept that men might be swearing within.

It gave my father a taste for politics that would see him elected as the mayor of Newark several years later.

Fear infested our house. When we did not greet him like the returning hero, he fell back into that familiar, permanent rage. Even my mother started to avoid him, and I can only recall spending any time at all with him once during that period. I broke my arm falling off my moped, and was taken to hospital by ambulance. That was at about 7pm. My father finally arrived to give me a lift home, pissed, at 11pm. Neither of us said a word, and when we got home I hurried straight off to bed.

A few days later, he walked out again, for good – he even took *Frankie Laine's Greatest Hits* with him. This time, mum suffered no nervous breakdown. She was upset, but she had a part-time job and a social circle of her own. She bought herself a copy of Gloria Gaynor's *I Will Survive*, dusted herself down, and got on with her life.

And I got on with my life on the Pedigree Wholesale fork-lift – though not for much longer.

* * *

IT ALL CAME TO an end one Monday morning in the summer of 1978. I was helping Sandy the Hayman unload his lorry load of hay, and will forever be grateful for the advice he gave me that day. I was glad to be out in the sunshine, but it was quite a time-consuming task and, as my tummy started rumbling, I asked Sandy for the time.

'It's half-past eleven,' he said.

'Damn,' I muttered.

'What time would you like it to be?' he said.

'Half-twelve,' I said, with a grin. 'Dinner time!'

'If you could click your fingers and make it half-twelve, would you do it?'

'Too right.'

'What if you could click your fingers and make it clocking-off time? Would you do that?'

'Like a shot.'

'What about clocking off on a Friday?'

'Better still,' I grinned back.

'I don't know,' he said, shaking his head. 'What the fuck's a young lad like you doing working here, wishing your life away?'

As I ate my sandwiches, I looked at Crombie and the others. Was it my imagination, or did they look a little older and greyer? At ten-to-one, I got to my feet. Crombie glanced up.

'Hooter hasn't gone yet,' he said. 'Where are you going?'

'To hand in my notice,' I said.

It's the only time I recall him being lost for words.

Horace wrote over two thousand years ago that men do more from habit than reason, and the call of habit certainly tempted me to stay in the rut into which I had been born. I agonised over my decision during the four-week notice period, and on more than one occasion I found myself halfway up the stairs to Derek Slater's office to tell him that I'd changed my mind. Like an institutionalised prisoner, I had got used to the stability and security of my life. I was striking out for the shore, but I felt like I was being swept into the open sea. What on earth had I done?

Eventually, though, reason won out, I stuck with my decision and, much to my mother's dismay, I was soon unemployed.

I woke up on the Saturday morning after my last day at work feeling unbelievably happy, and utterly free. By a quirk of fate, I actually know the date. I remember lounging on the sofa, watching a documentary on the Egyptian Queen Cleopatra, who had – it was said – committed suicide on that particular date in 30AD. Thanks to the wonders of modern technology (i.e. Wikipedia), I have been able to establish that Cleopatra died on August 12.

The Glorious Twelfth! The day that my life began to have

purpose! The day when – in spite of my mother's protestations to the contrary – everything would start getting a whole lot better!

Crazy, naïve fool that I was.

* * *

I HAD A PLAN. I was finally going to make something of myself, finally going to *be* someone.

I had resolved to become a fireman.

I enrolled immediately, but was left kicking my heels before my training course started in November, three or four months away. To tide myself over, I started work at Bell-Fruit Games as a gaming machine tester. My job was to play fruit machines all day and check that they were paying out the required eighty per cent. It would have taken forever to do this by feeding coins laboriously into the machines, so they were left open and I simply clicked up credits on the meter by repeatedly pushing down a metal wire which lay across the coin chute. It was while engaged in this task that I realised how easy it would be to defraud them.

At home that evening, I drilled a hole in a 10p piece and tied a length of fishing line to the coin. Next morning, I dangled it into the slot until it hit the wire which crossed the chute.

It clocked up a credit!

Instead of letting the coin drop down, I pulled it back slightly and released it onto the wire again.

It clocked up another credit!

I could clock up unlimited credits, *gratis*, but that was in laboratory conditions. I resolved to try it out in the pub that night. In twenty minutes, I'd won all the money in the machine, about eight pounds. After a couple of drinks, I moved on to another pub, and took my magic coin with me.

Clearly, I could make more money out of Bell-Fruit illegitimately than I ever could by working for them, so I resigned and went travelling round the country with a chap called John, the father of a friend of mine. He drove me from pub to pub, and we played on and won from fruit machines with monotonous regularity. It was great fun, but after a couple of months it came to an abrupt end in a pub in Southwell. I knew something was wrong about the pub almost as soon as we walked in – there were too many eyes looking too closely, and not enough hubbub and drinking. But John wouldn't have it, and, since he was in his forties, and was driving, I felt I had to stay. Just as I had feared, as we were leaving the pub the long arm of the law, attached to a very large undercover police officer, tapped me on the shoulder.

'Could I have a word please?' he said.

My first instinct was to run, and I duly followed it, but as my pockets were weighed down with about two hundred pounds-worth of 10p pieces he was able to overtake me at a reasonably brisk walk. I was taken to the police station and interviewed, and although I later told everyone that my confession had been beaten out of me with truncheons I was actually so scared that I admitted everything in about two minutes flat. I think that disappointed the officers: as soon as I was locked in a cell, the fellow who had arrested me grabbed my ear and started to twist it, implying that unless I told them everything they wanted to know they would kick it out of me, but before he'd completed half a twist I was singing like the proverbial canary.

So was John, apparently, because a few minutes later the police came back and started asking questions about people I had never heard of. It turned out that John had passed on my method to others, and that a large gang of fruit machine defrauders was operating across the Midlands.

The police were worried that, if we were bailed, we would alert the others, and thus thwart their attempts to capture the whole gang, so the following morning they applied to the court for a remand in custody. The magistrates didn't need much persuading, and ordered us locked up until the following Monday, five days away.

I was held at the police station, rather than on remand, and spent my time in a tiny cell, twenty-four hours a day. All my meals were served through a hole in the door by a policeman, and other than that there was no-one to talk to. There was also nothing to do, and nothing to read – Kevin visited me, but helpfully forgot to bring any books. At least the lights were left on all night.

It was hell, and if you think I exaggerate then try locking yourself into a bare room, with only a light bulb to look at, for five days, and see how it goes.

I remember thinking at the time that I had surely hit rock bottom in life.

How wrong I was – I had barely started sinking.

When we went back to court I was *desperate* for bail, but the police still hadn't caught the rest of the gang and were granted another remand in custody. This time it was for a week, though at least I was taken to a prison, which was a major improvement on the solitude and boredom of the police cell. Still, the week passed more and more slowly until, the night before my next court appearance, the clock practically stopped. If I'd been remanded into custody again I'd have been on suicide watch but, to my relief, the prosecution confirmed that they had rounded up the other suspects and did not oppose bail.

The night of my release was amazingly uplifting. I drank in the air of liberty like the chap from *The Shawshank Redemption*, and almost skipped down to Cotgrave Youth Club (where I was greeted like a minor celebrity). I can't begin to describe the wonderful feeling that came over me; I vowed that I would never again take my freedom for granted, and that I would never waste another day.

That vow lasted almost a whole week, until the intoxication wore off and I slipped back into my everyday life.

There was light at the end of the tunnel, though. A few weeks later, my Fire Brigade training began at Leicester.

I don't know if I'd ever have made it as a fireman. I was physically fit and strong enough for the job, if perhaps a little corpulent, and I found the academic side of it facile, but it was such an anal and disciplined environment that I doubt I could have hacked it for the three months of training, never mind as a career. As it was, this was not a question I had to confront.

On our first day, we were issued with a brand new uniform – all nicely pressed – and told to change and report for an inspection. We all had the same shiny shoes, crisply-ironed white shirts, and Fire Brigade suits, and you might assume there could be absolutely nothing to choose between us on our first parade. But then you were not the examining officer.

'Bell,' he bellowed, as we stood at a loose approximation of attention. 'Look at the state of you, man! You look like a sack of shit tied up with string!'

I couldn't fault him: clothes don't hang well on me. And it was downhill from there. I couldn't iron, and I certainly couldn't polish shoes, and I ended up taking a tip in that regard from an ex-Army chap called Scotch Mick, who advised me to spray them with Finish furniture polish. The effect was amazing. My boots were suddenly shiny all over, after three seconds' effort! I muttered my thanks to my saviour as we walked out to the next parade but he waved them away – with an ominous aside.

'We'll be alright,' he said, 'as long as it doesn't rain.'

I heard the first clap of thunder as we walked across the yard.

My footwear earned the lot of us a three-mile cross-country run, after which everyone else was allowed to go off duty whilst I cleaned all of their boots. Three hours it took me, and my hand still aches at the memory of it. I considered resigning, but in the event I didn't have to.

Shortly afterwards, I had to take a day off to go to court. My solicitor had warned me that I faced a possible prison sentence, even if I pleaded guilty, so I had to inform the Fire Brigade and hope they showed mercy.

They sacked me on the spot (though they dressed it up as a resignation):

memorandum   **Fire Service**

to Fm. Bell G.T., from Chief Fire Officer
   33 Hickling Way,
   Cotgrave,
   Nottingham

please ask for **S.A.O.**
int tel 135
date 18th December 1978
your ref
our ref ML/SC/BPers.

CONFIDENTIAL

RESIGNATION

I have your memorandum dated 15th December 1978, and accept your resignation from the Fire Service, which will take effect from midnight Sunday 31st December 1978.

... Will you please complete and return the enclosed Form SU/2 for refund of your superannuation contributions.

CHIEF FIRE OFFICER

Please arrange to hand your kit in to Stockhull Stores as soon as possible.
SAO.

NCC/FIRE/0614/9.75

* * *

I TURNED UP, trembling, at court in my next-door neighbour Rob Allwood's dad Horace's forty-year-old demob suit, and was herded into the dock with John and four other men I didn't know.

CHAPTER SIX: MOVING ON

We all pleaded guilty to conspiracy to defraud. The prosecutor outlined the facts and our barristers put our mitigation to the judge. As the youngest by about twenty years, I was the first to be sentenced.

'This was a serious and far-reaching conspiracy which was only made possible by your criminal genius,' said the judge.

That was a nice touch, I think, though at the time I was too busy trying to stop trembling to appreciate it.

'If it hadn't been for you devising this system in the first place, the crimes would never have taken place. I take into account the fact that this is your first offence, but only a prison sentence is appropriate. You will go to prison for six months.'

I almost swooned, and two very large gaolers took my arms. *Six months!* How was I going to manage that? *Twelve days* on remand had almost killed me.

Whether the judge could see these thoughts etched in my face, or whether he had always intended a last-minute reprieve, I shall never know. But, as the gaolers were about to lead me down the stairs to begin my incarceration, he spoke again. 'But, in view of your age,' he said, 'I am prepared to suspend that sentence of imprisonment for two years.'

The gaolers let go of my arms, slightly reluctantly.

'You're free to go,' whispered my solicitor.

I did, at great speed. If ever anyone had learned his lesson *vis-à-vis* a life of crime, it was Gary Terence Bell.

I was going straight. Forever.

But I needed to sort myself out. I had now been a coalminer who never saw any coal, a mechanic who never saw an engine, and a fireman who never saw a fire.

I bought a *Nottingham Evening Post* and studied the situations vacant page. Martin's Builders were looking for a bricklayer's labourer. I rang up expecting to have to go for an interview, but they were absolutely desperate.

'The job's yours,' said the chap. 'Can you start today? The labourer who was on the job has gone off sick with a bug. We need you at The Meadow Covet pub in Edwalton at one o'clock. I'll let them know you're coming. It's seventy quid a week, and I'll pay you a full day today.'

'I'm on my way,' I said, gleefully.

In one bound, etc. I hurried home, changed out of Horace's suit and rushed over to The Meadow Covet.

My job was simple enough. I had to mix the 'muck' for the bricklayer and keep him supplied with that and bricks as he built an extension on the rear of the pub.

At Toot Hill Comprehensive, the school hero was a boy two years older than me called Michael Merrill. He was an incredibly funny guy, he always nabbed the lead role in the school play, he had plenty of girls after him, and he was a good sportsman, too. In the American tradition, he'd have been voted 'Most Likely to Succeed', hands down. I often wondered what had happened to Michael Merrill.

Now I knew. He was a bricklayer at Martin's Builders.

Not the next day, he wasn't. He succumbed to the same bug which had laid the labourer low. The boss turned up tearing his hair out. Apparently, there were severe penalty clauses in operation if the job wasn't finished on time, and he was desperate.

'Do you know how to lay bricks?' he said, with a sort of hunted look about him.

'No,' I said.

'But you saw how Michael was laying them yesterday?' He was clutching at a water-logged straw.

'Er… I suppose so.'

'Just do the same as he did, then.'

'But it's a skilled job,' I protested. 'I'll be useless. It will look terrible.'

'It's only the damp course,' he said. 'The trench will be back-filled and no one will see it.'

And that was it. With four-and-a-half hours' experience as a bricklayer's labourer under my belt, I had been promoted to bricklayer. I believe it is normally a five-year apprenticeship.

I managed to lay the bricks in a reasonably straight line, though the cement between them was at least two inches thick and it did look terrible. Still, as the boss had said, it was only the damp course. He came back to see me at the end of the day, and I'd be lying if I said he didn't wince when he saw my handiwork. But he made no mention of it. He had something else on his mind.

'This wouldn't be you would it, Gary?' he said, holding a copy of the *Evening Post*. My case was front page news, and my details were plastered all over it.

'Yes,' I said.

'I'm sorry,' he said, with a sigh. 'We can't employ blokes with criminal records. I'm going to have to let you go.'

That was the second job I'd lost in three days.

I went back to the agency who had sent me to work at Bell-Fruit. I was still registered on their books, so I didn't have to fill in another form, which was just as well, because it contained the question, 'Do you have a criminal record?'

Practically all job application forms ask the same question, and you can only write 'No' once your conviction is 'spent' under the Rehabilitation of Offenders Act 1974. For my offence, I would be entitled to answer 'No' after seven years had elapsed following my conviction. But the employment agency didn't ask, so I didn't tell. Not – as it happened – that it would have made much difference.

The way it worked was, you turned up early and waited until a job came up. Sometimes there would be nothing, but that day I was lucky. There had been a heavy snowfall overnight, and a local company wanted the snow clearing from their car park. I couldn't believe it when I got there. The car park was about the size of Wales and was covered in snow six inches thick. The personnel director gave me a shovel when I arrived at the reception and simply left me to get on with it. I had no idea where I was going to put most of the snow, but at least I could shovel the stuff at the far end over the fence into the car park next door. An hour later I had cleared approximately one car space, which left some two hundred to go. I had no feeling in any of my fingers or toes, and my trousers were sodden up to the knees. It was impossible. Wearily, I plodded back to the reception. The personnel director was there.

'How are you getting on?' he smiled.

'I'm sorry,' I replied. 'It can't be done.'

'What do you mean?' he said. 'We had an Irish lad from the agency last week and he cleared it all in less than two hours. Of course it can be done!'

'Not by me,' I said, and, handing him the shovel, I trudged out and went home.

He complained to the agency, and when I turned up the next day I was told that my services were no longer required.

Three dismissals in four days.

Now I really *was* in trouble.

* * *

EVERY JOB I APPLIED for I had that blasted form, with that nosey question about one's criminal antecedents. I always answered truthfully, and the reward for my honesty was to be turned down, repeatedly.

In desperation, I even went 'on the knock'. 'Knocking' involved going door-to-door, selling household tat made by a rogue who employed only disabled people. This entitled him to market the goods as being sold for 'the handicapped', and it did provide some disabled people with work. But I felt they were really an excuse for emotionally blackmailing housewives. For everything sold, we received forty per cent, the van driver twenty per cent, and the rogue the remaining forty per cent. I believe the disabled got everything left over after he had purchased his country mansion, his Rolls-Royce, and his boat.

My fellow knockers were mostly lice-ridden tramps. Some were clearly mentally ill, others mere alcoholics; all were unspeakably filthy. I earned between ten and fifteen pounds a day, tax-free, a very reasonable income for a young bloke, but it was soul-destroying and shameful. I did it for about a month, though it seemed very much longer.

I'd like to say I left on a point of principle, but it was because I got a job at Pork Farms.

Pork Farms is a large factory on the outskirts of Nottingham which manufactures a number of pork products, the most famous of which is their pies. Their attraction to me was that they didn't seem to mind that I had a criminal record. Certainly, I wrote mine down on my application form, and was still taken on. I suppose they reasoned that – criminal genius or not – there was nothing I could steal except pork pies, and they were sold so cheaply in the staff canteen that there would have been no point.

They were magnificent pies, too. The factory was scrupulously clean, as were the people who worked there. And the wages were good, the hours were short, and the heavily-subsidised canteen was heaven-sent for a growing boy – I was now nudging seventeen stone – who was fond of his grub.

But it was inhumanly tedious.

I worked on the production line with another new recruit, Chalkie White. Chalkie was on one side of a conveyor belt, I was on the other, and two girls sat either side of the belt a little further up. Chalkie and I would take an empty tray out of a mobile rack, line it with the greaseproof paper, and take it to the girls. The girls would take raw pies off the belt, and put them onto our trays. By the time they had finished loading the first tray, we would be ready with a new one; as they began loading up the second tray, Chalkie and I would pick up the full one, put it into another rack, and collect a third empty tray, line it with grease proof paper, and take it to the girls on the conveyor belt...

When the mobile rack was full of trays of pork pies, someone would take it off to the baking section, replacing it with a new one full of empty trays.

This continued, for ninety mind-numbing minutes at a stretch.

After a short break, it was back to the conveyor belt to start again.

Repetitive work is alright if the conversation is good, but this job actually required a surprising level of concentration, and there was no time for chat whilst the belt was running. During our breaks, Chalkie and I would go off to the canteen together, to eat subsidised sausage cobs, drink mugs of tea, and moan bitterly.

'I can't stand much more of this,' I said one morning.

Actually, it was our first morning, and I'd put in precisely ninety minutes.

'Yes,' he said. 'I won't be here much longer.'

Every break, we had the same conversation – me saying how much I hated the job, him replying that he wouldn't be there much longer. But the morning became a day, the day turned into a week, and before we knew it we'd been there a month. We received our first pay packet and, to celebrate, we went to the pub for a lunchtime drink. There were about a dozen of us there, and, as we sat supping our pints, the conversation was all about how monotonous the job was. By general agreement, Chalkie and I had drawn the shortest of a lot of short straws.

'Well, I won't be there much longer,' said Chalkie, with a rueful shake of his head.

'I won't be there *any* longer,' I replied, finishing my pint. 'I'm not going back.'

This caused general consternation, though not of the negative type. They treated me like a man trying to escape from Colditz, and all patted me on the back and shook my hand in wonderment before scurrying off back to the factory.

Chalkie was the last to leave. 'Well done, Gary,' he said, shaking my hand warmly.

'Don't go back, Chalkie,' I said, almost begging him. 'Stay and have another pint.'

'I can't,' he said. 'I need the money. But don't worry – I won't be there much longer.'

CHAPTER SEVEN: EUROPE

Thirty-three years to silk

I LEFT PORK FARMS with a month's wages, around £200. The Fire Brigade had also returned my pension payments – another £200.

I was as rich as Croesus! I ought to have saved the money, but instead I bought a tent in Milletts on a whim.

'Going camping, are you?' said the shop assistant, with a smile.

'Yes,' I said.

'Anywhere nice?'

'Yes,' I said, thinking fast. 'I'm going around the world.'

I'd always enjoyed poring over maps and atlases, and dreaming of seeing exotic locales when I was a grown-up. Well, now I *was* a grown-up. And I'd always wanted to go camping. My bedwetting had stopped me – but if it was my own tent…

A week later, on a crisp, early spring morning in 1979, a new passport and £120 in my pocket, I set off in search of fame and fortune. The evening before, my friends and family had joined me in the Welfare for a farewell drink. Some doubted my staying power, including Chad Forrest, a fat Geordie who spent every night sitting in the same chair playing dominos with his cronies.

'See you next week!' he had cackled.

'No, you won't,' I had replied. 'I'm not coming back.'

One of the few teachers who had managed to drill anything into my thick head was Mr Pierce, the French teacher, so I was heading for Paris. By early evening I had hitched my way to Dover.

'How long are you going for?' said the woman at the ticket desk.

'Forever,' I said.

'I'll do you a day return, then,' she smiled. 'It's cheaper than a single.'

Half an hour later I was on the ferry, watching the brightly-lit white cliffs receding. I left the deck for a few minutes to change my pounds into francs and then walked to the front of the boat to await my first glimpse of France.

* * *

TO MOST PEOPLE, Calais is a grimy hole, good only for cheap booze and fags, but to me it was the gateway to the world. I was the first member of my family ever to travel abroad, if you don't count wars. Most of them had barely been outside Nottingham. So it was with genuine pride that I took my first steps on foreign soil.

It was late, so I found a camp site, pitched my tent, badly, and tumbled inside, falling into a deep sleep. I woke at about five, freezing cold and soaked to the skin. My first night away, and I'd wet the sleeping bag. By then, I was only suffering this indignity a couple of times a week. Why did it have to happen on my first night away?

I trudged through the rain to the camp site sinks, washed the bag and squeezed it as dry as I could, and rolled it up into a plastic bag. After a shower, I packed away my tent. The rain had become a light drizzle, and I was feeling more positive about life as I began walking. I spotted an English-registered truck at an all-night garage, and the driver said he could take me to Paris.

'Did you come over with a lorry?' he said, as we headed off.

'No, as a foot passenger. Why?'

'Drivers are allowed to take two people on the ferry, free of charge.'

'I wish I'd known,' I said. 'I could have saved myself a tenner.'

'Remember it on the way back.'

'I'm not going back,' I said.

Four hours later he dropped me at the Port D'Asnieres, and I thanked him and walked into the famous French capital. It was a great culture shock for me. I had been to London many times (admittedly only for football matches), and it's a wonderful city with many beautiful buildings and monuments. But Paris is truly spectacular. I walked for hours, seeing the Sacré-Coeur, the Eiffel Tower, the Arc de Triomphe, the Champs Elysee, and Notre-Dame. At lunchtime, I committed the blasphemy of eating stale beef-paste-and-margarine sandwiches, washed down with Dandelion and Burdock, in the Tuileries.

With a damp sleeping bag, and having £103 left, a shade over eleven hundred francs, I treated myself to a hotel room in the Pigalle, the vice quarter. It was a chilly evening, but I sat at an outdoor table with a beer and steak-frites, watching the prostitutes sauntering up and down, and men ducking in and out of seedy bars. I would find a job in the morning. And I still had £90.

The next morning I walked the length and breadth of Paris, but found there wasn't much call for an English forklift driver with almost no French. I slunk back to my hotel in the late evening, slightly disheartened, and settled for a more frugal supper of a baguette with 'La vache qui rit' cheese spread.

Two days later, my money ran out. The hotel manager agreed to give me another night and a hundred francs for my tent; it had cost fifty pounds, and I'd only used it once, but I had no choice. Despite spending sixteen hours tramping around every bar, restaurant and hotel in the city the following day, I was again unsuccessful; that night, I slept beneath the stars in the Jardin de Luxembourg.

I spent the next week or so nursing my money and desperately looking for work, but each night sleeping rough left me filthier and filthier, and my prospects of getting a job diminished commensurately. Eventually, I admitted defeat, packed up my belongings and caught the Metro to the Porte De La Chappelle for the Autoroute north. At Calais I found a trucker who would get me onto the ferry for nothing – he even changed my remaining thirty-five francs for three pounds – and I cadged a lift in a car at Dover, Chad's mocking 'See you next week!' echoing through my mind. I'd be back for last orders in the Welfare.

The driver dropped me off near Westminster Bridge. I was going to make my way to Staples Corner, at the bottom of the M1 and a hundred and thirty miles from home, but on my way to the tube station I passed a couple of teenaged tramps.

'Spare some change, mate,' said one.

'I was going to ask you for some,' I said, with a laugh.

'Where are you staying tonight?' he said.

I was about to explain that I was on my way back to my mother's, my tail between my legs, but instead I just said, 'I don't know. Why?'

'We kip down at the Bull Ring,' said the tramp. 'Come with us if you like.'

That seemed preferable to slinking home so soon; a night in London would give me time to think.

'Sure,' I said. 'That's very kind of you.'

The Bull Ring was a huge open-air space near Waterloo. It's now the site of the British Film Institute Imax cinema, but it was then full of homeless people dossing on the concrete in cardboard boxes or sleeping bags, or gathered in groups drinking cheap cider and smoking discarded fag ends. The stink was awful. My new friends drifted off, and I got my head down somewhere, using my backpack as a pillow. People talked late into the night, but I finally fell asleep. I woke up shivering, and desperate for a wee, in the small hours, and managed to stagger twenty feet or so to relieve myself against a wall. As I turned back, I saw a shadowy figure walking away with my backpack.

'Oi!' I said. 'That's mine!'

He turned to look at me, and I stopped. He was a fierce-looking fellow.

'It fucking *was* yours!' he snarled, in a drunken Scots brogue. 'It's mine now.'

I was scared to death, but the bag contained everything I owned: passport, clothes, and my last £2.50.

'Give it back,' I demanded, in a quavering voice.

He dropped it and threw a long, slow punch towards my face. I was no Muhammad Ali, but I could certainly cope with this: I swayed back, it swung harmlessly past, and I smacked him on the nose with a stiff left. I was about to follow it with a big right, but he went straight down. With a rage entirely born of fear, I jumped on him and grabbed him by the throat.

'You thieving bastard!' I screamed.

'Please,' he begged, 'don't hit me again.'

I dragged him to his feet, where he stood, shaking. 'If I see you again,' I said, 'I swear I'll kill you.'

I didn't dare close my eyes after that, in case he came back with a knife. After a few minutes another chap came over to me.

'Well done mate,' he said. 'That bully's always stealing things off the other tramps.'

'But I'm not a tramp,' I said.

'What are you doing here, then?' he said.

'I'm only here for the night.'

'We all are, mate,' he said, with a sad smile. 'We all are.'

After daybreak, the same man came back over.

'We're off begging,' he said. 'Want to come?'

'Begging?' I said, disdainfully.

'Yes,' he said, looking surprised. 'Haven't you begged before?'

'No, I have not!' I said.

'First time for everything,' he said, clapping a hand on my shoulder. 'You can make a fiver just sitting around. Where else can you get a job like that?'

'What about your dignity?'

'You can't eat dignity, mate.'

He had a point, but I would not beg. As he wandered off, I assessed my situation. I didn't want to go home, and I couldn't get a job in France. Maybe the streets of London were paved with gold? I packed up my possessions and set off like a twentieth century Dick Whittington. I didn't do as well as Dick. I tried agencies, bars, fast-food joints… But I couldn't get a job without an address, and I couldn't get an address without a job. I couldn't even sign on for the dole without an address. I was caught on the horns of the classic homeless person's dilemma.

That night, not wanting to give my Scottish pal the chance to stab me in my sleep, I wandered off to another well-known doss spot, Lincoln's Inn Fields, where I wearily laid myself down with a bag of chips and my thoughts.

When you become a tramp, you don't start out filthy, it catches up with you. I'd been spotless when I left Nottingham, and – after a shower on the ferry – cleanish upon my return to England. But I was soon as grimy as everyone else, except that I shaved, wore deodorant, and cleaned my teeth. It didn't help my search for work. Every evening, I sat and watched the others drinking cider and eating food bought with the proceeds of their begging. My mouth watered, but I'd have died of hunger before I stooped that low.

The weather turned bitterly cold, and a Salvation Army van turned up with bread and soup. I refused it: I didn't need charity. Starving hungry, I slept in all of my clothes, with my sleeping bag wrapped in rolled-up cardboard and a huge sheet of polythene. I was still freezing. I hadn't wet myself since getting back, but it was probably because my urine had frozen overnight in my bladder.

Then, one morning, a monster stroke of luck. I found a five pound note! If I'd called out, 'Has anyone lost a fiver?' I'd have been inundated with liars, so I snatched it up. I went straight to a launderette and washed everything I owned, other than what I was wearing. Then I went to a swimming baths (as an optimist, I had packed trunks), where I swam, showered and changed into my clean clothes. Then I went back and washed my dirty stuff. I felt like a new man. *Now* we'd see about a job.

Outside the launderette, I paused, wondering whether to turn right or left. Shivering, I looked at the billboard opposite. It featured a huge palm tree, a golden beach, and the legend, 'Leave your winter blues behind and come to the South of France.'

Paris might not have worked out, but what about the Med? It had to be better than this. At least it would be warmer.

Three-pounds-fifty in my pocket, and tentless, I set off to hitch to France again.

* * *

A LORRY DRIVER on the A2 agreed to take me aboard as a free passenger. Once parked up, we went into the drivers' canteen, where a waitress brought us a menu.

'I'm not hungry, thanks,' I said, embarrassed by my impecuniosity. 'But how much is a cup of tea?'

She looked at me, quizzically. 'It's *all* free for you drivers, love,' she said.

'Everything?' I said.

'Yes.'

I quickly re-evaluated. 'In that case, I'll have the soup, please, then steak and chips, then apple crumble and custard.'

'I thought you weren't hungry?' said my driver, grinning.

'Just a bit peckish,' I said.

A basket of bread came with the soup, and I palmed most of it into my pockets for later.

We reached Calais around midnight, and my driver pushed on, keen to beat the morning traffic in Paris.

'It's nice to have someone to talk to,' he said. 'Helps me stay awake.'

I tried, I really did, but I allowed my eyes to close and the next thing I knew, it was 6am and we were pulling into a service station on the A6 south of the French capital.

'I'm turning off to Fontainebleau soon,' said the driver, 'but this takes you straight to the Med.'

Kindly, he changed my £3.50 for a fifty franc note – claiming, over my protests, to have no change – and I said my thankyous and goodbyes, and off he went. Under a sign reading *Vous êtes sur l'autoroute*

93

du soleil, I turned up my collar against the chill and went inside. Over a breakfast of French vending machine coffee and ferry bread, I studied a free map for familiar names, narrowing it down to Monte Carlo, Nice, or Cannes. I'd watched a programme about the Cannes Film Festival a couple of years before, and that made up my mind.

I made it to Lyon, three hundred miles south, by lunchtime, the French tending to regard speed limits as suggestions, and found it noticeably warmer on the south side of the old A6 tunnel. I sat in the sun under a palm tree by the river Rhone, and ate a hot baguette and drank a bottle of ice cold water, putting another of each into my rucksack before setting off again. That would last me several days if I was careful.

I wasn't. It was a great mistake buying hot bread and cold water, and it taught me a valuable lesson: buy your bread and water a couple of days before you set off, so the bread is stale and the water is warm. Then you will only eat and drink for reasons of hunger and thirst, rather than gluttony.

The afternoon took me down to Orange, and then east along the Côte D'Azur with an English trucker on his way to Naples. He dropped me off outside Cannes just after dawn, and I walked down to the town. It was as I turned onto the great Boulevard Carnot that I caught my first glimpse of the sparkling Mediterranean. Half an hour later, I was standing on the famous white sands of the Croisette, my bare feet soothed by the tideless waters. Elderly locals were hurrying past in furs and hats, but it felt like Skegness in July to me. Under their startled gaze, I changed into my trunks, dived into the water, and struck out for the horizon. After a blissful half-an-hour, I swam back to shore, where I dried in the gentle breeze as I stood looking dreamily out to sea.

Two days earlier, I had been a tramp in London. I had been right: this was a *lot* better.

I was in luck, too. Cannes was gearing up for the summer, and there was plenty of work to be done. It all presented me with an opportunity to re-invent myself. I was no longer a failed coalminer/mechanic/fireman, nor a football hooligan/convicted fraudster from tiny, grey Cotgrave. I was an international jetsetter, lothario, and all-round man-of-the-world. That night, in The Swan, an English pub on the Rue Georges Clemenceau, I found a chap who needed his yacht painting. It was the first of many jobs that I got, and quickly lost, invariably for my ineptness.

Generally, my bosses and I parted on good terms, though on one occasion I accidentally ate the captain's lunch, and on another I inadvertently spilt white paint over the owner's Ferrari.

I accept all of the blame for my third dismissal, too. Two pretty backpackers from Mississippi, one lad from a Nottinghamshire pit village who somehow manages to convince them that he owns the boat he's scrubbing, out comes the Bollinger, back comes the skipper, and the rest is history.

Not that I was always successful with the ladies. Girls did seem to find the new 'me' reasonably attractive, but I was not terribly experienced and I struggled to deliver the required goods. I wooed one girl from Hull, and made love to her on the beach. She tore off all her clothes in passion, lay down naked in the sand, and said, 'Make me come, Gary!' She might as well have asked me to make her a soufflé.

I slept on the beach, too, with dozens of other itinerants. Many begged and some stole, but I stayed on the straight-and-narrow. I turned down one request to take 'packages' back to the UK (I later discovered the man involved was one of Europe's most unpleasant drug smugglers), in favour of starting my own business as an ice cream seller with a cool-box. It went well when the sun shone, but I lost all my stock and my money in an unseasonal downpour, ending up penniless and queasy after eating my own body weight in melting ice creams and lollies.

The beach was soon overflowing with rough sleepers and ne'er-do-wells, which was not allowed in the tourist season. This led to a number of arguments with the *gendarmes*, which I tended to lose. The last time, an officer prodded me awake with his baton and ordered me to leave.

I sat up angrily.

'Why?' I said, in what was, by now, reasonable French. 'I'm not doing any harm.'

Reasonable as my French was, it was Nottingham-accented.

'You English tramps,' he snarled, pushing me again with the baton. 'Get off the beach.'

'You were happy having us English tramps on your beaches in 1944, weren't you?' I said.

I don't think he found it funny, and neither did his colleagues who didn't smile once on the way to the police station. But although they were a little rough with me, they let me go free in the afternoon. Back at The Swan, as I nursed a pint of water and wondered what to do about somewhere to live, fate intervened. A French couple at the table next to me started arguing – so quickly and furiously that I couldn't follow them. I ignored it until the man finally silenced the woman with a Geoffrey Boycott cover-drive across the face. As he went to strike her again, I jumped up and gripped his wrist.

'You shouldn't hit a woman,' I said, calmly.

He shrieked with rage and made to strike me with his free hand, but I twisted his arm and he fell to the floor. He scurried out of the pub, cursing, and the woman stayed put, sipping her wine tearfully. I couldn't help noticing that she was extremely pretty, with that sultry French look about her… and no wedding ring. As I tried not to stare, she whispered a demure, 'Merci' and went to leave. She turned back in the doorway.

'Il est en attente pour moi,' she said, with an embarrassed smile.

'Pardon?' I said.

'He's waiting for me outside,' she said, in accented English.

'Sit down and have another drink,' I said, pulling over a chair.

Her name was Aurélie. She was twenty-seven, she worked as a hostess in a local nightclub, where her job was to sit around looking pretty and smiling while men plied her with expensive champagne, and the chap had mistakenly assumed she was a prostitute. She lived in Le Cannet, just north of Cannes, and I walked her home that night. I felt a very grown up nineteen-year-old, indeed, and my mates back in Cotgrave would have goggled at her, as did all the men who passed by.

She invited me in for coffee, and I ended up staying for two months. It was a perfect way to spend the summer. At first, the relationship – surprisingly – was based on mutual attraction, but as the novelty wore off it turned into a more practical arrangement. I had no work, no money, and nowhere to live; she had all three, but she also had two children, Étienne and Céline, by different absent fathers, whom she struggled to fit into her hectic lifestyle. So I was a kind of house husband, she earning the money to keep us and me improving my *midi* accent, learning to cook and looking after the kids.

Some evenings we went busking; Aurélie had a guitar, I had a decent voice, and we actually made good money with our medley of old Beatles hits, although I suspect it was more to do with her legs than my singing. It was cosy and secure, but after a while I began looking for a way out. It arrived with a French friend I'd made, Henri, who desperately needed a secretary-cum-bookkeeper. I introduced them; within two days he was moving in and I was the gooseberry. I bid her a fond farewell, and went back to dodging the *gendarmerie* on the beach.

It was high summer now, so I quickly got a job in a fast food restaurant on the Rue D'Antibes.

I had money in my pocket, lots of new friends, and I was living in a sub-tropical paradise. As the dog days drifted by, I often had to pinch myself. Life was wonderful, and the horizon was bereft of storm clouds.

Until September came.

* * *

CANNES IS HEAVING in the summer, and dead – apart from the music festival in February – during the rest of the year.

One by one, the bars and restaurants closed down, mine among them. The cannier casual workers went north to the ski resorts, or south onto the cruise ships, while the clueless – like me – wondered what to do next. I looked everywhere for a new job, but there was nothing. One particularly miserable day, spent trudging around hopelessly, ended with me sitting under a wild orange tree, hungry, thirsty, and tired. I looked up and saw that it was laden with fruit. At least I could eat! I picked an orange, peeled it, and took a bite. It was more bitter than a grapefruit, and I spat it out. It was a taste of things to come.

I wandered off to The Swan – not for a drink, I had next to no money – but to see if there was news of work. I got talking to a group of English people, including a chap called Doug, the captain of a yacht in Antibes.

'Do you need any crew?' I asked him.

'No,' he sighed, 'I'm lucky to have a job myself. There's not much on this time of the year.'

He was right. That afternoon I went around every boat in Cannes, to no avail. Over the next few days, I walked west along the coast to La Napoule, and east to Juan-les-Pins and Antibes. The story was always the same.

My money was soon all gone, and food became a memory. For the first couple of days I was ravenous, but the hunger disappeared as my body adjusted. Sometimes I'd snaffle a crust of bread, or palm a few sugar lumps; but, in one stretch of nine days, I had nothing at all to eat. By the end of it, all my lager-and-Chinese-takeaway fat had gone, my clothes were hanging off me, and I was feeling light-headed. I was only kept alive, barely, by the potable water in the loos at The Swan.

Early on the ninth day, I walked back to Antibes, where I'd heard rumour of a job. It turned out the rumour was false, which was a great disappointment as it had taken me two hours to get there. I slumped on the grass by the side of the port to rest before, gathering my strength, I tried to get up. But I swooned and fainted dead away. When I came to, I had terrible hunger pangs in my stomach. I dragged myself to my feet and set off, on very weak, wobbly legs, to walk back to Cannes.

I was at my lowest ebb. Enfeebled, desperate, close to tears, I was a beaten man, literally starving to death.

I had only taken a few steps when someone called my name.

'Hello, Gary, what brings you to Antibes?'

It was Doug, the chap from The Swan.

'A rumour of a job,' I said, 'but it was a load of bollocks.'

'Can I buy you a drink?'

'That would be great.'

We walked together to the Bar de Port, where Doug ordered himself a beer.

'What do you fancy, Gary?' he said.

'If it's all the same to you, Doug,' I said, 'do you mind if I have a sandwich instead?'

'No, fine,' he laughed. He ordered me a ham sandwich and, bless him, another beer. The ham sandwich arrived and I tore into it ravenously. Then I hesitated. It contained tomatoes. I detested them – I'd been caned at Cotgrave Infants by the terrible Miss Norman for stuffing them down my pants to avoid eating them at lunch. But, with a shrug, I carried on.

'How've you been getting on?' said Doug, watching me devour the sandwich.

'Still looking for work, Doug, but, like you said, it's not a good time of year.'

'I might have something for you,' he said. 'Only a couple of hours-worth, but I'll pay you fifty francs?'

I could have cried.

'Great!' I said. 'What is it?'

'I need the bilges clearing out.'

No boat is wholly watertight, and the 'bilges' is the area at the bottom where any water which leaks or splashes in collects. All decent yachts have a pump, but there's always some left which needs getting out by hand. It's a pretty smelly job, but somebody has to do it.

'Fine,' I said. 'I'd love to.'

I got filthy, wet and stinky, and it took me more than two hours, but I was glad of the work. When I had finished, I took my change of clothes from my backpack and Doug's girlfriend made us a cup of coffee, which we drank on deck as we watched the sunset.

'Will you stay for supper?' she asked.

'Yes, he will,' said Doug, on my behalf.

I ended up staying the night, and I slept like a baby, lulled by the soporific rocking of the boat. Lately I had been countering my bed-wetting by sleeping with a towel wrapped inside my pants like a makeshift nappy; oddly, since I'd developed this safety net I hadn't had a single incident, and this night was no different, thank goodness. I awoke feeling snug and well-fed, and within an hour I'd had my breakfast and was on my way.

I'd been as low as I'd ever been, but now I had a fifty franc note in my pocket, and a plan.

CHAPTER EIGHT: ON THE WAY UP

Thirty-two years to silk

BY CONVENTION, ONE attracts the attention of a yacht's captain by standing at the gangplank and calling out the name of the vessel. I stopped at the first boat along, and called the skipper out.

'Don't suppose you have any jobs which need doing?' I said.

'Nah, sorry,' he said, shrugging his shoulders.

I put my plan into operation.

'What about your bilges?'

'Nah,' he said. 'I was going to do that myself.'

'I'll do it for you,' I said. 'You won't have to pay me. All I want is some lunch.'

'Go on, then,' he said, laughing. 'You're on.'

In the event, he gave me lunch *and* fifty francs.

There are hundreds of yachts along the Côte D'Azur, most of them owned or crewed by Britons, and I found a job every day – always using my bilges-for-lunch *entrée*. Most of the time I got cash as well as food. As the weeks passed, I travelled further and further afield to find new boats, usually travelling ticketless on the coastline train towards St Tropez or Menton. And just when it was looking like I'd work my way through every port in the area, I came across that creature of myth, spoken of only in hushed tones by my old friend Crombie Thornton at Pedigree Wholesale: 'A job that's twelve-till-one, with an hour's dinner.'

I was on the jetty at Monaco, walking past an eighteen-metre vessel called *The Claudia Quinta*. Two men were arguing on the deck – you could have heard them in Nice. I inferred from the discussion that the older of the two men had just bought the yacht, while the younger was her captain. The owner was telling the captain that he (the owner) was off to America for two months, and that he would then be back to sail the yacht to Boston, Massachusetts. In the meantime, he wanted the captain to give her a complete overhaul – repainting, varnishing, re-fitting, the works. It was all music to my ears, and I imagine it would have been to the captain's, too – but for the fact that he was being sacked after the overhaul.

'Who's sailing it to Boston?' he yelled.

'An American crew,' replied the owner, forcefully.

'You said my job was safe!'

'You've no work permit for the States,' said the owner. 'I can't employ you as an illegal. I'm sorry, but I have to let you go.'

'Well, I think it stinks!' screeched the captain.

'Hey, pal,' said the owner, his voice rising in turn. 'Leave now, if you want to. I'm giving you plenty of notice. You'll find another job easy enough.'

I lingered, earwigging; neither side was happy, but the upshot was that the captain would work out his notice before the US crew arrived. Both men were still bristling as the owner left, and the captain called him back as he walked down the gangplank.

'If I'm going to get all that done in two months, I'll have to take on extra staff.'

'How many?'

'Three, at least.'

'Okay – three it is,' said the owner. 'But you pay them no more than a hundred francs a day.'

As soon as he left, I was at the bottom of the gangplank and was hired on the spot. I went aboard keen and eager to do my pitiful but level best.

'What do you want me to do?' I said.

'Sit down and have a beer,' he said, 'and I'll introduce you to the rest of the crew.'

The 'rest of the crew' ended up being a lad from Manchester called Nick. He came up on deck and we chatted for a while until the beer was finished.

'So… what shall I do?' I said.

'Nothing.'

'Nothing?'

'That's right, nothing. I'll give you a job for two months, seven days a week, at a hundred francs a day, and I'll throw in your own cabin, on condition that you do absolutely *nothing*. I'll sack you if I catch you doing any work at all. Clear?'

'Crystal clear,' I grinned back.

The next two months were heavenly. The captain never did take on the other two labourers, but he drew their wages from the owner's bank account so we had plenty of cash. On Thursdays I would do the shopping at the market in Ventmiglia, just over the Italian border; most other days I would take the speedboat for fresh milk and bread. But they were my only duties and, onerous as they might sound, I coped with them admirably. During the day we drank beer, water-skied, scuba-dived, and generally loafed around. At night we hit the bars and casinos, trying – with some success – to lure girls back to our yacht. It was a good job for anyone, but for me, who was really only any good at loafing around, it was nirvana.

All good things come to an end, of course, and in mid-December I left town in a hurry, and with a heavy heart, on the day before the owner was due back with his American crew. I doubt the skipper was there to greet him.

* * *

CANNES WAS EMPTY now, most of the casuals having moved on. I spent my evenings in The Swan, but I did feel a little homesick and lonely: I spent most of Christmas day 1979 sitting in the sand, reading a copy of Dickens' *Barnaby Rudge* that I had borrowed from the pub. It's a good book, but I'd have preferred watching *Morecambe and Wise* and The Queen's Speech on the telly.

January was similar, but February brought 'Midem', Europe's

biggest music festival. If you're English in Cannes in February, everyone assumes you're there in some professional capacity and it's easy to blag your way into parties. On the first night, I strolled brazenly aboard *The Sophisticated Lady*, a yacht hired by RCA. The only food provided was caviar, but there was plenty of champagne with which to wash it down. I hadn't eaten for several days, so I gobbled down about three pounds of the stuff before taking a look around. It wasn't an 'A list' affair: I only recognised Eddie Grant, The Village People and The Buggles. Eddie left all the talking to his brother Rudi, and The Buggles were rather stand-offish, but The Village People were very friendly, and I had a lengthy and discursive chat with the Cowboy and the Policeman, during which I attempted to establish how many members of the band were actually gay. (They convinced me that only one was, but wouldn't say who.)

Me in France with some friends: we'd borrowed someone's villa for the weekend

Things turned slightly ugly when a friend of mine called Pat, a bellboy at the Carlton Hotel who was posing as a top record producer, asked Trevor Horn for his autograph. Horn told him to piss off, Pat responded by punching him, and a couple of large bouncers quickly escorted him ashore. In the melee, concerned that some busybody might start asking people to show their invitations, I slipped away and laid low in a cabin. There was a telephone next to the bed, and it occurred to me that I hadn't spoken to anyone back home in almost a year. My great adventure had been built one day at a time, and I'd put off getting in touch until I had some good news to tell. Well, now I had good news. I was phoning from a yacht in the South of France, with a bellyful of caviar and Bollinger, and a fund of interesting tales – obtained first-hand, note – about New York's premier disco band of the 1970s. It doesn't get much better than that.

Mum still not having a phone, I rang a neighbour, Nick Murphy, to fetch her. She was delighted to hear from me, having given me up for dead. I fed her the aforementioned semi-truths, left out the bits about being broke, unemployed, and sleeping on the beach, and promised not to leave it so long next time. As I left the cabin, the party was wrapping up. Caviar is not filling, so I dodged into the darkened galley and, fumbling around, stumbled across a cupboard full of tins of food and a bottle of something. I grabbed what I could and concealed it in my jacket before sneaking off the boat to the beach. It was still fairly early, but I was glad of that; I had sorted out a couple of days' work on a yacht called *The Brave Goose* in Juan-les-Pins and, that being three miles away, I had an early start.

At a safe distance, I examined the purloined tins. They all contained salted anchovies. I'd never tried anchovies before, but I gave them a go. They didn't taste too bad for the first half-a-dozen tins, though their richness did begin to make me a little queasy. But my starving tummy kept calling out for more so I ploughed on, heroically. It was only when they were all gone that I noticed my raging thirst. All I had was the bottle I had pilfered, which turned out to be Pernod. There being no other liquid available, I was forced to drink it, neat.

It was a very sickly G. Bell who eventually retired for the night to his sleeping bag. I got up in the early hours of the morning feeling queasy, and still unbelievably thirsty. I staggered up to the Croisette, where the only water I could find was flowing from a fountain clearly marked, 'Water not drinkable.' Still, I drank about a gallon of it before shambling back to the beach.

I woke up with a small thermo-nuclear device detonating inside my head, but that was the least of my problems. My bedwetting was now the exception, rather than the norm – but this was one of the exceptions. Even that was only the half of it, or more accurately a third: I had also defecated and vomited copiously all over the place.

I got up and limped to the sea to sluice myself and my disgusting sleeping bag, before dragging myself back to my backpack, wrapping myself in a towel, and falling fast asleep. I eventually made it to Juan-les-Pins by a quarter to five, by which time the job was no more. In fact, the captain paid me a hundred francs just to go away. I didn't blame him: *I* didn't even want to be anywhere near me.

I spent an hour or two in a launderette before dragging myself back to The Swan, where – to my delight – The Village People were supplying drink for everyone. The first couple went down a little shakily, but after that I felt marvellous and in no time I was standing on a table to lead the pub – and the band – in a rendition of *YMCA*. After last orders, we moved on to the fabulous Carlton Hotel with Bellboy Pat and some of his mates, and the party continued into the small hours. When it finally wound down, Pat sneaked me upstairs into one of the hotel's most luxurious suites.

Before I went to bed, I sat on the balcony of my fabulously opulent £200-a-night room, drinking a gin-and-tonic from the minibar, and watching the Mediterranean glittering behind the palm trees in the moonlight. How one's fortunes can change in twenty-four hours!

I took advantage of another bedside phone to call people back in England. One of them was my old school *bête noire*, Fred Brown – the chap with whom I had tried to ingratiate myself by means of a naked lady found in a hedge. He and I had gone on to become good friends, and now he told me of his dissatisfaction at life.

'You ought to see where I'm calling you from, Fred,' I said. 'I'm having the time of my life. Pop stars everywhere.'

'Why don't I come out?' he said.

In a flash, we had agreed to meet in Amsterdam, where Forest would be taking on AFC Ajax in the 1980 European Cup semi-final. Then we'd travel back to the Côte d'Azur together.

* * *

I SPENT A FORTNIGHT in luxury in the Carlton, but as ever I was on shifting sand. The hotel filled up with spring holidaymakers, and I was back on the beach.

Before Cannes woke up properly, I headed off to the Netherlands. I had nearly six pounds in various currencies – easily enough for an 850-mile journey. I went via Florence (where I got a job washing plates in a restaurant – I was fired for breaking too many of them) and Zürich (where I found work in an ice cream factory, but was fired for absent-mindedly tasting the wares – I did have rather a large taste). From there, I hitched north for Amsterdam and my rendezvous with Fred Brown.

I had reached Brussels inside a day, and, with Fred still a week away, I decided to see the sights. On your travels, you meet a lot of people, and everyone happily swaps names and addresses, knowing that no-one will ever actually visit. As I sat in one of the city's many beautiful public squares, I got chatting to a lad from Stevenage called Ray Grange, and turned to the letter 'G' in my address book to enter his details. To my surprise, they were already there from some earlier time… and underneath was another name, 'Gino'. Gino was a gay chap I'd met in Cannes, and now I saw that the commune in which he lived was near this very spot. I remembered his enthusiastic insistence that I should – no, *must!* – look him up if I was ever in town. So I did, and he was delighted to see me.

'Gary!' he yelled, kissing me on both cheeks. 'Come in! It's great to see you! Guys? Come and meet Gary!'

They all made me extremely welcome and insisted I stay for a few days, despite the fact that I had no money.

'Just help with the washing-up, darling,' said Gino. 'Nobody will mind.'

They were all fabulously good-looking, and, to be honest, I was a little psyched out by the whole thing. On the second or third day, I took Gino to one side.

'Everyone does realise I'm… heterosexual?' I said, nervously.

'How could you *not* be?' he said, looking at my scruffy attire and unkempt hair, and chuckling. 'But don't worry. No-one fancies you, anyway!'

That was a weight off my mind, and I enjoyed their hospitality for most of the week before heading to Amsterdam.

It was my first trip to the notorious Dutch fleshpot, and I was not disappointed. The splendid, gothic revival Rijksmuseum and the ancient Oude Kerk, the rows of tall, thin, townhouses, the incredible matrix of canals… it was unlike anywhere I'd been. There's much to see for even the highest-browed tourist – I particularly recommend the Van Gogh museum, the Royal Palace on Dam Square and the Anne Frank house – but once you've seen those make immediate haste for the red light district. I am always drawn to the seedier parts of town, and there is none seedier than De Wallen, an acre-and-a-half of bars, cannabis cafés, sex shops, fast food restaurants, and lingerie-clad hookers staring out of brightly-lit windows. Pouting women from the four corners of the earth called out details of what they were prepared to do to me, and how much it would cost, and I stopped and gawped at a few – much as a rabbit is transfixed by the headlights of the onrushing car. I was down to my last two pounds, converted from francs into guilders, which I don't suppose would have bought me much.

I made my way, slack-jawed, towards the Bulldog Café on Oudezijds Voorburgwal, where I had arranged to meet Fred, and hung around outside until he arrived. He was startled by my appearance.

'Bloody hell, Gary!' he said. 'You've lost a lot of weight!'

I suppose he was right: I'd been well over sixteen stone when I'd left Cotgrave, and now I was hovering around twelve.

The match was the following night, and Fred – who wasn't exactly flush, but was generously paying for everything – booked us into a hotel in the red light district called Fat City. It was extraordinary – one giant dormitory, packed with bunk beds taken on a first-come, first-served basis, and occupied by the world's flotsam and jetsam, all of whom were filthy and broke but allegedly leading fabulously glamorous lives as minders to the stars, secret agents, and suchlike. One small, bearded Canadian claimed he was a Shaolin monk who had learnt kung fu from Bruce Lee himself, and he had an opportunity to demonstrate his prowess that night. His bladder had clearly been manufactured in the same batch as mine, because he swamped his bed at around 3am. Unfortunately, he was in the top bunk, and a torrent of urine hissed down onto the man below. Doubly unfortunately, this turned out to be a huge Turk with an aversion to being pissed on. With a curse, he leapt out of bed, grabbed the Shaolin monk by his beard, pulled him to the floor, and beat him to an unconscious pulp. I watched the giant Turk get back into bed, and gingerly climbed down from my own bunk to go to the loo, just in case. I was taking no chances, even with Fred sleeping underneath me.

* * *

THE NEXT MORNING we got up late, and went out to the nearest pub. A few Forest fans were already there and we enjoyed a beer or two before heading off to the Amsterdam Arena for the game. The Dutch fancy themselves a bit, and were out in force to prove a point to the English. But they had become carried away by their minor successes on the Medway in 1667, and had forgotten the lessons of history. Seeing Fred in a Forest shirt, a group of thirty Ajax charged him, but the Dutch are lovers, not fighters, and they quickly retreated when they realised there were two of us.

I remember the game as a dull, nil-nil draw, but in fact – on carrying out some research – I see that it was actually one-nil to Ajax, after a sixty-fifth minute goal by their Danish midfielder Søren Lerby. Anyway, we were in the final, on aggregate, having won two-nil at home in the first leg. That meant a trip to Madrid in a month or so, but that had to wait for a few celebratory beers, and then for some means of scraping together some cash. As I finished my eighth pint of Heineken that night, I got talking to a chap called Steve who was working on a building site in Herford in Germany. There was plenty of work available, he said, so I eagerly jotted down his phone number, told him we'd be in touch, and retired shortly afterward for the night with Fred. We didn't fancy Fat City, so we spent an uncomfortable night on the benches at Amsterdam railway station before setting off to hitch south to Rotterdam. We made slow progress, and it was dusk when we arrived. We ended up dossing down in a playground sandpit. I took some time to get to sleep, but Fred was snoring peacefully away in a few moments. I marvelled at how quickly he had adapted to being a tramp; just being away from Nottingham was glamorous enough for him.

We were awoken early by a tremendous downpour, and spent the whole day sitting in the railway station waiting in vain for it to stop. Eventually, not fancying a wet sandpit, we queued to get into a Salvation Army Hostel, and then queued again for a compulsory shower, alongside all the other local homeless. We didn't mind the shower, we welcomed it, but the indignity of being ordered to have one was unsettling. We found our way to a dormitory with about fifty other souls and, dog-tired, I dropped off almost immediately. Just as I was going, Fred leaned over and whispered, 'So, Gary… When are we going to meet all these stars?'

Next morning we headed due east for Herford, in search of Steve and his building site of dreams. It took two days and nights, through eastern Holland and over the German border, and I've never known cold like it. At Enschede, we slept in the open on pallets filched from a garage, and awoke to find ourselves buried under several inches of snow. Mick Randall would have been in his element, but Fred and I were lesser men; I felt like Captain Scott, my Oates by my side, as we trudged our weary way east with not a hint of feeling in our fingers or toes. Occasionally, a car would pass, and on the odd occasion when someone took pity on us we did our best with our very pidgin German. I had an ancient European phrasebook with me, but most of the German section had fallen out. Only one page remained, dealing with the purchase of foodstuffs. I defy anyone to hitchhike through The Fatherland while limited, linguistically, to, 'Haben sie karotten?'

We eventually got to Osnabrück, where we took refuge from the cold in a supermarket café and spent several hours drinking coffee and soup with most of what was left of Fred's money. We left at dusk, just about thawed out, but it was too late to start hitching so we found a bar and ordered a couple of beers while we pondered where to spend the night. As we sat down, a group of German lads spilled boisterously inside and took the place over. It turned out that they had just finished their national service, and were planning to drink the pub dry; the whole place was soon awash with jugs of beer, and Fred and I were glad to help them drink it. A debate broke out about football, and the forthcoming European Cup final between Forest and Hamburg. To my initial discomfort, I soon realised that a lot of them were from Hamburg, but hooliganism hadn't really arrived in Germany and nothing more ensued than good-natured banter.

At midnight, we staggered out of the pub and into a club, but at 2am the club closed and Fred and I were turfed out onto the freezing streets with everyone else. Hands were shaken, and hearty goodbyes said, the national service gang disappeared into the steadily-falling snow, and Fred and I began bumbling aimlessly along the road. I realise now that things could have gone seriously wrong for us. But then, out of nowhere, appeared a very attractive young German girl.

'Are you lost?' she said, in English.

'No,' I slurred back. 'We don't know where we are, but we're not lost.'

'I see,' she said. 'Where are you going?'

'Herford,' I replied.

'What?' she said, eyes widening. *'Tonight?'*

'I don't know,' I shrugged.

'Come with me,' she ordered, and we followed her to her apartment. 'You can sleep in here,' she said, opening out a sofa bed.

We crashed out immediately, and were awoken the next morning by this vision of a girl bearing coffee and croissants. My head was not happy with me, but she brought painkillers and I was soon up, and fully revived.

'Thank you for putting us up last night,' I said. 'I don't know how we can ever repay you.'

'There's no need,' she laughed. 'One day you'll find a German in your country who needs a bed for the night, and you can pass the favour on.'

If she hadn't taken us in that night, I shudder to think what might have happened. Her prophecy came true, too – about a German needing a bed in England – but I'll come to that later.

We arrived in Herford in the afternoon, and I called Steve to find out where to go for our jobs. But all I got was the 'number unobtainable' tone. We'd travelled hundreds of miles, and spent most of Fred's cash, and it came as a bit of a blow. We passed a chip shop, and treated ourselves. That left us with about a pound left, in guilders. We stopped at a British Army base, to ask if anyone knew Steve, or where we might find some work. The sentries were friendly enough, but couldn't help.

'We're desperate, lads,' I said. 'Is there anywhere on the base we can doss down?'

'No chance, mate,' said one of them. 'Sorry.'

'What about Dave's tent?' said the other, grinning.

It turned out that Dave was a member of the squadron, and that he had recently bought a tent and set it up behind the barracks. As a reward for doing so without an officer's permission, the whole squadron had been confined to barracks. The sentry in front of me had missed a hot date with a local girl because of it, and was anxious for revenge.

'If you wait over there at midnight,' he said, 'I'll lob the tent over the fence.'

We were there as arranged, and the tent came flying over as promised. We picked it up and ran, and we didn't stop running until we got to the top of the hill overlooking the camp, and then we ran a bit more, off into some woods – the tent was bright orange, and we didn't want to be seen by Dave, or anyone else. Two hundred yards in, we found a clearing in which to pitch it, and were soon inside and fast asleep, cosy and warm in spite of the weather. But when we eventually crawled out the following morning, a most unpleasant surprise awaited us. The 'woods' turned out to be very threadbare indeed, and I could already see people at the base peering up at us and Dave's Day-Glo tent through binoculars, and pointing. We tore it down and ran for it. I was sure I could hear whistles and barking dogs, and we stumbled for miles until, exhausted, we stopped underneath a bridge.

The following day, we were back on the road. Before long, a chap in a Ford Capri stopped. Luckily for us, he was an English soldier, headed for Amsterdam; we gratefully accepted his offer of a lift, and that evening we ended up back where we had started out a week earlier. We were hungry, obviously, but Fred had that pound's worth of guilders, so he went into a shop while I guarded the bags. He came out with a packet of cigarettes, and no food. I was as angry as Jack and the Beanstalk's mum.

* * *

SOMEONE HAD SAID there was tomato-picking work in Rotterdam. I had a niggling feeling that the tip had come from Herford Steve but we were prepared to clutch at any straw, so we went back there. I need not have worried: our first lift was a huge rescue ship driven by one Billy De Koning, an eternal student, scion of a wealthy family, member of the O.C. Hooeymayer Blues Band, and one of the nicest men I've met.

He immediately volunteered to put us up overnight, and the following morning he drove us around every tomato grower in the Greater Rotterdam area. But Herford Steve's job tips were about as reliable as an England penalty shoot-out, and no tomatoes whatsoever required picking.

We ended up staying at Bill's for three weeks, playing football or *Risk* with him and his mates, and going to clubs. Fred's mum sent him all the funds remaining in his Post Office account, £112, and he borrowed a hundred pounds from Bill against it. When the cash arrived, we reimbursed Bill and set off for Cannes, our pockets bulging with all of twelve pounds. It took us two days to get there, just in time for the start of the film festival, and I immediately found a job stripping and respraying a yacht. As I worked, Who singer Roger Daltrey – in town to promote his new movie, *McVicar* – lounged about on the next-door boat, handing me regular cold beers and generally chit-chatting in a most unaffected way.

Fred was too busy wandering around Cannes watching starlets and the occasional film to think about work, but we met up every evening, blagging our way into some premiere or other, or getting drunk in The Swan. My old mates The Village People had flown over to launch their own new film, *Can't Stop The Music*, and they were in the pub on our first night, and hailed me like a long-lost seventh member of the band. On one level, Fred was impressed, but – being an unreconstructed working class Englishman – I think he was mildly concerned to be sharing a tent with a man on first-name terms with America's gayest pop group.

In fact, the film festival is fish-in-a-barrel time for celebrity watching. One day I was stopped on the Rue D'Antibes by Kirk Douglas, who addressed me in French, albeit with a heavy American accent.

'Excusez moi, monsieur, ou est le Palais des Festivals?'

'Go to the end of this road,' I replied, in English, 'turn left and it's two hundred yards up.'

'Merci monsieur,' he said. 'Vous êtes très gentil.'

The festival ended, and it was time for Madrid, and the football. The night before we left, we joined a giant throng on the beach, made up of the thieves and vagabonds, the lost and lonely, and the transients like me, who were merely walking the earth from place to place – like Caine in *Kung Fu*, only less inscrutably. By now, I spoke more or less fluent French, though as I'd never paid much attention during French lessons at Toot Hill ('Gary must make every effort to settle down to work, and not busy himself with thinking up witty comments') I was prone to making grammatical howlers. This would have been perfectly understandable in an Englishman, but I was cursed with a perfect accent. Thus, people took me for a Frenchman, but assumed from the gibberish I spoke that I was a simpleton.

Even so, I was, by English standards, a polyglot. But amongst my fellow Europeans I was still a complete non-starter. A Belgian called Luc was particularly impressive. As we sat around a fire deep into the night, he moved easily between conversations, chatting to people of all nationalities in their mother tongues.

'How many languages do you speak, Luc?' I said.

'Only Flemish, Dutch, English, German, French, Spanish and Italian fluently,' he replied, 'but I get by in Greek and Hebrew.'

'That's amazing,' I said, in awe.

He shrugged. 'I've spent twenty years travelling the world. I'm bound to have picked up a few languages on the way.'

'Well,' I said, 'if I end up speaking half as many languages as you I'll be happy.'

'Whatever you do,' he said, sighing, 'don't copy me. I'm thirty-five, I have no home, no money, no family. Go home, kid. Get an education. That's what I'd do if I had my time again.'

Early the next morning, we trudged our weary way up the Boulevard Carnot to the motorway. Night found us crossing the Spanish border, high up in the chilly Pyrenees, and getting dropped off in the middle of nowhere. We pitched Soldier Dave's orange tent, donned our spare clothes against the cold, and settled down for the night. I tried to scare Fred with tales of the ravenous bears and wolves which roamed the mountains, but he just went to sleep and I succeeded only in scaring myself. I lay awake, starting at every rustle outside, until, at around 3am, came the definite sound of something large moving about. I nudged Fred, and we listened in mounting terror.

Then we heard a cough.

'It's a person,' I hissed, under my breath.

'You don't say,' Fred whispered back.

'Go and see who it is,' I said.

'*You* go and see,' he said.

'Why not you?'

'I don't speak French.'

'Good point,' I conceded.

I gingerly unzipped the tent, and stuck out my head.

'Bonsoir,' I called out, as firmly as I could. 'Qui est là?'

'D'you speak English, mate?' a voice called back.

The nearby border was brightly lit, and as my eyes adjusted I saw a man huddled against a tree. He was wearing jeans and a cap-sleeved tee-shirt, and carried no baggage.

'Yes, I do,' I said.

'*Animal*?' said the voice. 'Is that *you*?'

'Who's that?' I said.

As he stood up, I recognised him immediately as a Forest hooligan called Pat Keegan.

'It's me,' he said. 'Pat! You haven't got room in your tent, have you? I'm freezing my bollocks off.'

'Bloody hell, Pat,' said Fred. 'Where are your clothes?'

'Bastard Spain,' he said, miserably. 'I thought it was supposed to be fucking hot!'

We opened up our sleeping bags for blankets, used our towels as sheets, and the three of us settled down for the night. Next morning, I arranged for a lift for Fred and me in a French lorry into Barcelona. The trucker had no room for Keegan, so we said our goodbyes.

Barcelona is a majestic place, but I didn't see much of it. We arrived in the middle of a terrible thunderstorm, and pitched the tent on a traffic island on the road to Zaragoza. The rain didn't abate for three days, and we stayed in the tent throughout. When it finally stopped, early on the morning before the game, we set off for Madrid, courtesy of a kind German couple, Hamburg supporters, who were going our way. They dropped us off before lunch in the great Spanish capital, which was already well on the way to being overrun by Brian Clough's red-and-white army. Fred had arranged to meet up with a bunch of Cotgrave lads who had driven all the way in a minibus, and we finally found them just before kick-off. It was lucky we did – they had his ticket.

I didn't have a ticket myself, and I was resigned to listening to the game from outside the stadium. But lady luck was smiling down upon me once again that evening. With five minutes to go, I came across a chap who was frantically trying to sell a spare. I had no cash, but he gave it to me on the understanding that I would send the money when I got home. (When I duly did, he wrote me a lovely letter of thanks admitting that he never expected to get it.)

The game was another dull affair, but the result was the right one, thanks to a solitary John Robertson goal. We spent that night celebrating on a camp site with our Cotgrave friends, who were much struck by the difference between myself and Fred – me looking exceptionally well, he resembling a concentration camp survivor – before cramming into their vehicle in the morning. The plan was that they'd drop us off near Paris, and we would then hitchhike south to continue our European adventure. But when we reached Paris, mutiny was afoot.

'I'm not coming, Gary,' said Fred, near the drop-off point. 'I've had enough.'

I could see from his eyes that it would be no use arguing. He looked in need of his own bed, a wash, and some British food.

'Okay,' I shrugged. 'If that's your decision, mate, I'll see you later.'

But as I went to climb out of the vehicle, Steven Savage grabbed my shoulder.

'Why don't you come back an' all, Gary?' he said.

I thought for a moment. I'd left in early 1979, and it was now the end of May 1980. I'd proved my point. My mates wanted me to come home with them.

Four hours later, I was on the ferry for England.

CHAPTER NINE: THE BLACK HOLE

Thirty-one years to silk

ON MY FIRST night back, I went into the Miners' Welfare. There was Chad Forrest, still sitting in his usual seat, playing dominos.

'Alright, bonny lad?' he said, like I'd never been away. 'Fancy a game?'

'Why not?' I said, with a grin.

'Where you been, then?' said Chad.

'All over Europe,' I said. 'South of France, mostly.'

'Fucking France and the EEC,' he spat. 'We should never have joined in the first place.'

'Why not?' I said.

'Bunch of foreigners telling us what to do? They won't let us catch our own fish, they're telling us we've got to let all these immigrants in... I heard the French want us banned from eating beef. We'll all have to eat horses and frogs' legs.'

'The French all eat beef, Chad.'

'Do they bollocks!' he said. 'The cow is a fucking sacred animal in France! No-one's allowed to touch them!'

'I think that's India.'

'What the fuck do you know?' he said, indignantly. 'You're only a young kid!'

'I've been in France for the past year,' I said.

'You know fuck all!' he shrieked. 'You're only a fucking baby! You should listen to the voice of experience!'

I shrugged and sipped my lager. I'd lived in Cotgrave for most of my life, but it suddenly felt alien to me.

That weekend, I was part of a pub crawl which ended in a quiet country inn. One of our number – a twenty-stone jelly mountain, whom I won't dignify by naming – launched into a vile song littered with gross obscenity. The pub was full of middle-aged couples who didn't want to hear this filth, and I was thinking of protesting when, to my horror, the rest of the lads joined in.

The landlord, a small man in his mid-fifties wearing extremely thick glasses, came over.

'Excuse me,' he said, politely. 'Could you keep the noise down a bit, please?'

'We're only singing,' jeered the jelly mountain.

'It's the bad language,' said the landlord. 'Sing if you want to, but can you keep it clean, please?'

'Fuck off!'

The landlord paused, wondering what to do next.

'What the fuck are you looking at?' said the jelly mountain, jumping to his feet.

'Nothing, nothing,' stammered the landlord, beating a hasty retreat.

'Spineless twat!' the yob called after him. 'We'll sing if we want, and there's fuck all you can do about it!'

And he led the lads on another chorus.

If there was nothing the landlord could do, there *was* something *I* could do. I left and walked the three miles home, feeling ashamed and embarrassed.

The painful truth is that, a couple of years earlier, I'd have been singing along, and revelling in the sense of power that comes with breaking social conventions in public. But now I was disgusted by this behaviour. I'd known these men practically all my life. They hadn't changed, but I was somehow, irrevocably, different.

I understood – and I still understand – the siren call of the familiar, of living in a place where everyone knows your name, where the community is always there for you. If you don't strive, you can't fail. If you don't search for something, you never suffer the disappointment of not finding it. If you hunker down, many of life's storms pass harmlessly overhead. A routine, humdrum life is like a comfortable pair of shoes. Why buy new ones? They'll only give you blisters. Many of those present that night were intelligent men – though the fat cheerleader is not among them. Given a glimpse of some far horizon, they might have discovered the ambition that lives inside most of us. They could have broken out and fulfilled their potential. As it is, the vast majority of the people I grew up with are still in Cotgrave now. I'm proud still to call many of them my friends, but I knew then that I could live there no longer. The door to the world had been opened to me. I had seen a faint chink of light.

Despite that, I was slowly sucked back. Lunch times I spent in the Rose and Crown, evenings at the Miners' Welfare. Friday, clubbing. Saturday, pubbing. Sunday, five-a-side, my mum's lunch, and a Chinese in the evening. Cotgrave was like a black hole, and I was trapped in its gravitational pull.

I *had* to get out: if I got too settled and comfortable – too fat, dumb and happy, as the Americans say – then I'd end up living and dying in Cotgrave. But if – *when* – I returned to Cannes, I wanted to do it properly, not dossing on the beach, but with a small flat, and a fresh start. The question was, how to fund it? Work had really dried up while I'd been away; the dole provided beer money, but even if I'd saved every penny it would still have taken years to scrape together enough.

One lunchtime, I walked to the library to look for jobs in the *Nottingham Evening Post*, and I saw a leaflet for a place called West Bridgford College. The words of Luc, the Belgian beach polyglot, came back to me: *Get yourself an education, kid.*

I stuffed the leaflet into my pocket and set off for the pub. But the heavens opened, so I dipped into a phone box until it passed. Absent-mindedly, I looked at the leaflet. It promised a wide range of O and A levels. I had 10p, so I called the number. In a few moments, I had established that the O level courses took a year, were free, and were open to anyone. I made an appointment to see the admissions tutor the following Wednesday afternoon, scribbled the details on the brochure, and promptly forgot all about it.

By coincidence, on the Wednesday I found myself in West Bridgford. It was sunny, and I'd gone for a drink at a riverside pub with five mates. After a couple of pints it was my round, but I didn't have any money. To raise funds, I bet my friends a fiver that I could swim across the mighty River Trent, and they all duly chipped in a quid each. It was choppy and fast-flowing, and I'm sure their eagerness to enter into the bet was fuelled by the fact that another Cotgrave lad had been drowned swimming across that very stretch of the river a few weeks earlier. Anticipation that I was *en route* to a watery grave was high, but I'm a strong swimmer and, stripping down to my Y-fronts, I made it there and back with ease. I collected my winnings and bought the round, and it was as I put the change into my pocket that, by sheer chance, I found the college brochure.

Bugger! I'd forgotten all about that appointment.

It was an hour off; I bought a round for the lads, made my excuses and left. An hour later, the admissions tutor, a small Scottish academic called Dr Magee, grilled me as to my motive for coming back into education. Eventually, he said, 'I'll let you enroll, Gary. But because you've been out of education so long you'll have to do a one-year pre-O level course before you start your O levels-proper.'

'Please don't make me do that,' I said. 'I haven't got time. Let me go straight onto the O level course.'

He looked at me, thoughtfully. 'Do you promise you won't let me down, Gary?'

'I promise.'

'Good lad,' he said, offering me his hand. 'Alright, choose your five O levels and I'll see you in September.'

It didn't take me long to choose. Maths and English were compulsory, history had always fascinated me and French was a given. That left one more. When I'd been at school, I had walked into Bingham one lunchtime and had seen a beautiful Jaguar car pull up near me. The driver had got out and walked through a door, next to which was a brass plate bearing the name of a firm of solicitors.

That's what I'm going to be, I had promised myself, as a boy. *I'll be a lawyer. Then I'll be able to drive a Jag like that.*

For my fifth O level, I chose law.

* * *

I BROKE THE NEWS to my mother that night.

'I'm not going back to France, mum,' I said. 'I'm staying here.'

'Oh, that's wonderful, Gary,' she said. 'Now you just need a decent job.'

'I'm not getting one,' I said. 'I've decided to go back into education.'

I might as well have said I was planning to be the first man on Mars.

'What do you mean?' she said.

'I'm going to college to do my O levels.'

'But you're twenty years old!'

'I know. I'm going as a mature student.'

'Don't be so daft!'

'I'm not being daft, mum. I need an education if I'm ever going to make something of myself.'

'Make *what* of yourself?'

'I don't know,' I shrugged. 'I quite fancy being a lawyer. A barrister, actually.'

'A *barrister?*' she snorted. '*You?*'

'Why not?' I said, slightly hurt.

'Because people like *us* don't become bloody barristers,' she said. 'Just get yourself a steady job, and then you can settle down and get married.'

'I don't *want* to settle down and get married,' I said. 'I want to be a barrister.'

'Well,' she said, folding her arms. 'I'm not keeping you whilst you're messing around pretending to be a student. Unless you get a job you can find somewhere else to live.'

123

That night I moved into the spare room at Colin Henderson's house. Colin was a friend who had recently split up with his wife, and that summer was a non-stop party. I was pretty much permanently drunk, though I managed to sober up sufficiently to drag myself into West Bridgford for my first day of college.

And what an ordeal it was. I was oddly intimidated by it all. The first lad I saw was an A level student with spiky green hair. Someone called out to him, 'David! I didn't know you'd turned punk!' It was a nothing incident, but it unsettled me for some reason I couldn't put my finger on. Perhaps it was because they all knew each other, and all seemed far cooler and more confident than I was, or could ever be. As I went to book-in for my various lectures, I avoided catching any stray eye. My nerves eased a little when, to my relief, I spotted a familiar face – that of Lance Flynn, a fellow member of The Mad Squad, who was of similar age and background to me, and was shuffling along a corridor looking similarly disorientated. I didn't know Lance well, but he seemed equally pleased to see me.

Over the next few days, my confidence grew, though in my first week I missed two days through hangovers from drinking with the lads. I wanted to do this properly, and that was no good. It was time to eat some humble pie. I asked my mother if I could move back in.

'Are you still messing about at that college?' she said.

'Yes.'

'Have you got a job?'

'Not yet.'

'Well, come back when you have,' she said.

It took me two days to find one, working four nights a week and Saturdays at Asda, and I moved back home.

It was very lucky for me that I did.

A group of us had got into the habit of going into town at weekends in Colin Henderson's car. The weekend that I moved back home, I was *persona non grata* – Colin being miffed at my decision – and my place in the car was filled by his brother, Clive. Clive had served in the Parachute Regiment, where he had earned from his fellow Paras the nickname 'Oddie'. He was incredibly insecure, had to be the centre of attention at all times, and would do anything to shock people. He used to go to the pub in his wife's wedding dress, until he set fire to it (he was wearing it at the time), and I often saw him tip the contents of an ashtray into his pint and drink it. One evening we were in a pub loo using the urinals when a man rushed in and started being sick. Clive cupped his hands, caught about half a pint of the vomit and quickly guzzled it down before turning to us with a grin of triumph.

At least most of the time he only hurt himself. But one night, when we'd gone round to his house to watch the football, he smashed his wife unconscious with a heavy brass ornament for daring to turn the telly over to *Coronation Street*. Then he dragged her out of the room by her feet, before coming back in and plonking himself back in his armchair.

'She'll make us a cup of tea when she comes round,' he said, but we'd seen enough and left.

He was forever talking about his unarmed combat skills, and habitually carried an arsenal of pointed weaponry with which, he claimed, he had killed terrorists in his Army days. But the truth was that he wasn't very hard – unlike Colin, who was one of the strongest, bravest, and most revered members of The Mad Squad. Colin's party piece was to perform a hundred one-armed press-ups with either arm, and I once saw him charge alone at hundreds of Middlesbrough hooligans, drop their leader and chase off the rest. Clive was desperate to get out of his brother's shadow.

On the evening that Clive took my place in the car, he had a particularly humiliating experience. As they left a nightclub in the early hours of the Sunday morning, their group became involved in an altercation with another lot from St Ann's. No-one could say who started the fight, but the main part of it involved two youths from St Ann's fighting against Colin and Clive. Colin quickly put his man on his arse, but Clive came off worst against his. The chap he was fighting knocked him down, but then ran off as Colin turned toward him.

There are few greater disgraces for men of his type than to lose a fight, and Clive was anxious to find his assailant for round two. He insisted that Colin drive around to see if they could find him. Unfortunately for all concerned, they did find the two men, walking quietly home.

The car screeched to a halt and Clive leapt out. The men made to run but Colin drove the car past them and the Cotgrave lads all piled out, blocking off any retreat.

'Right,' said Clive, beckoning to the man who had earlier knocked him down. 'It's me and you, one-on-one.'

With little to fear, the man handed his jacket to his friend and walked towards Clive. But as they closed with each other, Clive produced a knife from under his jacket and stabbed his opponent through the heart.

I was safely tucked up in bed at my mother's house, trying to learn which French verbs went with *avoir* and which went with *être*, so I escaped the fate of the six who were in the car that night. Clive was sentenced to life imprisonment for murder, and everyone else went to jail for two years for violent disorder.

Had I been in that car, my life would have gone very differently.

* * *

THE COLLEGE WORK wasn't taxing – apart from maths and, surprisingly, French – and there was time for plenty of extra-curricular activity.

I played tennis and squash and, with boots that fitted me, strolled into the football team, which I captained. I also started up a five-a-side team for the college competition. I had three excellent players – Lance, a box-to-box midfielder called Pete Magee (son of the college admissions tutor), and Stuart Coutts, a pacey attacker – but we needed a goalkeeper. Stuart recommended a mate of his, Simmo, whom he insisted was almost on a par with Peter Shilton, then the Forest and England No1, and probably the world's best keeper.

I was dubious – Simmo was seventeen, about 5ft 9in tall, and looked malnourished – but I put him in nets for the next game, against hot favourites 'Brazilian Blend'.

My fears were justified. By half-time, we were 4-0 down and Lance, who was being run ragged by his opposite number, could hardly walk.

'Lance'll have to swap with you,' I said to Simmo. 'If the ball comes to you, don't try and do anything fancy. Just pass it to me.'

Three seconds into the second half, the ball did come to him. He dropped a shoulder, swerved around an onrushing opponent, dribbled around the rest of their team, and then slotted it past the goalkeeper.

'Change of plan,' I told him. 'If the ball comes to you, just do that again.'

He did, four times, and we went on to win the game 5-4, on our way to becoming college champions. Simmo could and should have played professional football. He had serious interest from many clubs, including Forest and Manchester United, but every time a scout turned up at his house with an offer of trials, his mother told them to fuck off – literally. These days he works sorting rubbish into its various recyclable components.

The best thing about college was the social life. I quickly made lots of friends – many of whom, Lance and Simmo included, I'm still close to – and was almost drowning in girls. The girls somehow saw Lance and myself as the epitome of sophisticated cool, though their parents tended not to approve of me, boyfriend-wise. I liked to play up my plans to become a barrister; they insisted on focusing on the fact that I came from Cotgrave, was five years older than their daughters, and had a criminal record.

In the middle of the first term I ran for Vice President of the Students' Union and was triumphantly elected to that position of great authority. I was sitting very prettily indeed. It was all quite tiring, though. I left home at 7.30am to hitch-hike the six miles from Cotgrave to college. After college, Monday to Thursday, I went to the Asda warehouse where I drove a forklift truck from 6pm until 10pm, before hitching home. I was back at Asda from 8.30am until 5.30pm on Saturdays, and did my homework on Sundays. But I didn't mind the hard work, nor the miserable £25 or so I received for my twenty-four-hour working week. For the first time since the age of eleven, I felt I was getting somewhere.

Some time in my first term, I went to see the careers advisor, Arthur Kemp, to discuss my ambitions.

'A *barrister*?' he said, looking me up and down. At the time, I had a skinhead haircut and moustache, and was wearing the uniform of my class and gender – a short-sleeved, checked shirt, tight, stonewashed jeans, white socks and Dunlop Green Flash plimsolls.

'That's right,' I said.

'What are you studying at the moment?'

'My O levels.'

'Your O *levels*? How old are you?'

'Twenty.'

'*Twenty*?'

'Yes.'

'Er… did you take any exams at school?'

'No, I left at Easter.'

He sat back, scratching his head. 'And what have you been doing since then?'

'I started as a coalminer,' I said. 'Then I became a fireman.'

'Oh yes?' he said, noticeably perking up. 'Why did you leave?'

'I got sacked after I was convicted of fraud.' This was actually the part I was most nervous about – the part I knew could scupper my plans. 'I wondered… Can you still be a barrister with a criminal record?'

'Let's concentrate on passing your O levels first,' he said.

So I did. Christmas came around, and my studies were going well. I was paying my way at home, and I had a girlfriend called Anita. Even my mother started to take my ambitions to educate myself seriously, although she still laughed like a drain whenever I mentioned the old wig and gown.

Anita finished with me after the Christmas break – I think she'd been expecting an expensive Christmas present and a few meals out, and had finally realised how poor I was – but I soon took up with a new girl. She was a Muslim, and I won't name her, as none of her ten brothers approved of the relationship, and they may still be after me. Interracial dating was unusual in my circle. Although West Bridgford was a multi-cultural place, Cotgrave and its surrounds were not, and there had been not a single non-white pupil amongst the three thousand at Toot Hill during my five years there. Consequently, people of other races were treated with suspicion, at best. I remember visiting my paternal grandmother one day.

'Have you heard about our Lisa?' she said – Lisa being my Aunt Carole's teenaged daughter.

'No,' I said. 'What's happened?'

'She's had a baby,' granny announced.

'That's lovely,' I said. 'What is it?'

She looked around her sitting room, as though checking no-one was listening.

'It's a blackie,' she said.

'Is it?' I said. 'Who's the father?'

'We don't know,' said granny. 'He's buggered off. But we think he might be a blackie as well.'

'Well, he would be, granny, wouldn't he?' I said.

'Yes, I suppose he would,' she said, after a moment's reflection. 'If you think about it.'

'What does it matter what colour he is?' said my grandfather, who had been sitting quietly in his chair reading the *Daily Mirror*. 'There's good and bad in all folk!'

It was a rare philosophy round our way, though it was the right one. Liam grew up to be a lovely young man, and his mother and I have always been close; when they moved to Derby, I bought him a full Nottingham Forest kit and took him to watch them play, just to make sure he grew up properly. He still lives in Derby, but he remains a Forest fan.

I don't want to sound as though I was some sort of fanatical anti-racist, because I wasn't. I just took my grandfather's *dictum* to heart. One of my mates from college and Asda was a black teenager called Audley Stewart. Audley was a quiet and sensitive man, who was popular with everyone – well, nearly everyone. The Asda warehouse manager hated him for his race, and delighted in picking him up for anything and everything, all the while making what he thought were amusing observations on the colour of his skin. Within weeks, the bigot had administered two written warnings on completely trumped-up charges; one more and Audley could be sacked. His chance came shortly after Christmas. I sped recklessly round a blind corner in my forklift and collided with a pallet of biscuits that Audley was moving. There was a crash, and biscuits flew everywhere. The manager rushed over and I started to apologise, but he cut me short, berating Audley for his stupidity.

'No, Graham,' I said. 'It wasn't his fault, it was mine.'

'Shut up,' he shouted. 'I'll blame who I bloody well like.'

Five minutes later, Audley was on his way with his P45 unemployment slip. Our shop steward had no interest in the matter, so I rang the GMWU directly. I also called for a general strike of all workers, stood on a solitary picket line, and organised a union meeting to discuss the matter at a local pub. The only person who showed up apart from me was a fellow student, Andy Haywood, after the management let it be known that any part-timers attending the meeting would lose their jobs. The following day, I received a letter from personnel in which they claimed that I had lied about my criminal conviction on my job application form. I can't recall whether I had or not, but in any event I followed Audley out of the door.

Maybe I was a touch over-enthusiastic about it all, but I didn't regret my actions, futile as they were. I couldn't have gone back to work in the warehouse after what had happened, anyway.

* * *

NOT LONG AFTER my father left the second time, my mum had been diagnosed with breast cancer. She underwent a mastectomy, and two years of chemotherapy, radiotherapy, painkillers, and operations to remove diseased tissue. She did her best to care for us through it all – especially my youngest sister, Samantha, who was only six years old when mum was diagnosed – and carried on working, mostly as a barmaid at the Welfare. Her bravery and determination made her a much-loved figure in the village.

Finally, she received the news that she had prayed for – a test that showed she was in remission. But the fight had taken a huge amount out of her. Her teeth and hair had fallen out, she looked a great deal older than her thirty-eight years, and her confidence, as a woman, was very low. In this context, she began coming home at night with a succession of different men, and even got engaged to a couple of them, both utter wasters of about my own age. I think now that she did this to prove to herself that she was still attractive, but it was terribly difficult for we children to deal with. But, with some encouragement from us, both of the engagements were called off, and life slowly returned to normal-ish until, in January 1981, my maternal grandmother Gertie Corpe died, leaving a terrible hole in all of our lives.

As I said earlier, Gertie was my mum's adoptive mother. I don't know why, but my mum never met her birth mother, Lilian Corpe, despite the fact that Lilian was family and lived not very far away on the other side of Nottingham. Now, in the aftermath of Gertie's death, someone discovered that Lilian had herself died of breast cancer. This shook my mum up considerably, less from an emotional point of view than from the news that the illness was clearly in her genes. Still, she put it to the back of her mind; after all, she was due shortly to go into hospital for a final cancer scan that would confirm her full recovery. Although she was dreading it, there was nothing to fear; it was merely a formality.

It was the end of May, and I was preparing for my O level exams as mum caught the bus into Nottingham for the scan. She went on her own, but didn't come back. As night fell, and we began to worry, I sent Dawn on the next bus to the hospital to check that everything was alright. Several hours later, she came back on the last bus from town, alone and inconsolable, in floods of tears. The scan had not gone well. The cancer had come back, and it had spread to all parts of my mother's body, including her lungs. It was no longer treatable, and she had only months to live.

I thought they were wrong. My mother was incredibly strong; she'd survived being abandoned by her husband twice, she had beaten cancer once, and she'd beat it again. The newspapers were always printing stories about people with her prognosis who had gone on for twenty years or more.

The next morning I caught the bus into town and went to the hospital. I was shocked by what I found. She was lying in a bed with tubes sticking into her, and her breathing was terribly laboured. There was not an ounce of fight left. She took my hand and, with great effort, managed to gasp, 'Don't let your dad have Samantha.'

I didn't reply: what could I say? I gently took her hand from mine and went to find a doctor.

'I'm Maureen Bell's son,' I said.

'Your mother's very poorly,' he said, tenderly. 'I'm terribly sorry.'

He made to leave the room but I clutched at his sleeve.

'You've got to do something,' I said, begging him.

'There's nothing we can do,' he said. 'I'm afraid it's too late.'

I knew in my heart that he was right, and my mother soon lapsed into unconsciousness. Her breathing got shallower and shallower until, at just after nine o'clock on the evening of May 28, 1981, she died.

She was only forty, and a truly great woman, and I was left feeling a terrible guilt at how I had taken her for granted. One small example: just after I started at college, I turned twenty-one. Somehow, mum managed to scrape together five pounds for me. It may not seem a great deal but, given how poor she was, it was a true widow's mite. We had no luxuries, and our clothes were old, but they were always clean, and she always managed somehow to feed us and pay the bills. She always held back herself, and, as a result, had even less than we children. One day, not long after that birthday, her threadbare jeans completely fell to pieces. She had no money to replace them, whereas I had two pairs.

'Can I have one of your pairs of jeans, Gary?' she asked. 'If I take them in they'll fit me.'

'No,' I said, with astonishing selfishness, and to my eternal shame. 'I need them both. I wear them all the time.'

She didn't ask again, but simply wore a skirt until payday, and then treated herself to a cheap pair of trousers from a charity shop.

I still think about that most days: she never asked for much in life, and her eldest son wouldn't even give her a pair of jeans.

It was a tough and ineffably sad time for all of us. My mother died on a Thursday, four days before my O levels were due to start. There was little time for revision, in between organising the funeral, trying to sort out the tenancy of the house, our housing benefit, and Samantha's child allowance. I sat five exams that first week, and four more the following week, and somehow I managed to pass them all. Mum's funeral was on the Thursday morning, and I had to leave as soon as she was buried and hitch-hike into West Bridgford for my law exam that afternoon. But the main thing on my mind was Sam. She was then ten years old, and I am convinced that mum only lasted as long as she did because of her desperation to see her youngest daughter grow up. What was to become of her now?

To say the least, we were not well-equipped as a family to raise a ten-year-old. I was twenty-one, and back at school. Kevin was twenty, and in the Army and bound for Germany. Dawn was sixteen, and wholly incapable of looking after herself, never mind a child. My mother's last words to me rang in my ears, but I felt sure that they were motivated more by her hatred of my father, than by her love of her daughter. A couple of days after the funeral, having read about mum's death in the local newspaper's obituary column, he turned up out of nowhere on our doorstep to take Sam away.

It wasn't so bad. Being so much younger than the rest of us, she had never suffered from his black moods as we had, and he had never shown her anything but unmitigated love (albeit that he hadn't seen or contacted her, or any of us, since the day he had left). It was perfectly obvious to me that she should live with him. In any event, I knew the courts would insist if I resisted. She was asleep in bed when he arrived; he loaded all her things into his car, and away they went.

With Kevin away at Catterick in Yorkshire, my family was breaking up before my eyes. All that was left was Dawn and me.

I doubt two people were ever more unsuited to living together. With mum to mediate, we had maintained a sort of armed truce. Now there was no-one to keep us apart.

As a younger sister, Dawn had always been treated pretty severely by Kevin and me. It wasn't so much plain bullying, although there was plenty of that; it was more our little experiments, like testing the batcape. Not that we were not protective of her. I recall one evening when she was about fourteen, when I heard a suspicious noise in her bedroom and burst in to investigate. She had a boy in there, and they were both in a state of undress. I grabbed him by the scruff of the neck, marched him over to the window, and threw him out of it. He plummeted into our front garden, scrambled up and limped away as fast as his injuries allowed. He never came around again. Neither did any other local boys. Dawn may have seen my chivalry as misguided. Certainly, she was in no mood to submit to my authority.

Initially, we pulled together, too shocked to fight, but, under considerable pressure from many directions, I'm ashamed to admit that it stretched my normal belligerence towards her beyond breaking point. In my defence, it wasn't difficult to lose your temper with her. After leaving school she had got a job at Boots, and had managed to hold it down for almost a whole week before deciding to retire early for a life on the dole. She had a steady boyfriend, Rowland, who lived with us and who, if anything, was even more useless than she. Although he was only eighteen, he had spent more time behind bars than not, was covered in tattoos, and would eat only from a large dog bowl engraved with his nickname, 'Oggy'.

While I was revising in the college library, or sitting my exams, they would be lounging in front of the gas fire in our sitting room, smoking and watching television. They only got up to change channels or nip out to buy more cigarettes; certainly, they seemed to think that staples like coffee, bread, and milk appeared in the kitchen by magic.

A few days after mum's funeral, Dawn buttonholed me.

'Me and Oggy are always in the same room together,' she said, 'so we're only going to pay half the bills.'

Until now, we had gone thirds.

'No way!' I shouted. 'If anything, you should pay it all. You're the ones using all the gas and electric.'

A strong case, I felt, but she refused to budge. The following day brought the final straw. Coming home to find the downstairs loo window smashed, I let myself into the house with some caution, concerned that the burglars might be still there. Instead, I found only Dawn and Rowland, slobbing in front of the roaring fire, watching TV.

'Have you seen the window?' I exclaimed. 'Somebody's smashed it.'

'That was me,' said Dawn, without even looking up. 'I couldn't find my key.'

They left the following morning, heading for Nottingham to stay with some of Rowland's friends. I wasn't too worried about Dawn. She was the most streetwise sixteen-year-old imaginable.

CHAPTER TEN: A LITTLE BIT OF POLITICS

Thirty years to silk

AFTER ASDA SACKED me, I had signed on the dole again.

I remember the day I did it. A long line of glum people snaked around the dole office courtyard, and just ahead of me was a man waiting quietly with his young son. It reminded me of queuing at Cotgrave pit with my father to collect his wages, an honest day's pay for an honest day's work – all the men of my class ever asked. But the work wasn't there anymore, and I could sense the shame emanating from the man in front like a bad smell.

I'd become interested in politics after starting at college. Before then, all I knew was that I was a traditional Labour supporter. I joined the party, too, though I had no idea why, except that my father was solidly Labour. My mind was an empty jar, ready to receive whatever was poured into it, and I was easy prey for the more outré left-wing groups who dominated student politics. I joined the Militant Tendency (an unwelcome parasite on the Labour Party), bought a poster of Che Guevara, and started wearing silly hats.

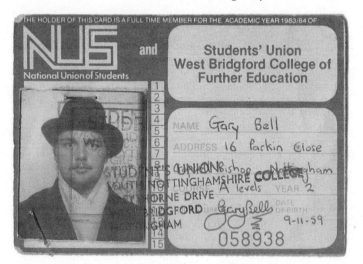

The staff, largely, were even more left-wing than the students. When my English language teacher wasn't deriding 'the system', he talked mostly of his plan to retire and start a sustainable garlic croft in central Wales (which he eventually did). The English literature teacher was hardly ever there: she spent two days a week educating the children of the Greenham Common protestors, *pro bono*.

By now into my A levels, I was elected President of the Students' Union and represented the college at the NUS conference in Blackpool. Many important issues were debated and settled, among them a vote to tell the Polish government that we students did not approve of them silencing Solidarity, and another to ban the playing of Kenny Rogers' *Ruby, Don't Take Your Love To Town* from college juke-boxes, on the grounds that it was offensive to disabled people.

Then, in April 1982, came the Falklands War. I still cannot understand the objections to that conflict. Islands belonging to Britain, populated by people who were to all intents and purposes British citizens, had been invaded by Argentina – a country ruled by a fascist dictator. There were no Argentineans living on the islands, there never had been any Argentineans living on the islands, and our claiming of the islands predated the very existence of modern-day Argentina. That country's sole and very flimsy claim to ownership rested on the fact that, at six hundred miles away, it was the closest mainland nation. People talked in dark tones about British 'colonialism', without apparently acknowledging that Argentina was itself founded on conquest. Perhaps they thought that the indigenous inhabitants had welcomed the Spanish *conquistadors* with open arms?

Mrs Thatcher immediately sent a task force to liberate the Falklands, while the Labour Party, the student left, and just about every idiot I knew came down firmly against it. Call me a cynic, but it seemed to me that some of them were so keen to attack the Tories that they were prepared, in effect, to support Galtieri's *junta*. They were not so much anti-war, as anti-Thatcher.

When the NUS denounced the war, I immediately – and with the full backing of the student body – withdrew our college from the union. When Michael Foot spoke out against the conflict on *Weekend World* I tore up my Labour Party membership card.

I wasn't the only one. The party no longer represented working people, and was – as it is to this day – led by a London-centric core of *bien pensant* trendies, many of them public school-educated, many of them very rich, some even titled. Their message to us was clear: know your place, *we* know what's best for *you*. Labour's main interest was no longer the pay and conditions of the working man and woman, it was the campaign for nuclear disarmament; in Cotgrave, our concerns were more prosaic, to say the least, and Margaret Thatcher took on Churchillian proportions to many in the village and millions of other working class voters.

There were plenty of criticisms of Thatcherism which could and should have been made, but it was hard to argue with her essential message, of self-help, hard work, and pulling yourself up by your bootstraps. People want dignity, not patronising handouts, and a lot of working folk were tired of paying high taxes to support those who neither worked nor – importantly – wanted to. Of course, many people *were* jobless through no fault of their own, but there were also plenty of scroungers in Cotgrave. Rich Hampstead liberals claimed such people didn't exist, and they didn't – not at Hampstead dinner parties. But we lived cheek-by-jowl with them. We saw their bedroom curtains firmly closed on cold, dark mornings when we left for work or college; we saw them partying and getting falling-down drunk in the pubs and Miners' Welfare every night.

In 1983, Cotgrave returned its first-ever Tory councillor.

In 1984, the year I turned twenty-five and went to university, Arthur Scargill took the men of the National Union of Mineworkers out on strike.

Perhaps he had fond memories of 1972, when all of Britain's miners had gone on strike together for the first time in fifty years.

Back then, they wanted a pay rise of nine pounds a week, up from twenty-five. That was not unreasonable. Mining was a filthy, dangerous job, and they were earning the equivalent of £14,500 a year in today's money, with inflation rampant.

Ted Heath's Tories were damned if they were going to get their nine quid, and so the miners stayed out for seven weeks. The country was beset by blackouts and lay-offs as the power stations ran short of coal, and it was a very hard time for all of us in Cotgrave. We children fared better than the adults. We had free school lunches during the week, and at weekends the NUM ran a soup kitchen at the Welfare. In between, we went to the village chip shop and begged for 'batter bits', which we smothered in salt and vinegar. NUM soup apart, my parents hardly ate at all during those seven weeks, but at least the miners won. Their pay was increased, and the Heath government (after a second strike in 1974) was doomed.

A decade later, in 1984, things were very different. Scargill had no democratic mandate for the strike which he called that year, but it must still have astonished him when the Nottinghamshire pits stayed open. Our lads had almost starved rather than cross the picket lines last time round, but Thatcherism meant everybody had bought their council houses, immediately sprucing them up with some stone-cladding and a new front door. People who had traditionally been paid in cash now got cheques, so they had to open bank accounts. Bank accounts meant overdrafts, and credit cards with which to buy luxuries – and run up debts. Scargill never had a chance. No other unions rushed to support him, and many of his own members were too worried about their mortgages to risk striking. The NUM was crushed, and Labour slid off the edge.

To this day, Nottingham Forest fans at away games in Yorkshire and on Merseyside can expect to be jeered at as 'scabs', and there are families where sons and fathers, brother and brother, haven't passed a word between them since the mid-1980s. That is tragic, and it reinforced in me the idea that politics rarely, if ever, has all of the answers. There are always many sides to any problem, and the pit closures were no exception.

The economic case was complex, and perhaps they were, in the long term, inevitable. Harold Wilson's Labour government, after all, had already shut more mines than Maggie Thatcher ever did. But I think few people now deny that they were handled badly. The entire *raison d'être* for Cotgrave, and many other villages and towns throughout Nottinghamshire, the north of England, and south Wales, was mining. Whole communities counted on men going underground and bringing up coal. It gave the men a purpose; it fed their families. To take that away with little apparent thought for what would happen next was verging on criminal.

And it happened to the 'scabs' too; in the early 1990s, Cotgrave pit closed – a bitter reward, perhaps, for supporting the government over the union.

* * *

OUR COTGRAVE TENANCY had been transferred into my name, but the house was a long way from college and held only bad memories for me so I swapped it for a two-bed flat in an enormous tower block in Radford.

It would not have looked out of place in Beirut, with broken windows, graffiti over all the walls, and urine, blood, and excrement in the stairwells. Many of the people who lived there – particularly the elderly – felt trapped, and didn't dare go out at night, particularly after the 1981 riots which took place outside my window.

But for me it was only a temporary arrangement. Lance Flynn moved in with me, and we enjoyed two halcyon, hedonistic years. We did the odd bit of A level studying, though it was only the odd bit. I had chosen law and history, which I taught myself from the source books in the library, and something called 'Communication Studies', to which I paid no attention whatsoever. Mostly, we messed about. We played football and rugby in the autumn and winter terms, cricket and tennis in the summer term, and squash all year round.

In the holidays, we would sign-on on a Monday (as you could in those days), collect and cash our fortnightly giros on the Wednesday, and immediately start hitch-hiking to France. It used to take us a couple of days to get to and from the Med, which gave us eight days lounging on the beach. During the long summer breaks, we would fit in three or four trips: for most of my A level years I was tanned and fit and – for the last time in my life, to date – thin, weighing in at an even twelve stone.

Partly, that was because I didn't eat much, because I was always broke, and partly it was because I tended to cycle to college, a hilly, four-mile journey which did wonders for my fitness.

Until one night, as I was coasting downhill towards home and I passed a stunning girl wearing a distractingly short skirt. I looked back, and rode straight into the back of a car which had stopped at traffic lights. I went sprawling, but there was no damage done – or so I thought. The following morning I set off again. I had a half-mile climb, followed by a welcome and extremely steep downhill of similar distance, and I was doing about 40mph as I approached a roundabout in the city centre. Unfortunately, when I applied the brakes it became horrifyingly apparent that the front set had been damaged the previous evening. As I pulled the lever, something went catastrophically wrong in the area of my front wheel, which locked solid and sent me flying over the handlebars and onto my face. Three of my front teeth tore through my lip and snapped off, and I needed about a hundred stitches to repair the wound. I looked like Plug of the *Bash Street Kids*; even worse, the wound turned sceptic and began to smell – right under my nose. About three hundred trips to the dentist later, I was back to my best, with a dashing scar to boot, but my cycling days were over.

We couldn't afford the bus, so Lance and I would walk the eight-mile round-trip every day. Even with this economy, we never managed to scrape together the money to pay our utility bills, or the rent. Whenever I received a demand, I left it a few weeks and then wrote back thanking them for sending a different, fictitious letter, on a made-up date, in which they had agreed to my offer of paying off my arrears at twenty pence a week. A few weeks later, they would write back querying my fictitious letter, and asking that I enclose a copy. I'd write back saying I'd thrown it away...

In that way, I managed to keep our gas and electricity on for eighteen months without paying a bill, and also saved us from eviction. Our only major crisis was when the picture tube blew on the TV one Christmas, leaving us with sound only. Lance went home to stay with his parents, while I had beans-on-toast on my own, listening to Morecambe and Wise on the telly.

I was growing up, slowly, though there were still moments when the old Gary reappeared. One night, I was in a bar in Keyworth with my new college friends and, as usual, I was hogging the limelight. A chap who wasn't with us, one Gary Robson, took exception to this. 'You've got a lot to say for yourself, haven't you?' he said.

'Yes,' I said, with a grin. 'Quite a lot.'

'Well, shut your fucking mouth,' he said, 'or I'll shut it for you.'

My slightly juvenile response was to open my mouth as widely as I could. Robson scrambled to his feet, and I gulped: he was massive, and built like Arnold Schwarzenegger. His friends held him back, and I made a show of going for him – once I was quite sure that *my* mates would hold *me* back. Then I allowed them to usher me outside.

'If I see him again,' I said, 'he's a dead man.'

Unfortunately, I *did* see him a few days later. I was running a college disco when a friend rushed over in a state of excitement.

'Gary Robson's here!' he said. 'He's looking for you!'

I followed his pointing finger, and my eyes met Gary Robson's. He stormed over as I stood my ground with heavy heart.

'We've got some unfinished business,' he said, prodding me in the chest.

Seeing no other way to avoid a beating, I replied via a head-butt to the face.

He collapsed in a crumpled heap on the floor, which seemed to settle our unfinished business. He didn't want any more, and I hadn't wanted the fight in the first place.

But such incidents were getting rarer. My A level tutor, a wonderful woman called Angela Green, had introduced me to classical music, opera, the theatre and ballet (we went to see Tchaikovsky's *Swan Lake* together), and had persuaded me to read Thomas Hardy instead of Frederick Forsyth. She also taught me to be less selfish. At her instigation, I rustled up a crowd of friends to help out at the old peoples' home next door to the college. We served lunch and tidied up, but the residents were desperately lonely and what they really needed was company. It became a regular thing, so popular that a rota system had to be introduced. To my surprise, I greatly enjoyed visiting the old folks, and would stay long after lunch was over, listening to their fascinating stories. But, mostly, the experience taught me that it was possible to influence others for good, rather than for mischief.

Angela also helped me apply to university. My plan was to take a year out and apply directly, rather than via UCCA (the forerunner of UCAS, the Universities and Colleges Admissions Service). I fancied Oxford, obviously, and wrote directly to Christ Church, but they had an entrance examination, and charged ten pounds to sit it; that was nearly half my weekly income, so I dropped the idea.

In the March of my final A level year, I was walking home from college when my sister Dawn stopped me in the street. We hadn't seen each other in a long time, and she had engineered the meeting.

'Hello, Gary,' she said.

'Hello, Dawn. How are you?'

'Not too bad, thanks. Yourself?'

'Alright. Are you still with Rowland?'

'Oggy, you mean.'

'Sorry, Oggy.'

'Yes.'

That was a good thing, because she was expecting his baby in a fortnight.

She lived nearby and invited me round for tea. I was pleased to see that Rowland had matured into a very solid and decent man (they're still together), but I was less pleased that they were living in a disgusting bed-and-breakfast slum – ten bedrooms, no electric sockets, and one shared bathroom. The landlord served breakfast, allowing him to charge the DHSS quadruple rent, but it consisted of toasted white bread with margarine and tinned tomatoes served by two of the tenants, both of whom were filthy and scabies-ridden and one of whom had a permanently weeping and pustulant sore on his neck. Unsurprisingly, no-one took advantage.

Dawn had been promised a council house after her baby was born, and fortunately Daniel arrived on March 15, 1983. There were complications at the birth, and he was kept in hospital for a few days; Dawn and Rowland moved into my flat, ten minutes from the hospital, to be near him until they were allowed to take him home to their new place in Cropwell Bishop, a couple of miles from Cotgrave.

I soon joined them, moving out of my own slum flat in a moonlight flit. By that time, the electricity and gas had finally been cut off, and the rent arrears made the Greek national debt look puny.

I duly sat my A levels, and left college that June. In my final report, the perceptive Angela Green wrote:

> Gary has, surprisingly, by native wit, managed to survive his three years here. He may or may not pass his forthcoming exams. I personally hope he does do well, but the staff need time to recover from his onslaught on the college so I hope there aren't any more where he came from!

I had no-one to show it to, sadly.

I went back the day the A level results came out. A sheet of paper was stuck on the notice board, and my surname was near the top.

Grade B in history, Grade C in Law and Grade C in Communication Studies.

I breathed a huge sigh of relief. Ten UCCA points – enough to get into a reasonable university.

As I left, clutching my certificates, Dr Magee hurried out of his room and stopped me with a hand on my shoulder.

'I knew you wouldn't let me down, Gary,' he said. 'Well done!'

I really needed that. *Someone* appreciated what I was doing.

Now all I had to do was apply to university and work out what I was going to do during my gap year.

* * *

THE ANSWER WAS supplied via a great friend from college, Sarah Dixon. Sarah was at South Bank Poly, and I would often stay with her at weekends. She introduced me to a girl called Julie Preston who was reading German. I took an instant fancy to Julie, and within a week we were going out.

There were only two problems.

The first was that her course took her to Germany for a year.

The second was that she already going out with a hulking German bodybuilder called Jorg.

But Jorg lived in Trier, and Julie was going to Stuttgart – several hundred miles distant – so it seemed a reasonably safe arrangement.

I went over for a short visit, to see the lay of the land, and as I was hitching back home through Aachen I met a hapless German physics undergraduate called Frank, who was heading to Scotland to find the Loch Ness Monster. Remembering the hospitality of the angelic German girl on that snowy night in Osnabrück, I invited him to stay with me and Dawn for a few days. It was a hard-lived few days, too, with thirty-six holes of golf every day, and pubbing and clubbing at night. Frank was astonished at the generosity of the English in one particular club, where the barman – Simmo – kept our glasses charged but simply refused to take our money.

When Frank finally headed off in search of Nessie, I went back to Stuttgart to move in with Julie. We had a marvellous apartment in Feuerbach, a short tram ride away from Stuttgart city centre. I got a job at the McDonalds on the Königstraße, but most of my time I spent growing exceedingly fat on German food and culture. I developed a strong love-hate relationship with the Germans. They are the most socially-responsible people I know, and Germany is clean, safe, and pretty much crime-free. But they do seem to be rather smug and formal. After a year working in the same office, Julie still had to call her colleagues – girls of her own age – Fräulein Schmidt and Fräulein Heidler. I told them to call me 'Gary', but they were horrified.

They are in my experience also terribly mean. We'd be invited to someone's house for supper, and, when it was time to leave, the host would first produce a receipt to indicate the cost of the drinks and the ingredients used in the meal, and then a calculator so as to divide that cost between those present.

But their worst trait – the one which got them into all that trouble with Hitler – is their obsession with obeying orders. One wintry Wednesday morning, I had gone out to buy some milk. It was -26°C, there was two feet of snow on the ground, and all of the roads were closed. As I plodded across a deserted street to get to the shop, a policeman sprang out from a doorway.

'Entschuldigen sie bitte!' he said.

'Ya, kann ich Ihnen helfen?' I replied.

'Oh, you are English,' he smiled.

I hate it when they do that.

'Yes,' I said, through gritted teeth.

'I regret to inform you dat you crossed der road when der red man was showing on der signal,' he said, pointing to a nearby pedestrian crossing.

'Well, yes,' I said. 'But the road is closed.'

'It is against der law to cross when der man is red,' he said. 'You must pay a fine of ten marks.'

'I know it's against the law,' I said. 'But the road is closed. There are no cars on it. Can't you see that?'

'Yes,' he replied, looking up and down the road to confirm it. 'Ten marks, please.'

I had to pay up.

Of course, in spite of the grim weather, our post arrived that morning at exactly the correct time. And in it was a letter with a Bristol postmark, forwarded to Germany from Dawn's house.

When I'd finally made my university applications, I had optimistically put Bristol – thought by many to be the best university at which to read law – as my first choice.

The letter was from Bristol Law Faculty: they would like to see me for interview, on Friday morning.

Forty-eight hours and some seven hundred miles away.

I set out ten minutes later. It was slow going in the snow, but I finally arrived in Ostend on the Thursday afternoon. I cadged a lift across the Channel with a lorry driver, and at Dover I hitched up the A2 into London and thence out west on the M4. I stopped off at Leigh Delamere services for a couple of hours' sleep in the canteen, before rousing myself for the short distance that remained.

I arrived at the Law Faculty half-an-hour before my interview, taking a moment to be suitably awed by the stunning Gothic revival building – paid for by the Wills tobacco dynasty, in order to train lawyers to sue them a century later. I was nervous. My ten A level points guaranteed me a place *somewhere*, but I was a shade light for a top university like Bristol, whose usual requirement was fifteen points, or A-A-A at A level. I caught sight of myself in a glazed door. Did I at least *look* the part? I wasn't sure. I was wearing jeans and a dinner jacket, bought from Oxfam in Nottingham for three pounds, set off with a bow tie – which was what you wore with a dinner jacket, after all.

Yes, of *course* I looked the part.

I waited anxiously, smoothing my moustache, as confident young men and women in sober suits, gleaming brogues, and immaculate hairstyles preceded me into the interview room.

Did I look the part, though?

'Mr Bell, please,' said someone.

Inside the room, I relaxed. There was a bust of Lenin on the desk, and a poster of Che Guevara on the wall.

Back at college, I had taken O level sociology in my second A level year, having bet the sociology lecturer Steve Broomhead a fiver that I could pass it by attending only one lecture. I got a grade C and, as Steve handed over the money, he asked me how I'd done it.

'When I was in doubt about what to write,' I explained, 'I turned left.'

I did the same with the two professors in front of me now. Not that it was difficult.

'I see that your father is a coalminer,' said one of them, approvingly. One's father's occupation was a compulsory question on the rather sexist UCCA form at that time.

'Yes,' I replied.

'Things must be very difficult at the moment,' piped up the other.

I was momentarily confused.

'Is your father actually on strike?' he added, fishing to see if my old man was a scab.

I hadn't seen my dad for a very long time, but he was old school, politically.

'He'd sooner die than cross a picket line,' I replied, truthfully.

'How did you get here?' the second interviewer asked.

'I hitch-hiked,' I said, taking out my rifle and blasting away at this barrelful of fish.

'Did it take long?' he said, a tear almost forming in his eye.

'Two days,' I said. I didn't mention that I'd come from Stuttgart.

'I suppose money must be tight?' said the first one, a quaver in his voice.

'A bit.'

They conferred briefly, and one of them took a twenty-pound note from his pocket.

'The university has a hardship fund,' he said, offering me the money, 'to assist with travel expenses.'

'I'm sorry,' I smiled, shaking my head. 'But I can't accept charity.'

'Thank you very much for coming,' he said, putting the note back in his pocket. 'We'll see you next year.'

So I was in – just like that!

If Arthur Scargill achieved nothing else in 1984, at least he helped me realise my dream.

CHAPTER ELEVEN: UNIVERSITY

Twenty-eight years to silk

I PITCHED UP at university that autumn, two months short of my twenty-fifth birthday.

My arrival was not conventional. Hitch-hiking back from Stuttgart to Dawn's place to collect my stuff, I had by chance got a lift from a van driver who was delivering something to the village next door to Dawn's and coming back south with an empty van. Somehow, I persuaded him to take me to Dawn's, help me pick up all my stuff, and then drop me at Milton Keynes railway station.

I don't know why I did that: it was a typically ill-thought out and naïve plan. I didn't have any money for my fare, and I didn't really know how trains worked. I foolishly assumed that, if you were travelling from A to B, you simply caught a train at A and it dropped you at B. It was with some dismay that I learned – at Milton Keynes – that a journey to Bristol involved travelling via Euston, and included taking the tube to Paddington where I would catch a whole different train to the West Country.

To get onto the Euston train, I simply borrowed a guard's trolley and brazenly pushed it onto the platform with my various bags and boxes. But at Euston there were guards at the barrier checking the tickets of arriving passengers. I decided the best policy was to tell the truth.

'I'm travelling to Bristol, and...' I said, to a guard.

'Bristol?' he interrupted. 'You're at the wrong station, mate – you want Paddington.'

'*Paddington?*' I said, swiftly abandoning the truth. 'But I was told Euston.'

'Well, you were told wrong,' the guard replied, forgetting to wonder how I came to be on the wrong side of the barrier. He opened the gate and let me through. I'd made it to London free of charge, but I was unlikely to be able to scam the rest of the journey. Praying she was in, I called my old mate Sarah Dixon, still in London and now living in Leytonstone. Within the hour, this wonderful woman arrived to save my life with enough money for a taxi to Paddington, a train to Bristol, and another taxi to my hall of residence.

* * *

BRISTOL UNIVERSITY EXISTED to provide a safety net for public school pupils who had failed Oxbridge, and I was just about the only student reading law in my year who hadn't been educated privately. If my working class northern credentials had impressed the interviewing professors, they didn't impress anyone else. My contemporaries affected floppy hair and wore salmon-pink trousers. I looked like this (you can't see the stonewashed Lee Coopers and white socks):

I stood out markedly from everyone else – not that they seemed to notice. They certainly didn't bother talking to me. I was used to being the centre of attention. Now I was an insignificant minnow in a giant lake. The whole thing was unsettling. I'm a gregarious sort, and I was very lonely.

CHAPTER ELEVEN: UNIVERSITY

It didn't help that I was deemed too old to live in the normal halls of residence, and was housed in a block for mature and overseas students. It was practically next door to the Law Faculty, which was good, but everyone else on my course lived miles away so I had no opportunity for evening bonding. Not that that would have been easy. I was miles out of my social depth. I had hoped it was true that all posh girls really fancied a bit of rough, but unfortunately it wasn't. Posh girls liked men with good looks, style, charm, breeding, and money. I wasn't *too* bad-looking, I suppose, certainly the right side of hideous, but I was struggling on the other fronts, and I felt distinctly inadequate, especially when comparing myself to the other male students.

People like Tom Purton, for instance. It was easy to hate Tom. An Old Westminsterian, he was tall, charming, and handsome, and all the girls loved him. He was also the first really wealthy person I had met. Living two miles from the campus, and not being much of a public transport man, he bought himself a shiny new moped, on which he could soon be seen zipping about the place. Until it rained. At which point he went into a Volkswagen dealer and bought a VW Golf convertible. The moped stayed chained to some railings, abandoned, until we graduated. For all I know, it's still there.

And when, after four lunchtime pints, he had to leave the Golf parked up and catch the bus home, he solved *that* problem by buying a flat a few minutes' walk from the Law Faculty, with breathtaking views over the Avon Gorge.

I quickly formed the opinion that Tom deserved a good kicking, but contented myself with ignoring him, and getting on with my studies. At least I wasn't intellectually intimidated. I quickly realised that this lot were no cleverer than I. They had just had more – a *lot* more – opportunity and encouragement. I threw myself into it like never before, was awarded firsts for my first three essays, and dominated my tutorials and lectures. I wasn't enjoying myself, but then I wasn't at university to make friends.

My problem with Tom Purton and his easy confidence finally spilled over in a tort tutorial – a 'tort' being a civil wrong, such as trespass, or defamation. We were discussing the implications of a very famous 1932 case, Donoghue v Stevenson, which revolved around a bottle of ginger beer sold to one Mary Donoghue at a Paisley café. The bottle contained a decomposing snail, and Mary suffered gastroenteritis and shock (she was easily shocked). She successfully sued the manufacturer of the ginger beer, one David Stevenson, and the judgment – that Stevenson could reasonably have foreseen that his failure to keep dead snails out of his pop might harm someone who drank it – created the modern concept of negligence.

Purton and I found ourselves in disagreement as to liability, and he dismissed my interpretation of the law in such a patronising manner that I thought the matter needed sorting out, Cotgrave style. I suggested that we take it outside to the car park.

Not only did he refuse to fight me, he found the very idea extremely amusing: the more I goaded him, the funnier he found it.

I was humiliated. I could just about have taken losing a fight – he was a big lad – but to be laughed off like that was something I'd never experienced. I now realise that this is one of the great differences between the working class and our brothers in the middle and upper classes. We fight in order to hold our positions in the pecking order; they don't, because their places in the world are assured.

I left with as much dignity as I could muster. Clearly Cotgrave rules did not apply at Bristol.

At least – not always. I recall an early law book sale, where second year students were selling their old textbooks to first years. I secured a copy of *Smith and Hogan's Criminal Law* for a tenner, but later found I had been ripped off – it was hopelessly out of date. I went to find the chap who had sold it to me and demanded my money back.

'*Caveat emptor*,' he replied, with a scornful laugh. 'Let the buyer beware.'

By way of reply, I grabbed the startled youth by the lapels.

'No,' I spat. 'Let the *seller* beware! If I don't get my money back I'm going to shove this book up your arse!'

He paid up immediately.

But this was a rare success for Animal. If I was going to get on, I needed a different strategy.

My next gambit was to stand for first year Law Club President. I had won every election I'd stood in at college, but when I saw the names of the other candidates – Vipal Desai (Wimbledon College), James Barnes (Rugby), and Clive Jeffries (Lancing) – I wondered whether I'd made a fool of myself. These people were about as posh as the Queen. But, to my great astonishment, I was elected in a landslide. I felt a little more sure of myself after that, though it didn't cure my general sense of anger and injustice, especially in respect of Tom Purton.

Until one lunchtime, when he approached me as we left a lecture.

'Hi,' he said, extending his hand. 'I don't think we've been formally introduced? I'm Tom.'

I took it, too surprised to do anything else. 'I'm Gary,' I said.

'I was wondering if you'd like a spot of lunch?' he said.

'Er… Yes,' I said.

It was the start of an enduring friendship. Far from the arrogant and condescending person of my imagination, Tom was – is – a kind and generous man, with a wicked sense of humour, and a tremendous thirst for life.

It proved a breakthrough moment. To my surprise, he and his set welcomed me with open arms and, if my first few weeks had been miserable, the rest of the first year was very different. I pushed my overdraft to gargantuan limits, and ignored my bank manager's entreaties. My studies went to the wall, too, as one of my contract law essays – written in the style of a ruling handed down by a Court of Appeal judge – suggests:

Garry Bell

Contract

I have read the essay of my colleague Lord Vickers of Somerset and I wish to concur with his judgement.

You may share his opinion but unfortunately you are not going to share his rank

But then I came across a lifeline – debating. This was to play a major part in my life, though it all started, as things often seem to for me, by chance.

I attended a presentation by the top London solicitors Norton Rose, at which they laid it on thick about the glittering careers that awaited us, before dropping a nasty bombshell.

'Of course,' said the chap, 'we only employ people with first-class honours degrees, or other evidence of outstanding ability.'

As things stood, I had about as much chance of getting a first as of joining the Chippendales. But did I detect a slight get-out in his words?

'What do you mean by "other evidence of outstanding ability"?' I piped up.

'If you excel in something like debating,' he said.

I rushed round to the Debating Union first thing next day and found, to my delight, that entries closed that very afternoon for an open competition. Needing a team-mate, I scurried off to Tom Purton's flat, but he wasn't interested.

'Come on, Tom,' I said, picking up the Norton Rose promotional brochure from his coffee table, and flourishing it. 'We're not going to get firsts. If we want a job at Norton Rose, we've got to do something like this.'

'That's true,' he said, 'unless your father is the senior partner.'

He went to answer a knock at the door, and I looked at the brochure. *Norton Rose – senior partner Peter Purton.*

Tom reappeared, followed by James Barnes.

'I'll join you, Gary,' said James. 'I did a lot of debating at Rugby.'

I was petrified almost to the point of speechlessness in our first debate, but James carried me through. I improved in the second and, in the third, we upset the form book by annihilating the tournament favourites. That put us into the knock-out stage – the only first-year students to qualify. We swept on through the next three rounds, only to come up short in the final in front of five hundred people. But runners-up felt pretty good; shortly afterwards, James and I were elected Secretary and Treasurer of the Debating Union respectively, with Tom Purton as Master of Ceremonies.

My public speaking slowly improved, but I was far from the finished article and not terribly confident in my abilities. As part of our law degree we had to take part in a competitive moot, where we would argue a point of complicated law in front of professors posing as Court of Appeal judges. James Barnes and I were drawn as a team against Tom Purton and Ronnie Vickers.

James was entirely convinced that our natural flair would overcome the incredible amount of preparation put in by our opponents. I didn't share his optimism, especially as I watched Ronnie and Tom carrying a huge number of heavy law books into the mock courtroom, with colour-coded Post-it notes tagging the relevant pages.

But I needn't have worried. Even as Tom reached for his first authority, a complex landmark tort case called *The Wagon Mound No.2* which concerned breach of duty of care in negligence, the wheels started to come off his carefully-prepared moot. As he turned to the page flagged by his pink Post-it note, he found to his dismay that it didn't identify the Wagon Mound Case he had expected, but an entirely different matter called *Brown*, about the lawfulness or otherwise of sado-masochists nailing their testicles to a coffee table.

Unaccountably, Ronnie Vickers experienced similar confusions with *his* Post-it notes, and these mix-ups unsettled the pair of them sufficiently that, hopelessly underprepared as we were, James and I stormed to victory. (Tom later accused us, wholly without justification, of sabotaging his and Ronnie's authorities. If there's one thing I can't stand, it's a bad loser.)

My life of partying like a sort of low-rent Charles Ryder was interrupted during that year by terrible news from home. My brother Kevin had had a difficult life. In a family of generally short stature, he stopped growing at seven, and underwent unpleasant human growth hormone treatments at Great Ormond Street hospital during his teens. He eventually reached average height for our family – a shade under five feet – and to his great credit he overcame that hurdle to join the Royal Corps of Signals as a technician. He had left the Army and settled back in Nottingham with his wife Margaret and their son, Richard, and Margaret had recently given birth to a daughter, Rebecca. But I received a call one day to tell me that Rebecca had died in her sleep. She was three months old, and I never met her.

The sheer injustice of it made me weep. Margaret had lost her mother as a child, and had been raised in various foster homes; surely she and Kevin had suffered enough grief, between the two of them.

The funeral was held in Radford, with a cremation at West Bridgford. I was trying to work out which buses Dawn and I would need to catch to get there, when Tom Purton spoke up.

'I'll drive you, Gary,' he said. 'Don't worry.'

It went as smoothly as it could, and we finally retired to a small wake. Apart from a few friends of Kevin and Margaret's, the only others present were my Auntie Eileen (mum's adoptive sister) and her husband, Uncle Harold. Harold was a builder with hands like shovels, who had fought at Monte Cassino in the war, and was not shy of mentioning it. I hadn't seen him for a long time, and he was full of advice and concern for my welfare.

'Hey up, our Gary,' he said, beaming.

'Hey up, Harold,' I said.

'Are you married yet, me duck?' he said, looking suspiciously at Tom.

'No, not yet,' I said.

'You want to get a move on.'

'But Harold, I'm only young.'

He sighed, and changed the subject. 'Have you got a job?'

'No,' I said. 'I'm a student.'

Like Shania Twain, that did not impress him much.

'I don't know, me duck,' he said. 'I *knew* you'd never come to anything.'

'But Harold, I'm at university doing a degree,' I said. 'In law.'

'I don't know,' he said again, and then he fell silent for a few moments. He seemed to be having some sort of internal debate with himself; he would sigh, then tut, then raise his eyebrows, and then shake his head. Finally, he set his jaw at me. 'I'm probably being an idiot to meself,' he said, 'but your mother would have wanted me to help you if I could.'

'What?' I said. 'How?'

'There's a job going at our builder's yard,' he said, taking my hands in his and boring into me with his pale blue eyes. 'If I have a word with the gaffer, I reckon I can swing it for you.'

'But Harold,' I protested. 'I'm studying *law*. At *university*. I'm going to be a *barrister*.'

'I don't know,' he said, releasing my hands and admitting defeat. 'There's no helping some people. You're that stubborn, it's like fighting the bloody Jerries at Monte Cassino.'

* * *

THE FACT WAS, Harold just could not understand what I meant. I might as well have been talking French, or trying to explain the concept of non-violent protest in the Cotgrave Miners' Welfare bar.

159

My mum had said it to me, years earlier: people like us did not become lawyers. People like us didn't even take our O levels. You got a job, you got married, and you settled down. As it had been, so it would always be – except that it wouldn't. The pits were closing, the factory work was going to the Far East, everything was being mechanised and automated and computerised. The jobs-for-life, which had fed, clothed, and housed men of my class and their families for centuries, were disappearing. I may not have articulated it in that way at the time, but I could see that the world was changing, and I was determined to change with it.

I'm not ashamed of my roots by any means – I wouldn't be laying them bare in this book if I were – but I'm not particularly proud of them, either. To my mind, you should have pride in things you have achieved, things you have worked for, sweated for – not something you are by a mere accident of birth. It wasn't a popular view in some quarters. My old O level sociology lecturer Steve Broomhead had asked us during the single lesson that I had attended what class we were from. Most people said middle class, but Lance Flynn was clarity itself.

'Working class, and proud of it,' he said.

'Proud of what?' I said. 'Proud of the fact that our families have worked their fingers to the bone to make other people rich?'

'What about the dignity of labour?' said Steve, a middle class revolutionary if ever there was one.

'I don't see *you* getting your hands dirty,' I said.

'You're talking bollocks,' said Lance.

'If labour is so dignifying, why are you planning to go to university?' I said. 'I assume you won't be going down the pit when you get a degree?'

'Just because you get an education, it doesn't mean you have to turn your back on your class,' said Broomhead.

I wasn't going to turn my back on anyone – certainly not my family or friends – and indeed I have not. But while I stayed in touch with my roots, my horizon was obviously widening. This is natural. You make friends at school, then new friends at college, then new friends at university. Each time you move on, you're further from your past. The deeper I immersed myself in my new university crowd, the more I realised that many of these people would be with me for the rest of my life.

Tom Purton had a new girlfriend and we saw less of him, and by now I was spending most of my time with the Old Rugbeian James Barnes. He was to become my greatest friend, the best man at my wedding, and Godfather to my son, Harry. But if my daughter ever comes home with a man like him, he's going straight out of the bedroom window. James was bitter ugly, with bad skin, dandruff, and a wardrobe consisting mostly of a raggy, lime-green jersey. He was also extremely dirty in his habits. He never bathed, held what I believe to be the world record for the most consecutive days spent wearing the same pair of boxer shorts and socks, had terrible breath, smoked forty cigarettes a day, and was rarely sober. But he was also wholly irresistible to women. I was astounded at the quantity and quality of his conquests, and by the stylish way in which he would end relationships when he felt they had run their course. I recall one girl, Camilla, who had been seeing James for a couple of weeks – long enough, in his view. Camilla had come over to his flat, and was waiting for him to get ready – which meant putting in his contact lenses – when she noticed a handwritten *aide-mémoire* on the table.

'What's this, James?' she said.

'Just a list of things to do,' he said.

'Oh,' she said. 'Do your washing, buy some milk… what's this? Dinner with Valerie? Who's Valerie?'

'She's the girl I'm taking to dinner tonight,' he said.

'What about me?'

'I think you'll find that's next on the list.'

She looked down. 'Pack Camilla in!' she yelped.

He strolled over, took the list from her, and ticked the item in question. 'There you go,' he smiled, and opened the front door.

It was James who first suggested the metamorphosis.

* * *

IT HAPPENED TOWARDS the end of my first year. *The Official Sloane Ranger Handbook* had not long been published, detailing the *minutiae* of social acceptability – what to wear, how to speak, why you should eat jelly with a fork, read Dick Francis novels, and live in the country ('or, failing that, Kensington Square'). A moment's study would confirm whether you were PLU (people like us), one of the *nouveaux riches*, or a mere prole (there was no doubt into which bracket I fell). It had quickly become Bristol's bible, and was being followed slavishly by everyone who was anyone.

I happened to be at Tom's flat one day, and was admiring the photograph of Princess Diana, the Sloane's Sloane, on the cover, when James arrived.

'Hello, Gary,' he said. 'Thinking of becoming a Sloane?'

'Am I not one already?' I said, with a laugh.

'Not quite,' he said, grinning.

'What's the difference between you and me?' I said, putting the book down. 'Give it to me straight.'

I'll list his main observations.

Hair: I wore mine close-cropped, whereas Sloanes tended to the floppy, Hugh Grant look.

Moustache: A huge *faux pas*. Sloanes were clean-shaven.

Shirts: Lumberjack shirts were out, and Thomas Pink stripes were in, worn with a silk tie.

Jerseys: I didn't have any. I needed at least one, preferably from Benetton.

Coats: I didn't have one of those, either. I needed a Crombie, and a Barbour.

Trousers: I would have to swap my tight, stonewashed jeans for baggy green cords (worn without a comb in the back pocket).

Pants: Y-fronts were also a no-no; Sloanes wore boxer shorts, preferably spotty ones.

Socks: My extensive collection of white socks would need immediate binning; Burlington Argyles were the thing.

Shoes: Ditto my comfy Dunlop Green Flash, in favour of Church's brogues.

'Anything else?' I said, a little dispirited.

'Your name could do with changing.'

'What's wrong with Gary?'

'It's very working class,' he informed me. 'Probably second only to Kevin.'

'That's my brother's name.'

'And one more thing,' he said. 'You absolutely have to get rid of that awful northern accent.'

I spoke like everyone else from Nottingham, with flat vowels and 'th' sounds pronounced 'f'. I dropped every 'h' and 'g', and called everyone 'duck'. It sounded fine to me. But James got me thinking: could I succeed as a barrister if I didn't come from the same *milieu* as most of the rest of the Bar?

And – given that I didn't – could I fake it?

The more I thought about it, the more I realised that it would be a big help if I became upper-middle class.

* * *

THE UNIVERSITY YEAR ended with my attire, accent, and bearing unchanged. Needing to pay off my overdraft, I headed off to a camp-site near Montpellier, where I got a job picking up litter with a stick with a nail in the end of it, and an evening job as a barman.

The bar was frequented entirely by French people, and it was while chatting with them one night that it struck me that I pronounced the word 'France' with a flat 'a' when speaking English, but with a longer 'a' when speaking French. I was equally comfortable with both, and started experimenting quietly to myself with English words. For instance, 'bath' was 'baff' in Nottinghamese, but 'barth' in the style of James Barnes; the more I said 'barth', the more I liked it. It sounded… more barristerial.

One morning, I looked in the mirror and saw a Rubicon which needed crossing. With a squirt of foam, and a swipe or two of the razor, my moustache was gone, never to return. For the rest of the summer, I made a deliberate and conscious effort to change my accent. Mostly, I would practise in my tent; it must have sounded absurd for a while, but by the time September rolled around I had arrived at a fair approximation of a BBC newsreader from the 1940s. I had also grown my hair and, as soon as I got home – having thought for a moment about paying off my overdraft – I invested the £700 I had saved up on a variety of brogues, cords, and striped shirts.

Before going back to university, I went up north to visit my sister and some of my Cotgrave mates, and it was while I was strolling through the village that I happened across my old school friend Mick Pringle. He was working on a car outside his parents' house, where he still lived, and he invited me in for a coffee, having first remarked that my painfully-cultivated BBC accent made me sound like 'a cockney'.

We chatted about old times for a while, and then he suddenly stood up and announced that he needed to get ready because he was going out to a 'posh do' that night. His house wasn't very big, and it was easy for me to conduct a conversation with him whilst I sat in the kitchen and he busied himself with getting ready upstairs.

'It should be a good night,' he called down. 'D'you fancy coming?'

'I can't,' I said, apologetically. 'I'm expected somewhere else.'

'Come on,' he said. 'There'll be loads of people there that you haven't seen for years. You'll have a great time.'

'I can't Pring, I'm sorry.'

'Course you can,' he said, forcing the issue. 'Mind you… have you got any smart clothes to wear?'

'Yes, I have,' I snorted. 'I'm wearing them.'

'Let's see,' he said, peering over the banister.

I stood up to reveal my new Sloane Ranger wardrobe. 'This is smart, isn't it?' I said.

'No,' he said, tersely. 'Haven't you got a suit with you?'

As he spoke, he was descending the stairs, and now he walked into the kitchen.

His outfit was a classic of the period. He had a packet of cigarettes in the breast pocket of his shirt, the material of which was so thin that not only could I clearly read what brand they were, I could tell how many fags were left. The suit itself was made of grey, woven polyester with rainbow flecks so loud that they seemed to wink at you. His trousers were the regulation six inches too short, giving a tantalising glimpse of white sock, and his shoes were of such highly combustible plastic that they'd have been dangerous in direct sunlight. He'd topped it all off with a tie that resembled the tail of a kite.

The whole effect was so stunning that I completely forgot Pring's last question. He strode over to a mirror, ran a comb through his hair and moustache before tucking it into his back pocket, and then turned to me as he slid his sovereign rings onto his fingers.

'Well,' he said. 'Have you got a suit or not?'

'Er, no,' I said.

'I didn't think you would have,' he sneered. 'You always were a scruffy bastard.'

Back at university there was much hilarity at the new Gary Bell when I turned up for the first day of term.

The official university newsletter had a column, called *Nonesuch*, dedicated to gossip about the smart set. Everyone was desperate to feature in it, though this had been but a pipe dream for me during my first year. In the first issue at the start of my second year, there I was!

Meanwhile Gary 'Dumb' Bell must be congratulated on his contribution to raising the social tone. His wonderful efforts of buying a completely new wardrobe, including, we expect, Barbour and trimmings, must make him our leading contender to take over from Huge (sic) Elwes as President of the very exclusive 'I'd love to be mentioned in *Nonesuch* club.'

I never failed to get a mention in *Nonesuch* thereafter.

One chap, Dominic Sanders, saw an opportunity for even more fun.

'Gary,' he said, one day, 'why don't we go the whole hog and turn you into an Old Etonian?'

That sounded amusing, so I became Eliza Doolittle to Dominic's Henry Higgins. He and a bunch of other OEs spent hours tutoring me on the finer points of 'School'. I was fed – and lapped up – an entire, fictional backstory… which house I'd belonged to, who my contemporaries had been, the names and foibles of various masters, and so on. We took it so far that I was signed up to play for the Old Etonian team in the University football league, and went 'back' to Eton several times to play the Field Game against the current school teams – hence the vignette which opens this book.

Even now, I still amuse myself from time to time by adopting an OE persona, occasionally helping things along by wearing an Old Etonian tie – there's no law against it, after all, it's just a blue striped piece of cloth. I must be pretty good at it, too, because to this day I meet people who are *convinced* I was at Eton with them. Or Rugby. I do a pretty decent Cheltenham, too – Rageh Omaar certainly remembers knowing me there!

And, I must say, I enjoyed it all immensely. One afternoon, Radio Bristol turned up at the law faculty to do on-the-spot interviews with Sloanes about their extravagant lifestyles. Most people were tame and guarded, but I gave them exactly what they wanted.

'What car do you drive?' said the interviewer.

'Whichever one I feel like driving when I get up in the morning,' I said.

I became something of an overnight celebrity.

The real world has a habit of intruding, of course. Christmas came around and, far from being the son of a stockbroker or a minor aristocrat, with a country pile to return to, I had nowhere to go. My relationship with Julie Preston, of South Bank Poly and Stuttgart, had long since fizzled out, so going to stay with her was not an option. Dawn had given birth to a second child, Zoe, and Samantha – having enjoyed living with my father as much as we had – was now ensconced with her so there was no room for me.

I planned to stay on at Bristol on my own, but word got round and the offers flooded in. Dominic Sanders invited me to his family estate for the first week of the Christmas break, and James Barnes and his family offered to host me for the following three.

Dominic lived with his mother and step-father, a larger-than-life character called Dennis Lennox, on a large country estate in Shropshire. On the first morning, he and I went shooting – not something I'd done before – and I have to admit that a kind of primeval bloodlust came over me after I shot a rabbit. I know that they cause untold damage to farms and have to be culled, but I didn't care about that – to my eternal shame, I just enjoyed the killing. The local hunt met the next day, followed by the Shropshire Landowner's Dinner, an annual event which was being hosted on the Lennox estate and to which I was invited. I wasn't sure which spoon you used to eat the fish course, but I followed the conversation alright. Just like back home in Cotgrave, it revolved around desperate financial hardship: one poor chap had been forced to sell a Turner to meet a tax bill, while others had flogged off their estates in Scotland, or (like Dennis Lennox) the family castle.

After dinner, the ladies retired somewhere, and port and cigars were brought out for the gentlemen (in which number I was pleased to be counted). One of them, Lord somebody or other, turned to me.

'You're a friend of Dominic's, I understand?'

'Yes.'

'Were you at school with him?'

'No,' I said, figuring that I'd be unlikely to pull off my Old Etonian act in this company.

'So where *were* you at school?'

'Er… the school on the hill,' I replied, truthfully. Toot Hill Comprehensive *was* on a hill, after all.

'Ah,' he nodded approvingly. 'Harrow. A jolly decent school.'

From Dominic's, I hitch-hiked to James's. The Barnes family lived at Kington Grange, a grade II-listed manor house in a village near Stratford-upon-Avon, and were the sort of people about whom PG Wodehouse and Evelyn Waugh might have written. Indeed, in the years that followed, I was virtually adopted by James' family, and Kington Grange became my Brideshead. His mother, Greta, a veritable Lady Marchmain, was a world expert on asthma who hated drinking and smoking, both of which her son did to great excess. That she had her concerns as to my own health was made clear on our first meeting.

'Goodness me!' she said, by way of a greeting. 'You're fat!'

It was not an allegation I could deny, having by now regained all the weight I'd lost whilst starving myself to death in Cannes. I quickly learned that Greta was not one to beat about the bush. But in time she became – and remains – a very generous and supportive figure in my life, who encouraged me to aim as high as I could.

James' father David, the senior partner of a large firm of accountants, worked like a Trojan and played just as hard. He thrashed me repeatedly at tennis – they had a court in the garden, naturally – and introduced me to the more ancient and highbrow sport of real tennis, at nearby Leamington Spa. (Players of vastly different abilities can still play a competitive game of real tennis, thanks to its astonishingly complicated handicapping system. This was almost certainly the first such system to appear in any sport, and

– so the story goes – was brought in to assist Henry VIII in the sixteenth century. Once a formidable player, Henry gradually got fatter and lamer, and the handicapping became more and more extreme, culminating in Henry winning the All England Championship one year against an opponent who had to carry a chair in his left hand and play all of his shots whilst standing on it.)

In return, I introduced the Barneses to football, taking them to watch Nottingham Forest play Birmingham City at St Andrews on Boxing Day. Forest won 1-0, but it was a dull match. The only excitement came when fighting broke out beforehand. I spotted a couple of Forest hooligans taking a pasting from a large group of Blues fans, and realised to my dismay that one of them was my old mate Paul Scarrott. I was on the horns of a difficult dilemma; I couldn't stand by and watch a friend getting filled in, but I didn't want to drag Mr Barnes and James into it, either. Fortunately, as I watched, Scarrott broke away, the police moved in and he bounded over towards me, with a couple of vicious-looking chums.

'Hey up, Animal!' he said, wiping a bloodied nose.

'Alright, Paul,' I said.

'Right,' Scarrott turned to his mates. 'Let's get the bastards!'

'There's not enough of us, Paul,' said one of his sidekicks.

'What do you mean, not enough of us?' said Scarrott, incredulously. 'There's us three, plus Animal and his two mates. That's six!'

As he spoke, Birmingham charged us and another fight broke out. I did my best to avoid the fray, but we all got caught up in it and, amazingly, we won. The Birmingham fans retreated to lick their wounds, and I started to apologise. The Barneses laughed it off; they'd found the whole experience rather invigorating. I didn't know that Mr Barnes had been a schoolboy boxing champion.

The Barnes family also had two daughters, Joanna, a lovely, honey-blond eighteen-year-old, and Kate who was reading medicine at Southampton. Jo eventually married Tom Purton, but I had one utopian evening with her, after a ball where she was my date. Lots of drink was taken, we retired to Tom's flat, and Jo and I somehow found ourselves having a cuddle in his bed. James walked in by accident, but kept his secret until he made a speech at her wedding.

'Within a few hours of first meeting Tom, Joanna was in his bed,' he told the newlyweds' friends and families. 'Unfortunately, it was not with Tom.'

Kate has an astonishing mind which allows her easily to assimilate and retain the most complex information; sadly, it is slightly deficient as regards common sense. One day, her father was discussing an employee who had a glass eye.

'He's had a new one made,' he said, 'but while it was being done he was wearing a temporary one. Funny thing is, the temporary one looked much better than the new one!'

'What does it matter,' said Kate, then a third-year medical student and now a successful doctor, 'as long as he can see through it?'

Amid the laughter, James pointed out his sister's error.

'Well, how am I supposed to know you can't see through them?' Kate replied, indignantly. 'We haven't done eyes yet.'

Christmas came and went, and it was back to university. With my new identity, I finally started to make the breakthrough I *really* wanted. Among the girls I dated in that second year were the daughters of a cabinet minister and a Belgian diplomat – neither of whom had noticed me during my first year. In the frantic social whirl, my connection with the Law Faculty became more and more tenuous. I attended no lectures, and precious few tutorials. But I did drink and eat a lot, and got on first-name terms with the croupiers at the Beau Nash casino. My bank statements were horrifying.

I attended a large number of twenty-first birthday parties, mixing with posh people from other universities. I found it was a surprisingly small circle. If two students of roughly the same age met, and they had attended one of the major public schools, they either knew each other or had friends in common. I suppose I was unwittingly conducting my own anthropological experiment. To give just one example, among the most glamorous members of my new crowd was an Iranian called Sahar Hashemi, who went on to co-found Coffee Republic. Her parents had fled Iran after the Islamic Revolution, arriving in the west with nothing but the clothes they stood up in – apart from a house in Kensington, an apartment in New York, a villa in Cannes, and about ninety per cent of the Iranian GDP in a bank account in Switzerland.

After Ayatollah Khomeini's death, Sahar was allowed back to her homeland, and when she returned she wept openly as she told us of the horrors she had seen. 'Our house used to stand in thousands of acres of countryside with woods, lakes and rolling hills,' she sobbed. 'They've knocked it down and built schools and hospitals there instead!'

F Scott Fitzgerald wrote, 'Let me tell you about the very rich. They are different from you and me.' How right he was.

My major achievement that year was in debating. I entered every national and international varsity tournament I could, usually with James, but sometimes with other partners, with great success. I won the Middle Temple Competition with Nigel Marsh, while David Gottlieb and I took the ancient and prestigious Punch Debating Competition at Birmingham, and the Reid Shield at Lincoln's Inn. I won individually at the Inner Temple and Gray's Inn, and was invited as a guest speaker to the Oxford Union, the Cambridge Union, Canterbury and Durham. Gottlieb and I entered the world debating championships at Princeton University in the USA; he came fifth in the individual speaking class, and I came second in the individual world humorous debating championships. We won the English Universities Debating Competition at the Oxford Union, and, although we failed to win the Lloyds Bank Trophy at Cambridge, I was awarded 'best speaker' by Charles Kennedy. (This was a mistake; he hadn't realised I'd been knocked out. I have no evidence that whisky was involved.) I beat everybody on the debating circuit, all except one – an Oxford debater called Michael Gove, who remains a good friend to this day.

Given my past life, of pork pie manufacture, football hooliganism/criminality, and homelessness in a variety of European countries, it was all rather heady. But my fine words, be they ever so beautifully crafted and delivered, were buttering no parsnips whatsoever. When the summer rolled around, I was broker than ever, and desperately in need of funds.

The Barnes family kindly allowed me to spend the holiday in their London flat, and James and I found work with a company near Oxford Street which sold advertising space to businesses in trade magazines. James and I were employed on a brochure to accompany a forthcoming United Nations publication, *Development Business*. Our pitch was that foreign governments who had received UN funding for any given project would receive a copy of the brochure; anyone who advertised in the brochure then stood a very good chance of being approached to tender for the work.

We made a fortune, working on commission, by selling stacks of advertising space to major companies which frankly should have known better. To my embarrassment, particularly in hindsight, I made a very good salesman, but I couldn't match James. Thanks to his disarming telephone manner, the section of the brochure featuring the Aswan Dam Project contained a double-page spread for bouncy castles.

I earned enough to pay off my overdraft, but – during a glorious summer of suppers, drinks parties, and balls – I spent enough to double it.

* * *

IN MY THIRD year, a wonderful opportunity arose. The English Speaking Union and *The Daily Telegraph* sponsored two undergraduates from the British Isles to go on an annual ambassadorial debating tour to America, visiting thirty-five universities in thirty states on a three-month, all expenses-paid trip. To be selected would be a great honour – perhaps fortunately, I didn't realise *how* great. Past participants had included Michael Ramsey (later an Archbishop of Canterbury), Rab Butler, Michael Foot, Edward Heath, and Robin Day.

By now President of the Bristol Debating Union, I secured an interview. The first place had already been filled, which left one more. That was just fine, as far as I was concerned, as there was only one of me.

I turned up for the interview wearing cords and a jumper. At the end, the selection committee chairman said, 'Why didn't you wear a suit?'

'Because I don't own one,' I said.

'If you go on the tour you'll be expected to wear a suit,' he said, earnestly.

'If I'm selected, I'll buy one,' I replied.

'Well, you'd better take yourself off to Jermyn Street,' he said, with a wink.

The tour left in early September, so I quickly contacted Stephen Cretney, Dean of the Law Faculty at Bristol, for permission to miss the first term of my final year. I expected it to be a formality, it being to the credit of the university to have a student selected for the ESU tour. To my amazement, Cretney refused and insisted I drop back an academic year. I appealed to the Vice-Chancellor, who overruled Cretney – much to the latter's chagrin. He called me in and gave me a stern lecture.

'Since you're missing a whole term,' he said, sniffily, 'make sure you select easier course options like Roman Law, rather than Company or Revenue Law.'

Of course, out of sheer bloody-mindedness, I put myself down for the hardest options. Then I went back to London for lunch at the ESU, and met my debating partner for the first time. Mark Malcolmson was a very wholesome man, to say the least. A serious-minded Scottish Catholic, who valued punctuality, sobriety, and chastity above all else, he was twenty going on fifty. After lunch, I went out and bought myself a Sony Walkman and some tapes. (What they were is now lost in the mists of time, though I know that Tina Turner's *Private Dancer* was among them.) It was going to be a long three months.

A few days before we left, I was contacted by the organisers, who wanted Mark and me to come up with five debating motions to be submitted to the American Universities. I pondered Mark's likely choices for a moment. But only for a moment. Then I rang him.

'The ESU have just called with the five debating motions for the tour,' I said.

'Really?' he said, sounding disappointed. 'I thought *we* were supposed to come up with them. What are they?'

'*This House Believes American Foreign Policy Is Offensive, This House Believes A Woman's Place Is In The Home, This House Believes England Is The World's Greatest Country, This House Believes McDonalds Is America's Greatest Contribution To World Culture* and *This House Would Rather Be Fat Than Thin.*'

'Oh, dear,' he said. 'They sound a bit racy.'

'At least they might make for some lively debates,' I said.

'Yes,' he said, doubtfully. 'But remember, this is supposed to be an ambassadorial tour.'

You can probably imagine my state of excitement as, at the age of twenty-six, I boarded the plane at Heathrow for my first flight, my case packed with that new suit bought especially for the tour. The excitement did not diminish upon our arrival at Newark, New Jersey, or as we were driven off to Marist College in Poughkeepsie, NY, where the Marist debate coach, an eager Christian called Jim, welcomed us cordially to the USA.

It was all exactly as I'd imagined America to be – so dynamic and fresh, so vibrant, and so big. Over the next three months, I discovered just *how* big – and varied – the country is. From the mountains to the prairies to the oceans, goes the song; one day we were in New York City, the next in rural West Virginia, the next on a beach in South Carolina.

For Mark, the tour was an opportunity to visit local churches and museums. For me, it was a never-ending whirlwind of drinking, eating, general debauchery, and some debating. Our different interests were apparent from the outset. After the event at Marist, I discovered a fabulous invention – frozen strawberry daiquiris. I drank about a dozen of them over dinner, where I also ate my body weight in beef and French fries, and then I tagged along with the Marist students and hit the bars until the wee small hours. I was feeling a little the worse for wear when Mark woke me up early the following morning.

'I'm off to church with Jim,' he said, shaking me awake. 'Do you want to come?'

'No, I fucking don't!' I said, groggily.

'Oh well, Mark,' came Jim's voice, from the other side of the room. 'Just you and me, then!'

Upstate in Albany, where the maple trees in autumn were a truly magnificent sight, an even more magnificent sight awaited – a girl on the opposing debate team. For some bizarre reason, she seemed to have formed the same view about me. After the debate, we all retired to a bar, but I surprised Mark by leaving for the hotel after a couple of pints.

'Early start tomorrow morning,' I said, 'so it's an early night for me.'

My companion and I were barely down to our underwear when Mark burst in five minutes later.

'I think you're right, Gary,' he said. 'We *do* have a very early start.'

From New York we moved on to Massachusetts, then down the East Coast, then over to Chicago and then Missouri – by air, train, and Greyhound bus. It all went smoothly, apart from one unfortunate incident in Columbus, Ohio, where a young woman called Vaneta Meredith introduced me to Long Island Iced Tea before the debate; I found Long Island Iced Tea greatly to my liking, and in

175

fact went slightly overboard, to the extent that I fell off the stage as I leaned on the lectern for support. Luckily, as I staggered to my feet the organisers took my drunkenness for concussion.

We then headed out west, ending up in a small Texas town called Huntsville, which I very much enjoyed. There may be better hosts on earth than Texans, but if there are I've never met them: we stayed with a local doctor and his wife, the Conwells, and in Texas fashion I was given the use of a huge car (a Lincoln Continental) and a gun for the duration of my stay. As its reputation suggests, it is a big state, and it can be brash, but its people are utterly genuine. I ended up being made an honorary citizen of Huntsville, and I have nothing but fond memories of Texas and the Texans.

In California, something really strange happened. We debated at the UCLA, and afterwards I was approached by a woman.

'I work for Troy Casden Gould,' she said. 'We're a law firm in Beverly Hills. I was just wondering whether you'd be interested in joining us?'

'What… as a lawyer?' I said.

'Yes, of course,' she said.

I didn't know much, but I knew it would beat driving a forklift at Asda.

'I'd love to,' I said.

She picked me up the next morning for a lightning round of interviews, and they promised to get back to me within three days. By the next day I had forgotten all about them, as I celebrated my twenty-seventh birthday drinking champagne with Tony Curtis on Malibu beach.

A day later we were in Portland, Oregon, debating against an all-female team of outstanding beauty. During the debate, I made a flippant remark about wanting to marry one of them – a girl called Kimberly – which raised a laugh. The following morning, I received two letters in my hotel room. One was from Kimberly – who really was incredibly beautiful – accepting my marriage proposal. The other was from Troy Casden Gould, offering me a job from the following June, at a starting salary of $63,000.

I enjoyed my breakfast that day.

Then I went off for lunch with Kimberly and her mother. It was during lunch that I realised, initially to my discombobulation and then to my horror, that Kimberly was quite serious. I think it was when her mum – who seemed very taken with the idea of her daughter marrying an eligible English gentleman – started talking

about where we would live after the wedding. I hadn't even kissed Kimberly at that point, and extricated myself from this delicate situation as best I could (leaving her in floods of tears), and we moved on to Washington State.

I was living every day like it was my last. After a debate in Seattle, I was on my way to a student party when Mark – who had turned out to be a lovely man, with a very dry sense of humour – put a fatherly arm around my shoulder.

Mark and me at a fancy dress party in the States: I've always had great legs

'Why don't you get an early night, Gary?' he said. 'You look absolutely knackered.'

Quite out of character, I took his advice and had my first decent night's sleep for three months, before we left for snowy Iowa, then windy Chicago, and then Heathrow.

I didn't feel my best as I boarded the flight home to the UK. I'd drunk more booze in three months than in my entire preceding twenty-seven years, and had also eaten enough food to keep the inhabitants of a small African country happy. I had left England weighing 14st 7lb, and I was returning at 19st 5lb, my new suit bursting at the buttons with that additional 68lb – I suppose, in fact, that it made me a quarter American – but I'd had a truly fantastic time.

* * *

BACK HOME, MY life was in turmoil – even more than usual.

I was broker than I'd ever been, largely thanks to Professor Cretney having informed my local authority that, as I had not been physically at Bristol during the first term, they should stop my grant. None of my clothes fitted the new 125 per cent of me, and I was also a term behind with my studies.

But my biggest problem was a long-running battle with the political left of the student body, which was to plague my final two terms at Bristol. At the end of my second year, my erstwhile debating partner, David Gottlieb, was elected President of the Student Union. David was and remains a great friend of mine – I was best man at his wedding – but now we were thrown into great conflict with each other. Privately, we remained close, but, in public, particularly in the union building, we were at opposite ends of a bitter political divide. He was a leading light of the loony left, and – more for sport than anything else – I enjoyed winding them up by adopting an über Thatcherite stance on everything.

178

The problem started with a university debating competition which I organised and chaired. The motion in the final was, 'This House Prefers Sloane Square To Greenham Common.' It was a popular motion of the day, encouraging healthy and strident debate whichever side you were drawn on, but the leftie students had turned up in force, as they often did, to stifle any views which didn't concur with theirs. One speaker, a very liberal-minded Canadian called Christian Brasso, was disappointed to find himself proposing the motion, when his natural inclination would have been heartily to oppose it, but it was a debate and he had no choice but to play the cards he'd been dealt.

He warmed nicely to his task, and had just made the point that the Greenham women posed a far greater threat to the environment, through their lack of personal hygiene, than any nuclear winter, when one women's group onlooker could contain herself no longer.

'On a point of information,' she shrieked, 'that's a complete fallacy! Most women at Greenham are scrupulously clean… The media only concentrates on the dirty ones!'

One wag in the audience immediately yelled, 'Get your tits out, love!' – a comment which was later ascribed to me.

Actually, it wasn't me who said it, but what does the truth matter when the mob is roused? An astonishing motion was put before the Student Union Council to have me thrown out of the union – a motion only defeated because of David Gottlieb's casting vote. I resigned as President of the Debating Union, stood for re-election, and won easily.

As it happened, the next debate I organised was on the fur trade, and was to be screened live on BBC2. On the night of the debate, I was warned that a group of anarchists and Socialist Workers were in the Union building looking for me, and that they were going to give me a good kicking. About thirty of them duly found me, as I was strolling to the debating chamber wearing a suit and my Old Etonian tie.

'There he is!' they cried in unison, and charged towards me. 'Let's get the bastard!'

For a moment, I put the pseudo-posh Gary Bell back in his box, and let Animal loose.

'Come on then, you wankers!' I shouted back, walking towards them. 'Let's fucking have it!'

The effect was startling, and instantaneous. As one, they turned and fled, some falling to the floor in their haste to get away. As I'd expected, this bunch of *faux* revolutionary *poseurs* didn't have the stomach for battle: they'd no sooner have fought me than they'd have done an honest day's work.

There were no more attempts at direct action after that, but I was targeted in every possible university publication – though, as the privileged, often privately-educated children of lawyers, landowners, and captains of industry, they struggled for purchase. The humble reality of my background spiked a lot of their guns, and left them confused and impotent. This extract, from an extra-university magazine called *Venue*, demonstrates their dilemma:

> With Bell's buccaneering right-wingery and impeccable working class credentials, this son of a coalminer, who left school at sixteen and pedalled effortlessly to the top on his Tebbitcycle, arrived in Bristol three years ago, already in possession of a stack of glittering prizes and a painstakingly cultivated BBC accent, and proceeded to take the Debating Union by storm. His ascent to the upper echelons of power and influence seems assured, or does it? We hear talk of a romantic banana skin set to send him slithering back from whence he came. Apparently the poor lad nurses an unrequited passion for Claire D'Albertanson, the furthest left of the candidates for this year's union presidency.

Talk about snobbery! If anyone had got to Bristol 'effortlessly', it wasn't me. And as for this D'Albertanson woman, who was going to 'send me slithering back from whence I came', I didn't even know who she was – though the social climber in me liked the sound of her name.

The *Women's Group Magazine* was particularly scathing. It ran to only one edition, and featured me and my supposed misdeeds on three of its twelve pages, one of which carried this caricature of 'Piggy Bell':

PIGGY BELL PONDERS HIS SUDDEN UNPOPULARITY...

Amusingly, as with David Gottlieb, most of the left-wing element of the student body, who affected in public to despise me, were on friendly terms with me behind the scenes. In fact, the more wildly, insanely feminist they were, the better we got on. I ended up marrying one of them.

It was quite debilitating, spending your life being pilloried as an object of hate, but it wasn't until the Easter holidays of my final year that it suddenly dawned on me just how far I was behind with my work. From then until my finals in May 1987, I put aside childish things and locked myself away with my textbooks, Wagner's *Ring*, and a month's supply of the Cambridge Diet.

I got as close to mastery of the various subjects as humanly possible under the circumstances, but the information was not deeply embedded in my brain; and I couldn't afford to speak to anyone on the way to any of my exams lest the conversation drove important nuggets of information from my short-term memory. But the exams all went surprisingly well, apart from a tiny scare when I found I hadn't been entered for Company Law because my tutor hadn't realised I was on the course.

Finally, all that remained was English Legal History. It being the easiest of the various modules, and me being pressed for time, I hadn't even glanced at a textbook. Two days before the exam, I went to see the Roman Law professor.

'Can I change to Roman Law?' I said.

'But the Roman Law exam's in a week's time!' he cried, incredulously.

'That's the point,' I said. 'English Legal History's the day after tomorrow, and I don't know any more about that than I do about Roman Law.'

My request was summarily denied, so I wrapped a towel around my head – it doesn't really help – bought a packet of ProPlus caffeine tablets, and did the best I could.

I remember the day the results came out. They were due to be posted on the notice board at noon, and James Barnes and I walked up together. He'd been even less productive than me on the revision front, and was concerned that his Conflict of Laws exam hadn't gone too well. This was astute of him, because it turned out he'd got the lowest mark in the faculty's history. He'd only squeaked through his Revenue Law paper because we'd sat up all night, cramming our brains with tax formulae and scoffing ProPlus. On our arrival at the notice board, James employed positive thinking. Licking his finger, he reached high and obscured the first name on the list – some swot who had obtained a first. He then ran his finger slowly down the list, through the 2:1s… then the 2:2s (where my name was found)… and then onto the thirds.

There were only two of these, listed alphabetically. The first was Afridi, the second was Barnes.

His father called him later that day to ask if the results were in yet.

'No, we haven't had them yet,' James lied.

'Well, call me as soon as you get them,' his dad replied, 'and don't worry – even if it's only a 2:2.'

My father didn't call me – I don't think he even knew where I was – but I didn't care. I took stock of what I'd achieved in the last seven years.

On the plus side, I had nine O levels – having added sociology to my original five, and then American History, Spanish and German – three A levels and a law degree.

On the minus side, I'd become alienated from my roots, and could never again live in Cotgrave.

But who cared? I was off to Beverly Hills.

CHAPTER TWELVE: LA STORIES

Twenty-five years to silk

LOS ANGELES CITY itself is a dull place a long way inland from the coast, and I never went anywhere near it unless I was going to Dodger Stadium for the baseball, which I did regularly during the magnificent 1988 World Series-winning season. To me, and most Angelenos, 'LA' means LA County, particularly the western part close to the Pacific beaches.

Luckily, Troy Casden Gould's offices were on that side, at 1801 Century Park East, near the junction with Santa Monica Boulevard, five or six miles from the ocean. I was in commercial litigation – about which I knew even less than I did English Legal History – and had my own secretary, and a starting salary of $75,000 a year, mysteriously increased from what I had originally been offered, and approximately five times what I had earned at Pork Farms. I didn't have views of the River Trent or all the cheap pies I could eat, but I did have a seventeenth floor office overlooking the Los Angeles Country Club, and some of America's best restaurants on the doorstep.

I rented a condominium in Santa Monica, complete with swimming pool and jacuzzi, and I really did pinch myself. How on *earth* had *I* ended up *here*? The universe is a strange place.

Everyone drives in LA, so I got myself onto an intensive course which promised to get me through my test in a week. The theory test was multiple choice, and the questions were extraordinary. One that I recall was, 'You are angry and upset. Do you: (1) Get into the car and drive away your anger, or (2) Refrain from driving until you are in a calmer mood?'

I passed, and the following morning the world's most dishonest driving instructor turned up at my apartment to give me the first lesson of my $500 intensive one-week course.

184

'Listen,' he said, 'if I tell my employers you didn't show up, instead of paying them five hundred bucks you can pay me a hundred and I'll give you driving lessons until you pass your test.'

'Fair enough,' I said, and we set off for my first lesson.

An hour later, he dropped me at the test centre.

'I've booked you in today,' he said.

'What, after an *hour*?' I said. 'Are you serious?'

He was. Five minutes later, I was sitting in a test vehicle with a middle-aged woman.

'I'll be your driving examiner today,' she said. 'You start with 100 points, and you lose points for every infraction. The pass mark is seventy points.'

It was a disaster. I sailed through two stop-signs, I knocked a cyclist off his bike on a zebra crossing (I'm not joking – we had to get out of the car and pick him up), and, finally, after a ropey three-point-turn, I drove for several hundred yards on the wrong side of the road.

The whole thing took only ten minutes, and ended with me driving back to the test centre, shaking my head in glum resignation.

My driving instructor was waiting for me.

'Congratulations,' he said, after conferring with the examiner. 'You passed.'

'I *passed*?' I said, in disbelief. '*How*?'

Apparently, I had lost six points for the two stop-sign incursions, six for driving on the wrong side of the road, two for 'poor steering smoothness' and a mere thirteen for almost killing the cyclist. These deductions gave me a score of seventy-three.

I went straight to a used car lot and spent $600 on an eighteen-foot 1966 Cadillac Coupe de Ville weighing more than two tons. If I was going to have an accident, and it seemed there was a fair chance I might, I didn't want it to be my problem.

* * *

THEY WERE GREAT days, though it was hard work. People see LA as a laid-back city, but Troy Casden Gould was anything but. Some people billed 3,000 hours a year – the equivalent of 375 eight-hour days. Obviously, no-one worked only eight hours, and the really committed actually slept at the office. The minimum billable hours requirement was 1,800 hours *per annum*, but woe betide any associate whose figures weren't well over 2,000.

The head of commercial litigation was a tremendous man called Derek Hunt, who took me under his wing and made sure I had interesting work to do – although rather too much of it for my liking. Early on, I was assigned to a lawsuit over the film *Die Hard*. The case turned on the building where the movie was set. The owners claimed it had been all-but destroyed during filming, while the filmmakers pointed out that that is what happens when you let John McClane loose in a skyscraper, and they should have expected nothing else. As one of the team, I received tickets to the premiere and, as we queued to get in, I couldn't help but eavesdrop on a conversation between two people in front of me, a young man and a very attractive woman. It became apparent that he was one of the stars of the film, and I earwigged, fascinated, as he regaled his date with tales of his experiences with Bruce Willis and the other big names. When the film started, my friend from the queue was almost the first character to appear: he said one line, and then was promptly shot dead. The whole thing was, I gradually came to understand, very Los Angeles.

Despite having a well-paid job in sunny California, I still dreamed of a life bewigged. Fortunately, Derek thought that it would be a good thing for the firm if I became a qualified English barrister as well as a California State Attorney. After organising my sitting of the California State Bar exams, he approved a one-year sabbatical so that I could apply to Bar School in London.

First I had to join an Inn of Court, a prerequisite for a career at the Bar. There are four Inns: Gray's, Lincoln's, the Middle Temple, and the Inner Temple. As far as I can tell, it makes no difference which one you join, but there is an old rhyme: 'Inner for the rich, Middle for the poor, Gray's for the scholar, Lincoln's for the bore.'

For reasons of irony, I applied to join the Inner Temple.

On the application form itself, at box 4, came the question I had always dreaded:

> Have you, at any time, been convicted of a criminal offence? NB: The Rehabilitation of Offenders Act does not apply to this form.

I filled in the details of my fruit machine fraud, posted the form, and crossed my fingers. Two weeks later, I received a reply asking me for an interview to discuss the issue on the day before Bar School started.

The summer came and went, and it was time to go back to England to discover my fate. My job at Troy Casden Gould would be waiting for me the following June, as long as I returned as a barrister. The more I thought about it, the less optimistic I became. Surely criminals couldn't become barristers? In my darker moments, I wondered if Pork Farms beckoned, or Pedigree Wholesale?

I should have saved up a fair amount of money from my colossal salary, but thanks to my usual profligacy I only just had enough to pay my airfare. I couldn't even sell the Cadillac. I would have liked to have dumped it outside the condo as a final act of revenge against the persistently irritating tow-truck companies who had plagued my American sojourn. They had repeatedly towed my car from outside my apartment, until I stymied them with a cunning plan, which involved buying wreck after wreck for fifty dollars apiece and leaving *those* parked out front. After they had towed away the twelfth rusting, thirty-year-old Buick, and had a yard full of the things and no chance of anyone reclaiming them, they finally got the message, but I'd still have enjoyed leaving with a final flourish. Unfortunately, I needed the Cadillac to get to the airport. I was still intending to abandon it in the drop zone outside Departures, but that changed on the way to LAX when I pulled into a strip mall off Sepulveda Boulevard to buy a Diet Coke. When I returned to the car, there was a young black lad looking at it.

'Nice car,' he said.

'It's lovely, isn't it?' I said.

'They don't make them like that anymore.'

'Do you drive a Cadillac?' I said.

'Not me, man,' he said, with a rueful shake of his head. 'These are hard times. I ride the bus!'

'I'll make a deal with you,' I said. 'If you drive me to LAX I'll give it to you.'

'What?' he said, looking immediately suspicious, and stepping backwards.

'I'm going back to England,' I explained. 'I don't need the car. Drive me to the airport and you can have it.'

Two minutes later, he was sitting in the passenger seat – I decided I would drive – and stealing glances at me as though he feared I might be a serial killer, or perchance a gay rapist. Ten minutes afterward, I pulled up outside Departures, took my bag from the back seat, and handed over the keys to the still deeply-incredulous young man. As I walked into the airport, I looked back over my shoulder: he had slid into the driver's seat, looking extremely confused but very happy.

I was upgraded to first class because the flight was overbooked, and, as I refreshed myself via the courtesy champagne, I took glum stock of my situation. I had no money and, having been in LA, I had missed the deadline for applying to my local authority for a discretionary grant to cover my fourth year of higher education. More worryingly, I had nowhere to live. I had trespassed on the hospitality of the astonishing Barnes family for too long, though in any event they had sold their London flat and bought a villa in France.

It was probably all academic, anyway: I was sure that the Inner Temple would not allow a convicted criminal to be called to the Bar.

Fourteen hours later, I was on the Tube, and two hours after that I was being interviewed by a group of Inner Temple benchers. They asked me only one question: 'Do your referees know about your criminal record?'

'Yes, they do,' I said.

My referees were my course tutor at Bristol, and James Barnes's father, and I'd told both of them.

The Inner Temple Benchers asked me to wait outside, and I paced the corridor nervously whilst they decided my fate. My entire life, I felt sure, rested on their decision.

I didn't hold out much hope. The Fire Brigade had sacked me because I was too dishonest for them, as had Martin's Builders, and Asda. How could the Inner Temple be any different?

I clung to the fact that my offence was a decade old, and that I really had turned my life around.

After an age, I was summoned.

'We are greatly heartened that your referees, both professionals, a university professor and an accountant, have agreed to stand referee for you,' said the chairman. 'That was a matter of great importance to the benchers. We strongly believe that everybody is entitled to a second chance. Welcome to the Inner Temple.'

I was so happy I committed my first social *faux pas* as a barrister, by offering them my outstretched hand. Barristers never shake hands with each other: men originally shook hands in order to show that they were unarmed, and since barristers are obviously gentlemen it has historically been considered a slight on the other's integrity.

It was a mild September day, and with my final few pounds I bought myself a sleeping bag and walked back to Lincoln's Inn Fields. This splendid square – laid out by Inigo Jones in the seventeenth century, and once a popular spot for duels and home to Charles II's mistress, Nell Gwynne – is directly between Bar School and the Inner Temple, and was familiar to me. During my homeless period in the 1970s, I had occasionally slept out there. Now, as I squinted in the late afternoon sunshine, I saw a large group of homeless people playing football. I joined in, and I passed a very enjoyable hour kicking the ball and various tramps all over the field. After the game, we fell to chatting.

'What you doing here then, Gary?' said one chap.

'I'm a homeless trainee barrister,' I said.

'Yeah,' said another fellow, 'and I work for MI5.'

Tall stories are common in this fraternity, and cynicism abounds.

'No, seriously,' I said, taking my Bar School registration papers from my suitcase. 'Look.'

'Blimey,' said my first interlocutor. 'He's telling the truth!'

Later, I queued with everyone else for soup and a hunk of bread from the Salvation Army van, and then, dog tired and jet-lagged, I dossed down in a quiet corner of Lincoln's Inn Fields. I awoke early next morning feeling positive and refreshed, and headed over to the Inner Temple, where there was a large changing room nestling between the library staircase and a bust of Gandhi. I had a quick bath, changed my clothes, stashed my suitcase on top of the lockers, and strolled up Chancery Lane to enroll at Bar School.

I slept rough like that for my first week, doing my homework in the Inner Temple tea rooms and trying to work out where I was going to stay. In the end, the decision was made for me. I was caught one morning by the Inner Temple treasurer as I was getting dressed after my shower, and later that day the students' officer came to see me.

'Captain Sheehan asked me to have a word with you,' she said. 'He wants to know why your suitcase is stored in the changing room?'

With a sigh, I told her the truth, and, an hour later, I was summoned to the treasurer's office. I was expecting a serious bollocking, but I received a pleasant surprise.

'When Edward Marshall Hall KC died in 1927,' said Sheehan, 'he donated a substantial sum of money to the Inner Temple for the benefit of impecunious young barristers starting out on their careers. I think we can safely include you in that category.'

I was issued with a cheque for £500, which was a lifesaver, financially. But it meant much more than that. Marshall Hall was perhaps the greatest barrister who ever practised law, the 'great defender' who in one trial gave what is widely regarded as the best speech ever made at the English bar. He was everything I aspired to be: a great orator, a maverick showman, a criminal defence specialist, and, most importantly, a silk.

(Queen's Counsel, 'QCs' – King's Counsel, or 'KCs', when a king is on the throne – are senior barristers known as 'silks' because they wear gowns made of silk.)

With Marshall Hall as my sponsor, I *had* to succeed.

I moved into a flat in Clapton, east London, with a friend from Bristol, Philip Malcolm. Clapton, at least the part we lived in, was an extraordinary place. On the night London was practically destroyed by the famous hurricane of 1987, Clapton was completely unaffected: it *always* looked as though a hurricane had hit it. For once, I took my studies seriously. I hardly went out, and what little free time I had was taken up in 'dining' (all would-be barristers were then required to dine at their Inn twenty-four times during their year at Bar School, I think it's a mere dozen now). Moreover, I needed to save enough money for my airfare back to LA in June.

Fortunately, at Christmas, Nottingham's local education authority agreed to pay me a maintenance grant and to fund my tuition fees. I celebrated by joining the Inner Temple football team.

A few days later, we had a friendly fixture against Gray's Inn. Neither side had any kit so it was agreed that we'd wear red and they'd wear white. The unfortunate result of that was that I played as centre-half for the Inner Temple wearing a Nottingham Forest shirt, and the barrister playing centre forward for Gray's Inn – one Ecky Tiwana – wore a Derby County shirt. If he had been a member of what Roy Keane described as the 'Prawn Sandwich Brigade' there would have been no problem. But unfortunately he was from a similar background to mine, and it was inevitable that some form of hostility would break out. Just after half time, after some fearsome tackling by both of us, I blocked him as he went to chase the ball. He was incensed, and pushed me in the back, causing me to stumble forwards. I turned to face him, and he advanced towards me, his chin jutting out defiantly.

'What's your fucking problem?' he screamed in rage.

As he came close, he swung a punch at me with his right hand. It started at his hip and came in a huge arc aimed towards my left temple; I swayed back slightly, his fist sailed harmlessly past my head and I stepped in close and gave him three quick jabs in the face, knocking him to the floor.

By the time he had got to his feet, others were pulling us apart, which made me extremely happy, as Ecky was a great big bull of a man. He still is, actually – though we're now firm friends, and have been in the same chambers for years.

* * *

I FINISHED MY dining, spring brought the Bar exams and, before I knew it, I was on a flight out of Heathrow, bound for California. After a night in a grubby motel, I caught two buses to the office, where Sandy Locke, the accounts manager, advanced me my first month's wages. Ever the spendthrift, I rented a plush apartment with a swimming pool near Venice Beach, and bought myself a 1959 Cadillac Coupe De Ville.

It was like I'd never been away.

At Troy Casden Gould that year I met one of my great friends, a New Yorker called Gregg Missbach. It was fabulous for my social life, but not for my American career. I tried to work hard, I really did, but the joy of Los Angeles lay not in grinding out hour after hour on commercial litigation files, but in having fun. Gregg and I spent evenings at Dodger Stadium, cruising Sunset Strip, or drinking on Santa Monica Boulevard or in Marina del Rey. At weekends we'd swim in the pacific at Manhattan Beach, or drive to Tijuana for a weekend in Mexico, or gamble away far more than we could afford in Las Vegas, that incredible twenty-four-hour desert city.

When the Americans needed a rest from me, their places were taken by a steady stream of layabouts from Nottingham and elsewhere flying out for a cheap holiday. They'd drop me at work and then head off in my Cadillac to the beach, promising to pick me up later. Often they failed to show, and I'd have to cadge a lift home with Gregg; in the end, I bought another old Coupe De Ville, just for guests.

This was, I felt, the life I had been born to lead – it was the stuff of my fairly shallow dreams.

But it could not last. In October 1988, on the Monday morning after my appearance on the TV dating show *The Love Connection* (my appearance was orchestrated by Gregg Missbach, it did not go well, and I propose to dwell no further on it) I received two visitors into my office.

The first was senior partner Bill Gould.

'Gary,' he said. 'I've been keeping a close eye on you since you arrived.'

Oh bugger, I thought. *That's torn it.*

'You're one hell of a lawyer,' he said, to my great surprise, 'and we were lucky to get you! I just want you to know we appreciate the hard work you're putting in. Keep it up!'

Five minutes later, my second visitor arrived. It was Sandy Locke, from accounts.

'Hey, Gary,' she said. 'I was just dropping by to say we haven't had any timesheets from you in a while. We need to collate your billable hours for the partners' meeting on Monday.'

'Okay,' I said. 'I'll bring them over later.'

As she left, I took stock. By and large, I had adopted Mark Twain's approach – that work was a necessary evil, to be avoided where possible.

My billable hours timesheet would not be impressing those partners.

For once, my rent and other bills were all paid up to date. I owed no-one anything.

It was time to go. I went to see Derek Hunt.

'Derek,' I said, 'I'll come straight to the point. I'm not sure I'm cut out for a legal career in LA. I've decided to go back to England.'

'This is all very sudden,' he said. 'I thought you were happy here?'

'I am,' I replied, 'and I'll always be tremendously grateful to you and the firm for this opportunity. But I need to get on with the rest of my life.'

'Well, if that's the way you feel…' He tailed off with a sigh. 'When are you thinking of leaving?'

'I thought in about ten minutes?' I said.

I dropped my timesheets off with Sandy Locke on the way out.

I went home via Canada, where I visited the Brasso brothers. I'd met Christian and Pete Brasso at Bristol, along with their Canadian chum Scott Lamb, and the three of them had become (and remain) very good friends of mine. A little spell *chez* Brasso seemed a good way to round off my North American adventure.

The Brassos had emigrated to Vancouver from Denmark after World War II as the Petersons, but had changed their name because of prejudice against anyone who looked or sounded even slightly Germanic. Their grandfather chose 'Brasso' after seeing a jar of the polish in a store. His family was from the shores of Lake Brasso in Denmark! It was fate!

Peter and Chris's father Henning had scrimped a living doing up old cars and selling them from his front garden, until he saw an advert in the *Vancouver Sun* in the 1960s. The Japanese car manufacturer Datsun was seeking a sole agent in Western Canada, and Henning, the only applicant, took on the franchise for British Colombia and Alberta. It went slowly at first – in those days, real men drove big Cadillacs and Lincolns – but the oil crisis of the

1970s made his fortune. Suddenly, everyone wanted smaller, more economical cars, and within a few years Henning was a multi-millionaire who owned the franchises to Datsun, Nissan, Honda, Lexus, Porsche, Jaguar, and Range Rover.

I was closest to Pete, whose room in Halls was opposite mine, and I could tell many funny stories of him. One blackly amusing tale will suffice. We returned very much the worse for wear in the small hours one day, and George, the senior resident, was on the phone.

'Lads,' he said, cupping his hand over the mouthpiece. 'Could you go and wake up Nick in Room 47 and tell him there's a phone call? And try and be a bit sensitive. His dad's just died.'

Instantly sobering up, I crept up to Nick's room and tapped on the door. After a few seconds it was opened.

'Yes?' said a drowsy Nick.

'I'm sorry to bother you, Nick,' I said, 'but there's a phone call for you downstairs.'

'A phone call?' he said. 'But it's three o'clock in the bloody morning! Who the hell's calling me at this time?'

Pete stuck his head over my shoulder.

'I'll tell you one thing, Nick,' he said, 'it's not your dad.'

Anyway, I spent a lovely week or so with the Brassos at their Vancouver home, playing tennis and golf, ocean salmon-fishing, and sailing the family yacht (I got a speeding ticket in Vancouver Harbour) up to their 'cabin', a huge villa on an isolated peninsula north of the city, where I nearly drowned when a drunken Chris cut my rowing boat in half with his flat-bottomed speedboat. But that was a minor blot on an otherwise glorious holiday.

Holiday it was, though, and eventually it was time to head back to England, and begin my glittering career.

CHAPTER THIRTEEN: GARY BELL, PUPIL

Twenty-four years to silk

IT WILL NOT surprise those readers who have stayed the course to learn that I was, once again, homeless and practically broke.

I rented a boy racer's Ford XR2 at Heathrow, and roared up to Nottingham to collect my belongings from Dawn's house, before returning to London to commence my pupillage.

Like my hero, Marshall Hall, I had decided to specialise in criminal law, the prosecution and defence of those charged with committing criminal offences, as opposed to civil law, the much more lucrative business of representing clients engaged in fantastically dull arguments about who did what to whom, and how much compensation one is to pay the other.

But passing your Bar exams merely takes you into the finishing straight. Before you can call yourself a barrister, you must spend a minimum of twelve months – divided into two periods of six months – as a 'pupil'. The first six – which is unpaid – sees you shadowing an experienced man or woman, your 'pupil master'. The second sees you let loose on minor motoring matters and shoplifting in the magistrates' courts, earning small fees. After that, if all goes well, you may fly solo, as it were, and can soar as high as your ability, ambition, and luck allow.

Of nine hundred students in my Bar School year, only three hundred had found pupillages, and I was among the fortunate third, thanks to the chap from Norton Rose. With my debating record, I had obtained interviews in all the top 'sets' of chambers, and they all offered me pupillage. I selected the best two, dividing my pupillage year between them. My first six would be at Queen Elizabeth Chambers; my second six would be at 5 Paper Buildings, where – after seven-and-a-half-years of study (or, at least, attendance at institutions devoted to study) – I could finally earn some money. Each was stuffed to the gills with QCs: starting out at such prestigious sets was sure to give me a head start.

For the first few days of my pupillage I slept in the XR2 in the Inner Temple car park, and once again availed myself of the changing rooms, taking great care to avoid the Treasurer. But after a week the car was due for return, and thereafter I was stuck. I found a firm in Kensington which rented out lesser vehicles on cheaper terms, and persuaded them to allow me to store all my belongings in their offices while I took the XR2 to the airport and returned on the Tube. But when I got back there was bad news: unlike the Heathrow people, they required renters to have held a licence for two years, and I'd had mine for fewer than eighteen months. I pleaded, I begged, but to no avail: I was left, homeless, without transportation, and with all my worldly goods in an array of bags and boxes, at the side of the road in Kensington.

Just to ice my cake, it started to rain.

I dragged everything into a shop doorway and racked my brains. A bus went by and I absent-mindedly noted its destination – Notting Hill.

Sophia FitzHugh. Didn't she live in Notting Hill?

I'd been at Bristol with Sophia – everyone knew her as Sophie – and had fancied her on sight (as had everyone else). Unfortunately, she was an upper-class socialist, and I was a lower-class reactionary, and she made it perfectly clear that she loathed me from the first. We met at the flat of a mutual friend, Nick Nugent. She walked into the room as I was holding court and telling what are nowadays termed 'politically incorrect' jokes. I was toning them down by Cotgrave standards, but they were still extravagantly *outré* to everyone else there, and probably the entire student body. While the rest of those present were laughing fit to burst, the object of my adoration let me know in no uncertain terms what she thought of my so-called 'humour', and stormed out of the flat.

For a long time, Sophie would refuse even to be in the same room as me. The ice was broken *slightly* one day, when she came to watch the football at Nick's flat. The only free place was next to me, and so she perched frostily on the edge of the sofa. Ninety minutes spent in each other's company discussing the finer points of the game did not exactly make us firm friends, but there was some thawing. Sadly, Nick was the only acquaintance we had in common, and when he dropped out of university early on I didn't see much of her again.

Until, one night, towards the end of my final year, when I was sitting in my flat watching television with an attractive blonde on my lap. Sophie stormed in, drunk and animated, having been at a dinner party in the flat below.

'We don't like each other very much, do we?' she slurred.

'Don't we?' I said, raising my eyebrows. 'I don't even know who you are.'

My white lie took her aback.

'I'm *Sophie!*' she said. 'Sophie FitzHugh?'

'So what do you want, Sophie FitzHugh?'

'I want to go out for dinner with you.'

'My diary is on the table,' I said. 'Find a free evening and book yourself in.'

'What about Saturday?' she said.

'Fine,' I said. 'Just write in a time and place.'

She did so, and said, 'Well, I'll see you on Saturday, then.'

'I'll be there,' I replied, not looking up from the telly.

Goodness knows what Caroline – the girl on my lap – thought about it all.

That dinner is etched on my memory. Sophie was beautiful, I already knew that, but now I found that she was also very bright, very witty, and wonderful company. In fact, the only fault she had was that, in spite of having press-ganged me into a date, she didn't fancy me one jot – not even when I told her, sincerely, that we were destined to be married. Still, I saw a bit of her over the next few weeks, and we became good friends, despite the fact that we were polar opposites in every way.

An old girl of Godolphin and Latymer School, she was related to Clive of India and Henry the VIII's sixth wife, Catherine Parr, and her great-great-great-great-and-possibly-great grandfather was Sir Richard Arkwright, the inventor and entrepreneur known as the 'Father of the Industrial Revolution' whose development of mechanised spinning frames revolutionised the cotton industry of the middle seventeen-hundreds. His son, also Sir Richard, was in modern money the eighth richest man in history, and the family – Sophie included – are listed in *Burke's Landed Gentry*.

But in spite of – or perhaps because of – her privileged background, she was a committed socialist, and was absolutely fascinated by my lowly origins. I took her on a trip to Nottingham to meet Dawn, then onto the City Ground to see Forest v Derby, then for supper at the Cotgrave pit canteen, and she loved every minute of it. Sadly, her feelings towards me remained entirely platonic, and we had lost touch as I entered my intense, ProPlus-fuelled, eleventh-hour revision phase. I had not heard from her since leaving Bristol.

But now, as I watched that bus go by, I remembered: just before we all went our separate ways upon graduation Sophie had put a card through my door on which was printed her London address and telephone number, and a handwritten message:

I treasured that card, and always carried it with me – I carry it with me to this day – and now I realised that her family home was about a mile from where I was standing. I hurried to a phone box, and dialled the number, praying that she'd be in.

She answered the phone herself.

'Hello, Sophie here.'

'Hi Sophie, it's Gary Bell.'

'Hello, stranger,' she said, sounding pleased to hear me. 'To what do I owe this pleasure?'

I told her my predicament, and asked if I could borrow her car to take my stuff back to Nottingham. She was there in a matter of minutes, and took me, with all my belongings, to her parents' house.

I've never met kinder people than William and Gillie FitzHugh. I told them my tale of hire car woe, and promised to return Sophie's car in the morning after dropping off my stuff with Dawn.

'But won't you need your things in London?' said William.

'I need to sort myself out a flat, first,' I said. 'Then I'll hire a car and bring it all back down.'

'Where are you staying now?' he said.

'He's been sleeping in a car,' said Sophie, 'only now, he hasn't got one.'

'What about tonight?'

'I'll be at my sister's house,' I said, 'if Sophie lends me her car.'

'Oh, no,' said William. 'We couldn't allow that. No, I think it would be better if you stayed here.'

'Well, that would be very kind,' I said. 'But just for tonight.'

I ended up staying for several months.

William, who is sadly no longer with us, was without doubt the most generous man I have ever known. When I raised the question of paying for my board and lodging, he waved me away.

'I have plenty of money,' he said, 'and you have very little. It seems foolish to increase that inequality. Why not leave it, and if one day you're in my position, and meet somebody in yours, you can do the same for them?'

Sophie herself was no longer living at home – she had recently inherited a flat in Earl's Court from an aunt – but we saw a lot of each other. Of course, I was smitten. I might have thought I'd been in love before, but I never knew what it meant until I found myself suddenly, desperately, and – tragically – unrequitedly obsessed with Sophie FitzHugh. My every waking thought concerned her. If she ever mentioned another man, it was as though a knife had been plunged into my heart. I took to reading soppy books and poems. A passage from the *Extrait du Journal de Salviati* in Stendhal's *De L'Amour* (*On Love*) described the problem in the following terms. Imagine a bag containing a pair of tickets. Upon one is written 'Be loved by her'. Upon the other is written 'Die at once'. If you are truly in love, you will unhesitatingly plunge your hand into the bag and take out a ticket. I would have done so if 'Be loved by her' was written on only one of a million tickets.

She must have known how I felt, but she apparently enjoyed toying with me. She certainly made it maddeningly, abundantly, clear that ours was a platonic relationship. I suppose I had little right to expect anything else. I was then aged twenty-nine, and weighed in at 18st 10lb (I was, frankly, as fat as a pig). She was only twenty-one, a shade under nine stone, and spectacularly beautiful with it.

Girls like her do sometimes dally with men like me, I accept, but it always seems to involve the man having money. I was as poor as a church mouse, whereas Sophie was extremely wealthy.

It was going to take something very special for me to crack this nut.

* * *

UNFORTUNATELY, I WAS all out of ideas. In the end, I took the coward's way out, and decided to accept defeat and move on with my life.

I'd been out a few times with a very attractive woman called Becky, a fellow barrister, and she had invited me for dinner at her flat in

Streatham. That was miles away, so she had suggested I might want to stay over.

Then, out of nowhere, on the day of the dinner, came a chink of light on the Sophie front.

I was in the FitzHugh family kitchen, and we were discussing the note which Sophie had pushed through my door just before I'd left Bristol, and which had led me there, when she spoke up.

'How come *you've* never written *me* a letter, Gary?' she said.

I immediately put pen to paper.

Dear Sophie, I wrote. *I love you but you won't go out with me because I'm too fat, so I've decided to go out with Becky Littlewood instead. Love Gary x.*

For some reason, she seemed stunned by this news.

Later that evening, I was packing my overnight bag when she walked in.

'What are you doing?' she said.

'I'm going out for dinner,' I said.

'Who with?'

'That girl called Becky. You don't know her.'

'Why are you packing a bag?'

Was it my fevered imagination, or was she jealous?

'I'm staying over,' I said, 'so I'm taking a change of clothes for work in the morning.'

'You can't.'

'Why not?'

'Because you can't,' she snapped. 'That's why.'

With that, she stormed out of the room. Not knowing quite what to think, I finished packing, and I was just about to leave the house when she stopped me.

'You've got to ring this Becky now and tell her you can't make it,' she said, 'Tell her something came up.'

'Like what?' I asked her.

'Tell her you're taking me out instead.'

I called Becky and made my excuses, and that evening Sophie drove me to an Italian restaurant. I tried to make conversation, but was met only by a frosty silence. After the meal, she drove us back to her flat for coffee, but she was still uncommunicative. Finally, she said, 'You can stay here tonight, in the spare bed.'

The spare bed was in Sophie's bedroom, a few feet from hers. We lay there in the quiet dark, me wondering what was going on, until she spoke up.

'I hate the idea of you being with another woman,' she said.

'Don't you think that's a bit selfish?' I said. 'You don't want me, but you don't want anyone else to have me?'

'I'm sorry,' she said, 'but I don't want you going out with anyone else.'

'So what do you suggest?'

'Do you mind if I get into your bed?'

She is still there, twenty-six years later.

After that, I stayed at Sophie's flat every night, though I maintained a *pied à terre* at the FitzHugh family residence. Until one Saturday morning, when we were careless. Sophie had stayed at her parents' house, I had snuck into her room in the night, and we were still snuggled up in the morning when we heard footsteps on the stairs. Her father knocked on the bedroom door and then walked in, catching us.

He was carrying breakfast – for two. The crafty bugger had known all along, and was content to allow love to run its course.

He was a true old-fashioned liberal, and a man who paid absolutely no heed to a man's class or the colour of his skin. As far as he was concerned, the fact that his daughter was happy with me, irrespective of my origins, was enough. I feel bound to say that Gillie FitzHugh felt differently. She viewed with dismay the prospect of her daughter being with a coalmining fraudster called Gary – even one who was scrubbed up, educated, and had some sorts of prospects. For some time, she was hopeful that Sophie would ditch me for a genuine Old Etonian, but she mellowed as time went by, and finally gave us her blessing. She is an amazing woman; I could not wish for a better mother-in-law.

Not long after we started going out, Sophie swapped her Earl's Court flat for a house in Shepherds Bush, and we moved in together. I bought a place of my own, a three-bedroomed maisonette in Shepherds Bush, just to get my foot on the property ladder, but I never spent a night there. Instead, I let it out to two friends. One was Rob Manning, an old friend from West Bridgford College who had finished university and was himself just starting at Bar School. The other was Simmo, star of the college five-a-side tournament, who had come down to sample life in The Smoke. It was nice to have them near, but financially ruinous: I never received a penny in rent.

Sophie's house was a large, four-bedroomed affair, and we had a never-ending stream of weekend guests and full-time lodgers. Among the latter was a girl called Alice, to whom I had first been introduced, during a party in Oxford, as the girlfriend of one David Cameron (whose brother, Alex, had been a Bristol contemporary of mine). We ended up seeing quite a bit of the future Prime Minister. David was – and is – one of the nicest and most genuine men I've met, nothing like the wealthy hypocrite of his enemies' propaganda. He knew my real background and was as relaxed about it as I was about his – neither of us had much choice over which school we attended, after all. He is also very generous, and supported lots of charitable and worthy causes long before he entered public life.

But the Queen of Notting Hill charity was Sophie's mother. Gillie ran an organisation called Kids at Risk which helped underprivileged youngsters earn an honest day's pay for an honest day's work. Gangs of local youths were employed on the renovation of Sophie's house, with predictable results.

Predictable, that is, to me – coming, as I did, from rather less rarified circles.

Gillie's mother, Enid – who loved Jesus, sport, and Mrs Thatcher, in that order – was similarly sceptical.

'Surely you're not having those risky kids in your house?' she said, incredulously.

Her warning was prophetic. The painters stole my watches, the wallpaper hangers ruined the wallpaper, and pinched the TV and video, and the carpenter used the place for a daytime rave. And, after Sophie foolishly paid him in advance, we never saw the glazier again (though he did leave a big hole in the wall). The FitzHughs had had their own problems – including one of the risky kids plumbing the hot water into the lavatory – but Gillie could see no bad in anyone. And she did indeed save a lot of promising young people from life's scrapheap. In west London she is rightly revered for the good she has done; in 2001, she was awarded the MBE at the same time as J K Rowling, but there can be no dispute as to who deserved it more.

Sophie's younger sister, Rafela, was the exemplar of the FitzHugh worldview. Another extremely kind and generous person, she was also rather daft. She had joined KPMG as a trainee chartered accountant, but soon dropped out to follow her mother into the charitable sector. Her first job, at a prison charity, ended quickly, and badly, after she lent a prisoner some sort of headset which he promptly used as a weapon on someone. From there she moved to a halfway house which provided short-term accommodation for those recently released from sentences. Her view was that trusting ex-offenders and treating them with respect was the way forward, which was why she hung her coat and handbag on a hook just inside the front door on her first day. Six minutes later they had vanished, much to her amazement.

She bought a house, but instead of using gang members to renovate it she decided to use only female builders. The first job was to lay a patio, but on the first day she was surprised when only one builder turned up. Progress was extremely slow, an issue which Rafela raised, carefully.

'My mate's ill,' explained the woman, leaning on her shovel. 'Period pains.'

'Ah,' said Rafela. 'Well, couldn't you make a start yourself?'

'Oh, no,' said the builder. 'These slabs are far too heavy for me. Don't worry, I've got someone coming round to help me lift them. He'll be here in five minutes.'

As with many young people of her class, when Rafela wasn't pursuing worthy causes she was travelling. During the first few months I knew her, she went to Thailand, Burma, Sri Lanka, Prague, and Jordan, and those are just the places I can remember. One day she told me that I ought to see a bit of the world myself.

'I have, a bit,' I said. 'But sadly not Thailand, yet. Can't afford it.'

'It doesn't cost much if you stay in cheap hotels,' she said. 'I paid for the whole trip by working at the pub two nights a week.'

She neglected to mention that her colleagues behind the bar needed their wages to pay off loans and to meet bills, whereas her pay-packets went unopened into a drawer.

There are benefits, of course, to living in such rarefied company. Evelyn Waugh would have described my life in London with Sophie as being like drowning in honey. She introduced me to fine wine and expensive restaurants, and we went to the theatre more often than we went to the cinema (though most of what we went to see was very dull). Any given evening might have found me wandering around an exhibition of great impressionists at the National Gallery, or watching the London Symphony Orchestra at the Barbican. Sophie taught me bridge, and we entered a few duplicate tournaments as a pair. One of our regular playing partners was the *Spectator* bridge columnist and England ladies' team member Susanna Gross – Sophie's oldest friend, and much later Godmother to our first son.

To honour my roots, I started my own football team, AC Shepherds Bush, in Division Three of London's Sportsman's Sunday League. Even that was some way removed from my past, mind you; the side included four barristers, four bankers, a teacher, an actor and a graphic designer, and there were eight Old Etonians among them. The only team member who had been to State school was me.

Many of the other sides in our league sounded vaguely threatening – one was called 'Chopper', another 'The Brixton Raiders' – and I did wonder how my bunch of public schoolboys would fare. The answer, it turned out, was very well. In one game, against The Brixton Raiders, we were awarded a hotly-disputed penalty. Our centre-forward – a barrister and Ghanaian royal called Tunde Johnson – strode forward. As he did so, one of the opposition grabbed him.

'Before you take this,' he spat, angrily, 'I thought I'd let you know I've got a gun in my car boot!'

'Really?' said Tunde, calmly. 'I've got a set of golf clubs and a CD multi-changer in mine.'

Then he smashed the ball into the top corner of the net.

We finished the season in second place and were promoted, but the following year was a struggle. We were often short of players, to the point where we even tried to sign up one Nick Hornby, who trained with us on a Monday night – let's just say he was better at writing about football than playing it. We finished in mid-table and after that the club was wound down and my playing days ended with a few games for Wilf Kroucher FC, a side made up of expat Nottinghamites now based in London, and run by my old friend Tony Ryland.

Tony and I had lost touch after leaving Toot Hill, but somehow kept coming across each other. We'd met when I turned up at West Bridgford college (Tony was taking his A levels); we met again when I was at university (he was working in Bristol); and we met *again* when I moved to London (I bumped into him at a Forest v West Ham game; he happened to be living nearby).

We had started our football careers as toddlers, kicking a ball around in my grandparents' garden, and had played together in junior and senior school teams. My last game was with Tony, too, a few years ago for a Wilf Kroucher Old Boys side against the current team. Our partnership spanned nearly fifty years.

* * *

LIFE IN LONDON at that time was very good, but Sophie still maintained that she was a socialist, despite our incredibly privileged lifestyle. Curiously, most of our friends were also socialists – socialists who lived in large, mortgage-free houses, called their children 'Africa' or 'India', fed them nothing but organic kiwi fruit, and sent them to the best private schools.

One, Lucy, went on anti-road demos in her soft-top sports car. Another, Annabel, was going out with a Middle Eastern terrorist and never wore western dress. The most socially conscientious person it is possible to be without being certified insane (although I'd have signed the forms in a jiffy), Annabel lodged with us while working at Amnesty International. That ended when she ditched the terrorist for a hunting-shooting-and-fishing farmer; one morning she arrived at Amnesty and announced that she had shot her first stag at the weekend. She was drummed out of the organisation immediately. Eventually, Annabel married an Old Etonian, as did Lucy and Rafela.

When I met Rafela, she was going out with a big fat doughy German banker called Peter Kohl, whose only claim to fame was that he was the son of the big fat doughy German Chancellor, Helmut.

Sophie's mother was delighted by such connections, though William FitzHugh was less convinced. I didn't mind, until the relationship started to get serious and it seemed I'd have a German brother-in-law, and my children German cousins. But it ended after an evening at which Peter told bad jokes extremely badly, and Rafela moved on to a film director called Wilf.

Wilf had us all fooled for a while. He was introduced as 'Wilf Brown from South London', a revolutionary Communist and independent film maker for Channel 4's *After Dark* series, and I rather resented his appearance – *I* was supposed to be the token working-class member of the family, after all. But then I found out that he was, in fact, Andrew McDonald-Brown, Eton and Oxford, and I started to warm to him. He is now one of my favourite people in the world, although I'm not sure he reciprocates the feeling.

At our first meeting, over dinner at the FitzHugh house, he told us we should cycle everywhere to save the environment.

'Does anyone here drive to work?' he said, in what he clearly thought was a rhetorical question.

'I do,' I said.

He goggled for a moment.

'Well,' he said, recovering his composure, 'I think you should try cycling instead.'

'It would take too long,' I said.

'You'd be surprised. With the amount of traffic on the roads, cycling is much quicker than driving.'

I pooh-poohed the idea but Wilf was insistent.

'Why not try it tomorrow?' he said. 'Leave your car at home and borrow my bike. I'll bet you any money you get there quicker.'

'Okay,' I said. 'You're on.'

'Whereabouts *are* you tomorrow?' said Sophie.

'Leeds Crown Court,' I said.

'Wilf' really is the perfect husband for Rafela.

After Sophie and I had been together for a year, storm clouds appeared. I had always known that we would end up getting married, and so had she, which was why she was so reluctant to get involved with me in the first place. Being only twenty-one when we had begun seeing each other, she still had wild oats which required sowing, and in this she was egged on by Lucy of the anti-road demos. Lucy had dumped her Old Etonian for a while in order to spend a little time getting to know the Shepherds Bush locals, and she almost persuaded Sophie to follow her path. One evening, Sophie announced that she 'wanted some space'.

No prizes for guessing what for; I had to nip this in the bud.

'No,' I said. 'I think we should just call it a day. I'll move into my own flat tomorrow. It'll be good living with Rob and Simmo for a bit.'

I packed my bags, loaded up my car, and slept in the spare room. Next day I was up and dressed early, and waiting in the kitchen. Just as Sophie was coming down the stairs, I made a big show of walking to the front door, lugging my case.

'Well, I'm off then,' I said.

'But… when will I see you?' said Sophie.

'You won't,' I said. 'I've taken my stuff. You can keep our friends, they were mostly yours anyway. Goodbye, it's been great knowing you.'

She came to the door and called after me, but I walked down the street, got into my car, and drove away.

That afternoon I took a phone call in my flat from her father.

'Hello, Gary,' he said, tentatively.

'Hi, William,' I said.

'Could you come over? Sophie is in a bad state.'

'Why?'

'She's just very upset.'

I went round to the house, where Sophie clung to me like a limpet. I hid a grin as William advised her to stop playing silly buggers. And so it was that, after a break of around ten hours, we were gloriously re-united. It couldn't have worked any better if I had scripted it.

There were challenges ahead. I still had ambitions unfulfilled. But Sophie gave me the stability in my life which I'd so long craved, and the confidence to go out and try and achieve those ambitions.

* * *

THE FIRST OF THESE was to finish my pupillage and become a tenant in chambers – a tenant being a qualified barrister, appointed on a vote by the tenancy committee of a chambers, and 'chambers', often called a 'set', being where you are based with other barristers, with clerks managing your work and invoicing your fees.

My first six, at Queen Elizabeth Buildings, was a nightmare from the beginning. My pupil master was a nice, well-meaning chap, and anxious for me to learn, but I was a terrible pupil. It wasn't entirely my fault. The idea is that, by the end of your first six months, you should be able to conduct your own hearings in the magistrates court. But to do so you need to learn how to do basic bail applications, pleas-in-mitigation and to prosecute or defend in summary trials.

(There are three levels of court case. 'Summary offences' are minor crimes which can only be tried by magistrates, or a district judge, and attract commensurately lower sentences. 'Indictable-only offences' can only be tried by a judge and jury at the crown court, and are punishable by harsher sentences. 'Either-way offences' can be heard in either, and a mode-of-trial hearing is held to decide which forum will be used. If the magistrates decide to hear a given case, the defendant can still 'elect' a crown court hearing before a jury.)

I didn't visit a single magistrates' court but instead sat behind my pupil master in long trials involving serious charges, where my role was limited to keeping quiet and paying attention. One of them alone lasted three months, during which period I read the complete works of Shakespeare; interesting, and enjoyable, but of limited utility.

The relationship between us grew strained, and became irreparable after an unfortunate incident at the Old Bailey. My pupil master was prosecuting a rape, and part of the evidence involved a nightclub bouncer who had looked over a cubicle in the loos and had seen the accused inside. The case turned on whether or not the defendant's trousers had been undone. If they were done up, he was innocent. If they were undone, he was guilty.

During his closing speech to the jury, the defence barrister said that the nightclub bouncer couldn't have seen the trousers. 'As the witness said,' he intoned, 'he could in any case only see the defendant down to his chest.'

At that, my pupil master rose to his feet. 'I hesitate to rise during my learned friend's closing speech,' he said, 'but what the witness actually said was "down to his waist".'

'No, no,' said the defence barrister waving him down contemptuously. 'He most definitely said "chest".'

'Well, I can't help,' said the judge, looking at his papers. 'I'm afraid I don't have a full note of that part of the evidence.'

'I don't have a note of it, either,' said my pupil master. 'I was on my feet questioning the witness.'

'Well, my note says "chest",' said the defence barrister.

My pupil master turned to me, and uttered the words I'd been dreading. 'Have a look at your note,' he whispered, 'and check what he said.'

I froze, mentally. There were odd snippets from the case in my notes, but mostly they were lists… My best-ever Forest team, all the American Presidents since 1789, Oscar-winning best films since 1929… I couldn't admit that I'd just been sitting there, doodling. To the best of my recollection, he'd said 'waist'. Panicking, I found a likely spot and quickly wrote, 'I looked over the top of the toilet cubicle. I could see the defendant down to his waist.'

I then held up my notebook, keeping a tight grip on it, and showed the freshly-written passage to my pupil master.

To my dismay, he snatched it from me and flourished it high in the air.

'My pupil has taken a very full and accurate note of the proceedings,' he announced, 'and it is quite clear that the witness said "waist".'

'Well, there it is then,' said the judge, 'waist it is.'

'I'm sorry, my Lord,' said the opposing barrister, climbing back to his feet. 'I clearly recollect the witness saying "chest". Perhaps the tape could be checked?'

'What do you say about that?' said the judge, addressing my pupil master.

'I've no objection if my learned friend is insistent,' he said, crowing slightly, and snapping my notebook shut. 'But it's a complete waste of time. It's here in black and white. He saw down to his waist.'

He then sat down with a glow of triumph, turned to me with a great beaming grin covering his face, and winked at me. 'Well done!' he whispered.

It took about ten minutes to find the correct passage in the tapes, during which time my pupil master's confident wink did nothing to subdue my rising sense of panic. Finally, the correct passage was found, and a hush of concentration fell upon judge, barristers and jury alike, as the witness's evidence was played for all to hear.

'I looked over the toilet cubicle,' he said, *'and I could see the defendant down to his chest.'*

It could not have been clearer.

It took a few minutes to re-set the tape machine, during which time I sat, transfixed, as my pupil master, too embarrassed to raise his head and catch anyone's eye, thumbed through my 'notes' in what was clearly consternation shading into rage. Eventually, he picked the notebook up between forefinger and thumb, turned to me with a sneer, and dropped it on the bench in front of me. He never spoke to me again. (And I mean *never*. It's customary when one takes silk for one to receive a message of congratulation from one's pupil master of all those years before. Unconventional as ever, I had three pupil masters, and I didn't hear a dickie bird from any of them.)

Even professionally and personally embarrassing myself paled into insignificance against the events of April 15, 1989. Nottingham Forest had declined since their European glory days, but had reached the semi-final of the FA Cup, to be played against Liverpool at Sheffield Wednesday's Hillsborough ground. I went up from London with James Barnes on a beautiful spring day, expecting to watch a cracking game of football; in the end, we witnessed one of the great horrors of modern times, as ninety-six Liverpool fans were crushed to death against the fencing designed to keep supporters from invading the pitch. I will never forget the sight of dead people being pulled from the surging mass and laid out just in front of our stand before our unbelieving eyes. We watched in silence for a long time until we were finally told to leave and drifted silently home. I stopped to fill up my car on the M1. The then England football manager Bobby Robson was standing at the adjacent petrol pump and I caught his eye. Neither of us said a word, we just frowned and shrugged.

The venerable old Liverpool manager Bill Shankly once said, 'Some people believe football is a matter of life and death. I am very disappointed with that attitude. I can assure you it is much, much more important than that.'

If Shankly was looking down on that game from whatever realm exists beyond this one, I'm sure he regretted those words. Football was forever diminished for me from that day. I still support Nottingham Forest, and I go to the games when I can, but after Hillsborough the importance of the sport was very firmly put into its proper context.

CHAPTER FOURTEEN: GARY BELL, BARRISTER

Twenty-three years to silk

I HOPED THAT my second six, at 5 Paper Buildings, would prove more fruitful. But before starting it, I first had to be 'called' to the Bar.

You become a barrister by being 'called' at one of a few 'call nights' held each year. You can only be called before beginning your second six, and after finishing Bar School and having 'dined' the requisite number of times. Having been called allows you to use the title 'barrister', but you must complete your first six months' pupillage before you can practise.

Most of my Bar School contemporaries had been called in autumn 1988. It was now April 1989, and the next call night at Inner Temple was only a matter of days away, just before I was due to begin the new pupillage. One of the Bar's many ancient quirks, customs and practices is that aspirants need to be sponsored by a Bencher – a senior member of the Inn, invariably Queen's Counsel, who sits on the various committees that oversee the life of the Inn. I should long ago have written a grovelling letter asking one of the same to sponsor me. True to form, I hadn't got around to it. I was sitting in the FitzHugh kitchen one evening, poring over the Inner Temple handbook in search of a likely candidate, when William rolled in from the pub with a chum.

'What are you up to, Gary?' he said.

'Looking for a Bencher of the Inner Temple to sponsor me for call night,' I said, glumly.

'Look no further,' said the other man, with a grin. 'I'm a Bencher of the Inner Temple.'

He was Richard Clegg QC, and he did indeed sponsor me.

Once called, I was finally able to 'get on my feet' and work. There were still no guarantees that it would go anywhere: of those offered pupillage from my Bar School year, only a third secured tenancies, and I was one of three second-six pupils who started at 5 Paper Buildings on the same day, all chasing one spot. Ever the optimist, I was overflowing with confidence – until my first court appearance. It was a mode-of-trial proceedings, at Hampstead Magistrates Court. All I had to say was, 'Sir, the defendant elects crown court trial, he requires all witnesses to be fully bound, and asks that legal aid be extended to cover crown court proceedings.'

A straightforward task, I thought, but I was almost dumbstruck at the awesome responsibility on my shoulders. Eventually, I stammered my way through my three lines and left. I found the whole thing terrifying.

My next day was even more daunting. I was to provide cover for a senior junior member of chambers, Simon Spence, who was being led in a gruesome murder in Norwich by a top QC called Dan Hollis.

(You might be sixty years old and highly competent, with forty years at the Bar, but you are still a 'junior' if you have not been appointed Queen's Counsel. You charge lower fees, and take more cases, but they tend – or tended – to be less serious matters. In serious matters, such as murder, a QC would traditionally 'lead' a junior who worked as his or her assistant. In recent years, as money has tightened, more and more serious cases, including murder, have been briefed out to juniors, particularly on the prosecution side, because of the lower fees. This may or may not be a good thing, depending on your point of view.)

I made my way to Norwich Crown Court, introduced myself to Hollis and then slid into the bench behind him (only silks are allowed to sit in the front row at court) and began taking a (proper!) note of the proceedings. It was a Friday, and at lunchtime Hollis asked the judge if court could finish at 3.30pm, an hour earlier than normal.

'Why?' said the judge.

'I'm going to France for the weekend with my wife,' Hollis replied, 'and we've got a ferry to catch.'

The judge was not impressed and declined Hollis's application.

At 3.25pm Hollis turned to me. 'Are you fit?' he said.

'Well,' I said, 'I play football and squash, and I do a bit of swimming, but…'

He rolled his eyes. 'These are the witnesses you've got to call to give evidence this afternoon,' he said, handing me a couple of witness statements. 'I'm off.'

With that, he gathered up his papers and strode out of court.

The defence junior, who was about twenty years' call, turned to me. 'And some have greatness thrust upon them!' he said.

Somehow, I bumbled through, and at the end of the day the defence silk patted me on the back. 'Well done,' he said. 'One day you'll be a silk yourself, and you'll look back on this day and laugh about it.'

'Yes, like that's going to happen!' I said, chuckling.

Me – Gary Bell – a QC? Silks need at least twenty years' experience, to have built a practice of very serious cases, and to be recommended for the honour by judges, solicitors and existing Queen's Counsel. It's an honour visited on fewer than eight per cent of barristers. What were the odds?

The following day, I was instructed in a bail application at Southwark Crown Court in front of His Honour Judge Anwyl-Davies – or 'Judge Animal Davies', as my clerk called him, with a smile. Three bail applications were listed, in consecutive, ten-minute slots, from 10am until 10.30am, when the judge would resume hearing an ongoing murder trial. Two other pupils were handling the other applications, along with a more senior man to represent the prosecution. The other pupils appeared terrified at the prospect of facing Animal Davies but, being older and perhaps more worldly wise, I was honestly not. In fact, I was looking forward to it, and prepared to give as good as I got.

In the event there was a delay, and the court clerk told us to wait in the judge's room. We all shuffled in, and settled down to await his arrival. At 10.29am, he swept through the door.

'I've read your bail applications,' he scowled, 'and, in my view, all three of your clients are menaces. Bail is denied. Anybody got anything more to say?'

The other two nervously shook their heads. The judge glared at me. 'What about you, Mr Bell?' he snarled. 'Have you got anything more to say?'

'Er...N-n-no,' I stuttered, and slunk out.

I had fondly imagined myself as a combination of Marshall Hall and Cicero, dazzling judges and juries alike with my expert knowledge of the law and my dashing advocacy. As it was, I staggered from crisis to crisis, mumbling and muttering as I went. More than once I wondered whether I was at all cut out for this lark.

On one occasion, I was instructed by the prosecution to take charge of the entire day's list at Brentford Magistrates. I decided to drive there to make sure I arrived with an hour spare to read the papers – unfortunately, I had to pick them up at the court – but I didn't leave nearly enough time. The traffic was horrendous and I arrived with two minutes to spare. As I was tearing open the envelope containing the papers, the magistrates entered court. They saw what I was doing, and asked if I needed more time.

'No,' I replied, with a confident smile. 'I'm ready to proceed.'

The first case was called on, a mode-of-trial proceedings. I scrambled for the file.

'This case is suitable for summary trial in the magistrates' court,' I informed the bench. 'The defendant entered Marks and Spencer on Brentford High Street, and was seen by a store detective to remove a dressing gown from a rack and hide it under his coat. He was challenged by the store detective and pulled a... er... pulled a large knife from his pocket and... er... stabbed the store detective in the throat.' I paused, and wiped my brow. 'You know,' I said, 'on reflection, perhaps this case is not suitable for summary trial.'

The magistrates looked at me as though I was an idiot, and they probably had a point. There's a lesson there for all young barristers: if someone offers you more time, take it!

* * *

A FEW DAYS later, my luck seemed to change. I was instructed to seek bail for a young single mother I'll call Alison Smith at Clerkenwell Magistrates Court. She was accused of handling stolen goods, the proceeds of a number of burglaries committed by her boyfriend, a chap called Kelly. He was a co-defendant and was being represented by the aforementioned Simon Spence, a junior tenant in chambers. It was the perfect opportunity to impress someone who would, in due course, be part of the decision as to my tenancy.

The case was listed in front of a magistrate called Johnson, a large, ruddy-faced man of about sixty, who appeared permanently on the edge of violence. Simon made his bail application first, and Johnson frowned and scowled throughout his submissions. My application was next and, even though I say so myself, it went very well. I was eloquent, I was brief, and on one occasion I even made Johnson smile. After I had finished, he addressed the dock. 'I'll deal with your client first, Mr Bell,' he announced. 'Miss Smith, I'm prepared to grant you bail. You may leave the dock.'

The gaoler released Alison, who smiled broadly at me as she walked to the public gallery.

'But you, Mr Kelly,' Johnson addressed the co-defendant, 'will be remanded in custody.'

I was overjoyed – this couldn't help but impress chambers – but my joy was interrupted by a wail of anguish from the back of the court. My heart sank – it was my client making all the noise.

'You fucking fat bastard!' she screamed at Johnson. 'You should have given my boyfriend bail!'

'Arrest that woman,' Johnson ordered the court staff, 'and take her to the cells!'

She was immediately seized and carried below, kicking and screaming. As the door clanged shut, muffling her cries, Johnson turned to me. 'Mr Bell,' he said, calmly. 'Ordinarily, for a contempt of that nature, I would prescribe two days' imprisonment. But I understand that your client was caught up in the excitement of the moment, and an apology will suffice.'

I hurried downstairs with the good news.

'*Me* apologise to *him*?' shrieked Alison. '*He* should apologise to *me* – he's locked my fucking boyfriend up!'

If I went back to court and she was imprisoned for contempt, I'd be a laughing stock. I spent the next half hour begging and cajoling her into seeing sense. 'If you don't apologise,' I said, 'you'll go to prison for two days. What's going to happen to him if he doesn't apologise to you? Nothing!'

'I don't care.'

'But what about your children? Who'll pick them up from school if you're in jail?'

'Alright,' she said, finally. 'I'll do it.'

I dashed up to court before she could change her mind. Simon Spence was still there, waiting to see what was going to happen. My case was called back on, and I addressed the magistrate. 'Sir, Miss Smith has something she wishes to say to you,' I intoned, gravely.

'You can pass the message on,' he snapped. He was in the middle of a busy list, and anxious to dispose of my matter as quickly as possible. But I wasn't going to let him ruin the moment of glory. I wanted everyone to see that I could make even the most difficult client see sense.

'I think it would be better if you heard it from Miss Smith personally,' I said.

'Very well, then,' he scowled. 'Miss Smith can approach the bench.'

The gaoler unlocked the door to the dock and released her. She walked forwards and stopped directly in front of the bench.

'I understand you have something to say to me?' said the magistrate.

'Yes,' she replied in a whisper.

'Well?' he said, testily.

'Suck my pussy, you fat cunt!'

Alison Smith was sent to prison for a week, and I was, indeed, something of a laughing stock.

* * *

OF COURSE, TEETHING troubles are inevitable in any new job.

I had one client at Tottenham Magistrates' Court who was accused of shoplifting from Argos. After looking surreptitiously around him, he took a jemmy from under his jacket and prised open a display case of Swatch watches. He selected a trayful, slipped it in an inside pocket, and took a last look around to make sure that the coast was clear.

It wasn't – a large security camera was pointing directly at him, and he heard the rumble of onrushing feet. Thinking as quickly as he could, with the brain God gave him, he unzipped his coat, pulled out the tray of watches, and said to the approaching store detectives, 'How much are these?'

It was my first trial, and I lost it, but the following day I got a shot at redemption at Romford Magistrates' Court. The defendant was charged with burglary, but had an explanation. It had been the early hours of the morning, he said, and he had been out for a walk in a field which just happened to be behind some houses. He spotted a figure in a back garden shining a torch, so went over to investigate. It all looked very suspicious, so he challenged the man, who promptly dropped the torch and ran off. Being a public-spirited sort, my client climbed into the garden to see what he had been doing. Alongside the torch on the floor was a pair of gloves and a crowbar, which had been used to open the French windows of the house. My client went into the house, but only to try to secure the French windows, as any decent person would surely do. The lock was broken, so he needed something to tie the two handles together from the inside, so that he could then let himself out of the front door and leave the place secure. He was in the bedroom searching through the drawers for something with which to secure the French windows when the police arrived and, for some reason, arrested him.

I met him briefly to discuss his explanation.

'So why did you put on the gloves?' I said.

'I've got a large number of convictions for burglary,' he said, 'and if my fingerprints were found in the house I knew they'd blame me for the original break-in.'

'And why were you using the torch?'

'If I'd turned the lights on the neighbours might have called the police,' he explained.

'And why was the jemmy in your pocket?'

'Well, I wasn't leaving it outside, was I?' he said, wide-eyed. 'What if the burglar came back?'

He was convicted inside five minutes.

Next day didn't look any more promising. A police officer had tried to force his way into The Fridge, a concert venue in Brixton, to question a robbery suspect whom he had seen disappearing inside. Two bouncers – my clients – had refused him entry.

'I am a police officer executing my duty,' he said, superfluously given that he was in uniform, 'and I have the right to enter this nightclub to question a suspect who has entered the premises about an armed robbery.'

The bouncers didn't agree with his analysis of the law and when he tried to force his way past them there was a struggle, during which, in full view of other officers in a van outside, he was given a bit of a beating. To compound matters, the incident was captured on CCTV, and played to the outraged magistrates during the trial. They were clearly revving themselves up to give my clients lengthy prison sentences.

'When did you write your notes about this incident?' I asked the officer, when he took to the witness box.

'Later that night,' he replied, 'after I was released from hospital.'

'And are you certain that, after all you'd been through, you recorded the exact words used in your conversation with the defendants?'

'Yes.'

'So you said, "I am a police officer executing my duty and I have the right to enter this nightclub to question a suspect who has entered the premises about an armed robbery"? Those were your *exact* words?'

'My exact words,' he said, nodding.

'Thank you officer,' I said. 'No further questions.'

'Aren't you going to challenge the witness's account?' said the chairman of the magistrates.

'How can I?' I replied. 'It was captured on film.'

'So why are the defendants pleading not guilty?'

'They are entitled to put the prosecution to proof,' I said.

'And have you advised them that, if they are found guilty after a trial, the sentence will be much harsher than if they had pleaded guilty at the outset?'

'I have.'

'Very well, then,' said the chairman. 'Let's get on with it.'

Other witnesses were called and I didn't question any of them. Finally, the prosecution case rested, and it was my turn.

'Are either of the defendants giving evidence?' said the chairman.

'I need to make a legal submission first, sir,' I replied. 'I submit that there is no case to answer.'

'No case to answer?' he spluttered, staring at me.

I waited for him to calm down. 'The Police and Criminal Evidence Act of 1984 gives an officer, acting in the execution of his duty, the right to enter private premises to *arrest* a suspect,' I said. 'This officer was absolutely certain that he wanted to enter the premises to *question* the suspect, not to arrest him. Therefore he was not acting in the execution of his duty, and was a trespasser.'

'Question and arrest,' the chairman replied. 'It's the same thing, isn't it?'

'Are you asking me a question?' I said.

'Yes,' said the magistrate.

'Does that mean you're arresting me?'

'Even so...' said the chairman, finally realising the trap that I had set. 'The defendants' actions went well beyond what was permissible in preventing the officer from entering. They beat him up. It was a clear assault, which is what they are charged with.'

'Not exactly, sir,' I said. 'They are charged with assaulting a police officer *in the execution of his duty*. If they had been charged with a simple assault they would have been guilty – but this was not an assault of an officer in the execution of his duty.'

The magistrates had no choice but to find the defendants not guilty. It taught me the power of a legal defence, and gave me my first trial victory, and I felt like the king of the magistrates' courts as I gathered my papers together and left. The two defendants were waiting outside and engulfed me, hugging me in triumph and relief. It was a fantastic feeling to be so appreciated – but then the prosecution came out of court, followed by the police officers. The defendants immediately turned their attention to the crestfallen coppers. 'It's not an offence to beat up a pig,' they crowed. 'Not if you've got Mr Bell as your lawyer!'

I felt ashamed to be associated with them – though, after I'd pondered the matter for a while, the shame was replaced by a sense of vindication. Yes, by exploiting a legal technicality I had assisted two men who had prevented a police officer from getting to an armed robbery suspect. But an untrammelled police force is a truly terrifying prospect. The law, and its checks and balances, was designed by Parliament to control the police, and to hold them to certain standards. Parliament had decided that the police had no right to enter private premises merely to question suspects; therefore, the police officer in this case had no right to enter The Fridge. I hold no brief for armed robbers, but neither do I hold any brief for police officers who ignore, or do not understand, the law of the land.

CHAPTER FOURTEEN: GARY BELL, BARRISTER

* * *

AFTER THAT CAME a major breakthrough.

A person arrested for a criminal offence initially consults a solicitor who handles the police interviews and prepares the case for trial, which involves taking the client's instructions and obtaining statements from defence witnesses etc. The 'brief' is then sent by the solicitor to a barrister, and the barrister conducts the case in court.

For obvious reasons, solicitors tend only to brief those barristers whom they personally rate highly, or whom a client has specifically requested. For equally obvious reasons, neither of these situations usually apply to pupils, so most pupils can only dream of fighting a crown court trial.

But – once again – I was very lucky. I'd only been on my feet for three weeks when I made a successful bail application at Great Marlborough Street Magistrates' Court. The defendant insisted to the solicitor that I should handle his trial, and so the brief came in, in my own name – as opposed to a generic chambers brief which is then dished out by the clerks to whomsoever they favour – to appear at the Inner London Crown Court before a judge and jury.

It was a massive affair. The defendant had allegedly stolen a t-shirt valued at five pounds from Mr Byrite on Oxford Street. I felt the evidence was weak – not least because he wasn't caught with the t-shirt – but I was nervous as I addressed the jury for twenty minutes before they went out to consider their verdict. They were back within half-an-hour – not guilty! Not only had I won another case, I had won a crown court trial!

It was as I left the court that I learned to stick to my own job, rather than attempting to act also as a probation officer. Outside, I put a supportive arm around my client's shoulders.

'You've got fifty previous convictions,' I said. 'All for the same thing, and all from Mr Byrite. You're thirty years old, and after fifteen years of crime you're utterly penniless. Don't you think it's time you packed in shoplifting?'

A few days later the solicitor called me. 'Your shoplifting client has been arrested for an armed robbery,' he said. 'On Mr Byrite, as it happens. In his interview he said you advised him to do it.'

Since that day, I've never given non-legal advice to any client.

A week later, I had another trial, at Snaresbrook Crown Court. The defendant was charged with actual bodily harm.

'You'll love Snaresbrook,' said Simon Spence. 'They draw their juries from the east end, and they never convict.'

Fantastic news! I was about to win my second trial! The case went well, and, as I made my speech to the jury, I couldn't help noticing several of them were nodding in agreement. Victory was certain, and I was beginning to think that I would never lose. Then the jury came back, after lengthy deliberations of around ten minutes, with a unanimous verdict of guilty. I came out of court feeling utterly depressed – though not as depressed as my client, who left in a prison van.

That's a barrister's lot – you really are playing with people's lives. It can wear you down if you let it; the only solution is to take each case as it comes.

Much to the annoyance of some of the junior tenants in chambers, one particular solicitor, a chap called Paul Selby, started to send me a lot of work. The Bar is a terribly jealous place, full of gossip, sniping and backbiting, and is always awash with talk about solicitors briefing barristers purely because they are friends. I'm sure this happens, occasionally, but it must be very rare. Solicitors live or die by the results obtained by the barristers they brief. A solicitor who briefs a chummy but useless barrister, who in turn loses cases, is not going to retain his clients for long.

Where Paul Selby was concerned, my envious colleagues were highly suspicious as to his motive for briefing me. I cannot say what that motive was, but I suppose it did not hurt that I had known him while I was at West Bridgford College, and that we had also worked alongside each other at Nottingham Asda.

It also didn't hurt that I got his clients acquitted. Whatever anyone thought, we got some pretty spectacular results. I went on a run where I won seventeen cases in a row, and other solicitors started to brief me in my own name. By the end of my second six-month pupillage, I had conducted several jury trials, and my diary was pretty busy. It was mostly down to being in the right place at the right time, but was nevertheless very unusual for a pupil.

I still didn't get the tenancy. Many of the tenants, particularly the junior juniors who were my closest rivals, found me not sufficiently respectful. For my part, I found a couple of them enormously, and unjustifiably, arrogant. They were much younger than me, and were not exactly setting the Bar alight with their brilliance, and yet they tried to treat me like a skivvy. One of them came into chambers one day to find me reading *Troilus and Cressida*.

'Have you nothing to do?' she snapped.

I held up my book.

'If you've nothing to do,' she said, scowling, and handing me a brief, 'have a look at this and tell me if anything needs doing on it.'

I held it up in the air and looked at it. Then I handed it back to her. 'Looks fine to me,' I said.

I got on very well with the clerks – they tend to come from my sort of background – and they remain my friends to this day. But sadly it wasn't their decision as to whether or not I would be taken on.

* * *

SO I WAS OUT of 5 Paper Buildings, and looking for a third six. I hadn't expected not to have a tenancy by that stage, and now I realised how stupid I had been to apply to all the top sets at the beginning. I couldn't reapply to those I'd turned down, so I had to approach the second division.

In view of my earlier idiocy, I decided to apply one at a time, and was offered an interview at the first attempt. At the interview, one very short, jumped-up barrister flourished my CV. 'I see you've done some debating,' he said. 'Well, you can forget all that. Just because you were the English Debating Champion doesn't mean you'll make a good barrister.'

'I never said it did,' I replied, defensively. 'But it can't do me any harm.'

'Don't be so sure,' he hissed.

I was offered a pupillage 'with a view' – unless things went terribly wrong, I would be taken on as a tenant after six months.

Of course, things did go wrong.

But before we get to that, I booked a holiday. I'd actually made a fair bit of money during my second six, I had no outgoings to speak of, and I felt like a short break. What better than a month in Ecuador, followed by a fresh start in the New Year? Sophie and I flew off to Quito on a cold November morning, and arrived to brilliant sunshine. I suggested staying in the modern, five-star Hotel Colon, but Sophie insisted on stopping in the old town, in a hotel that was as bad as anywhere I had ever slept, including the snow-covered pallet in Enschede, and we set about exploring the capital.

It was our first holiday together, and it brought its own challenges, challenges that I had not foreseen. In spite of going out with a fat man, Sophie had made it clear – as she continues to do to this day – that I needed to shed some, or even all, of my excess weight. Back in London, with ample opportunity to escape her gimlet eye, I could maintain an apparently earnest dedication to controlling my eating, while finding the time and space to sneak the odd pie, or Mars bar, or Big Mac-and-fries. But I now found, to my horror, that discreating (discreet eating) was much harder.

I got my chance when she asked me to pop out from the hotel to buy a bottle of water. I stopped off on my way and purchased a delicious-looking cheeseburger from a local café.

I've tried most diets – Weightwatchers, Slimming World, the Atkins, the Cambridge – with varying degrees of success. None compares with Ecuadorian amoebic dysentery.

After a couple of unpleasant days, I had an idea. The general medical consensus, in respect of food poisoning, is that you should avoid food, and merely rehydrate yourself. This, the theory goes, gives your body's white blood cells time to take on the bugs which are rotting you from the inside out. But what if the entire medical profession was mistaken? Surely, if you eat nothing, the invading bugs can concentrate on fighting your white cells? Whereas, logically, if you eat food – a lot of food – the bugs will be busy dealing with that, and your white cells can attack them whilst they are distracted. It was an attractive hypothesis, and I found it helped to think of the bugs as Hitler, the white cells as the Allies, and food as Stalin. Even the formidable Nazi military couldn't win a war on two fronts.

With that in mind, I went straight out and treated myself to lobster thermidor and a bottle of Ecuadorian red.

I heartily suggest that if you find yourself suffering from dysentery in foreign climes you do not medicate it with lobster thermidor and a bottle of Ecuadorian red. If you really must, do not compound your error by doing so a mile from your hotel, while wearing white shorts.

Once I had recovered, we went to the coast for a week on the beach, and thence to a bus for a fourteen-hour journey to Baños de Agua Santa, a city in central Ecuador known as the 'Gateway to the Amazon'.

The trip was hellish. The seats were tiny, and the vehicle was crammed full of *campesinos* getting on and off the bus, often with chickens or sheep in tow. To escape the cacophony, Sophie and I rode on the roof, clinging on to the rails as we hurtled along pot-holed mountain tracks and stared, literally, into the abyss, a mere slip of the steering wheel from death.

At Baños, I persuaded Sophie to allow me to book us into a very nice hotel, and we had a lovely few days in this beautiful town which sits atop a smouldering volcano. We bathed in natural spa pools by day, and ate in a superb French restaurant each night, and it all had a rather soporific effect – so much so, that we clean forgot the hell of the journey in, and got ourselves onto another bus, this time for a sixteen-hour ride to the small Amazonian town of Misahuallí.

After another desperate journey, and a hellish night under mosquito nets in a sweltering pit of a hotel, we went to board a motorised canoe for a further nine-hour trip up a tributary to a remote jungle village where we were to stay for a few days. It was only ten in the morning when we set out, but it was already terribly hot; as we waited to clamber aboard the boat, I stripped down to my boxers and dived into the river, partly because I wanted to cool off but mostly because I needed a wee.

'Cuidado!' warned the canoe steersman. *Careful!*

'Por qué?' I said. *Why?*

He shot back a rapid-fire burst of Spanish... something about dangerous fish in the river, but most of it far too fast and complicated for me to understand.

'Lo siento,' I said, 'pero no entiendo.' *Sorry, I don't understand.*

There was a rather smug German couple with us, and the man helpfully translated the Spanish for me. It turned out that this stretch of water was teeming with tiny, spine-laden *candiru* fish. The *candiru* is attracted to heat, and – supposedly – if you urinate whilst swimming in the water it can follow the flow back to source, swim up your urethra, and lodge there. Because of the spines, the only way it can be removed is by slicing the penis in half, lengthways, removing the *candiru*, and then sewing the penis back together again.

I got out of the river as nonchalantly as I could – that is, in about a thousandth of a second – and lay down in the hot sun to dry off. After a few minutes, I caught the German's eye. He looked concerned. 'You must be careful,' he said, 'or you will get sunburned.'

'I'm alright,' I scoffed. 'I'm used to the sun.'

'The sun here is very hot.'

'I think you'll find it's exactly the same sun we have in England,' I said, fixing him with a steely glare.

I sat topless in the boat for the whole nine hours, whilst he looked on in consternation. What a fascinating nine hours it was, too, right into the heart of darkness. The sounds of the rainforest echoed from either bank, and numerous exotic creatures appeared at various points. Just when I was beginning to see myself as a latter-day Livingstone, bravely forging a path through wholly uncharted territory, we turned a corner and passed a giant advertising hoarding reading 'Drink Coca Cola.' The 'remote jungle village' turned out to be a sizeable town, Puerto Francisco de Orellana, with its own airport and oil refinery.

Not that I cared. Thanks to nine hours of merciless sun, I could barely move. Sophie had to carry both of our bags as I walked, glowing in the darkness, to our hotel.

That night was one of the worst of my life. We had chosen the best place in town because it was the only one with air conditioning, but the electricity was cut off at 10pm so it didn't make much difference. We ate at the hotel restaurant – the meat was so tough that when I bit into it I lost a crown – and then repaired to our bedroom. We were sharing it with many thousands of mosquitoes, and, although it was pure agony on my third-degree burns, I gritted my teeth and watched through one eye as Sophie covered every inch of me with mosquito repellent.

Watching her was foolish, as it turned out; it meant she missed that eyelid, and one of the buggers bit me on it during the night. It must have been watching me, too: I had hardly slept a wink.

I looked in the mirror in the morning, assessed my scarlet frame, my missing tooth and the enormous lump on my eye, and decided to get out of this hellhole. There was a booking office for the airport in town, and I arrived at 8am, just as it was opening. The woman behind the desk explained that there was a flight every two weeks, and that – praise God! – the next one was the following morning.

The only other way out was by the same canoe we had arrived on, followed by another insane, thirty-hour bus ride back to Quito.

Unfortunately, the flight was full. I could have wept.

But then she threw me a lifeline. 'There may be cancellations,' she said, 'but we won't know until the morning. The flight is at ten o'clock. If you come to this office at 8am sharp, you can buy any cancelled seats here.'

At lunchtime, Sophie and I bumped into the Germans in town.

'How are you today?' said the man, looking at my blistered, peeling flesh.

I thought I could detect a faint, Teutonic smirk.

'Fine,' I lied.

'Are you not burned?' he said, arching his eyebrows.

'No, certainly not.'

At his invitation, we joined them for lunch, and the conversation turned to ways to get back to Quito. They, too, had learned of the flight the following morning.

'I went to the booking office at 7am,' he said, with a shrug, 'but it was not yet open.'

'I went later,' I said, 'but the flight is fully booked.'

'That's a pity,' he sighed. 'So it's the canoe and bus!'

'They said there might be some cancellations,' said Sophie, innocently. I almost kicked her.

'Oh, really?' said our German friend, excitedly.

'That's right,' I said. 'They said we have to go to the airport first thing in the morning to find out.'

'The airport?' said Sophie, her brow furrowed. 'But I thought…'

This time I did kick her, and she fell silent. Later, she tackled me. 'Why did you tell him to go to the airport?' she said. 'I thought you had to go to the booking office?'

'They're Germans,' I said. 'Wherever they go, they'll be there long before us. It wouldn't surprise me if they were on their way to queue at the airport now.'

Next morning I was down outside the booking office a good half hour before it opened – and I was in luck. There were two cancellations, which I snapped up. After breakfast, Sophie and I got a taxi to the airport. As we were walking in we bumped into the German couple.

'It's no use,' he sighed. 'Your information was wrong. We should have checked at the booking office in town.'

'Oh no!' I said. 'That can't be right!'

'I'm afraid so,' he said, gravely. 'The check-in lady just told us that cancelled tickets go on sale in the booking office on the morning of the flight.'

'That's terrible,' I replied. 'They told me… Well, anyway. Have you been waiting long?'

'Since five o'clock this morning,' he said, with a frown. 'But if some people don't turn up for the flight, then we can purchase their seats.'

So we waited, but of course everyone turned up for the flight: who wouldn't have wanted to get out of Puerto Francisco de Orellana? The plane started to load, until only we and the Germans were left at the gate. The German chap had been seeking updates at the departure desk every two minutes, and now – with the plane moments from departure – he came back. This time a triumphant grin had replaced his despondent air.

'It is good news for us!' he said, beaming. 'But bad news for you, I'm afraid. Two people have not turned up. They are going to put out a last call for them, and if they are not here in five minutes we will have their seats.'

Sophie was absolutely squirming with embarrassment, but I was euphoric. Two minutes later, the last call indeed came out, and I pulled out our tickets, waved goodbye to the spluttering Germans, and we boarded the plane.

We landed back in England on Christmas Day, and immediately set out west on the A40, on our way to North Wales, where Sophie's family spend their Christmases. It was my first Christmas away from the Barnes family in five years, and I would never spend another with them. They remain saints on earth in my eyes; I can never repay the kindness they showed me.

CHAPTER FIFTEEN: TROUBLE IS WHAT YOU'VE GOT

Twenty-two years to silk

MY THIRD SIX, with a view, was at 1 Middle Temple Lane – an old-fashioned set, with an old-fashioned clerk called Mike Strong who ran the place with a rod of iron. Everyone was scared of him, from the lowliest pupil to the loftiest silk. The notice on his office wall said it all. 'If you have nothing to do,' it read, 'please don't do it in here.'

Professionally, things couldn't have gone any better. It all started when I was prosecuting the court list at Guildford Magistrates, and a solicitor asked if I had any information on a case he was defending.

'I've only got my case file,' I said, 'and, as you know, I'm not allowed to show you that.'

His face fell.

'Only kidding,' I said. 'Bring it back when you've finished. You might want to start on the second-to-last page.'

Two minutes later he was back with my file and a beaming smile. His case was called on, his client pleaded not guilty and, as a result, I dropped the case – as I had been instructed to on the second-to-last page, the main prosecution witness having retracted his statement.

Later, the solicitor came over. 'Hi,' he said, 'I'm Neal. I like your style. Have you got a card?'

'No,' I said, 'I'm only a pupil.'

'Well, give me your name anyway,' he insisted, 'and I'll send you some work.'

I wrote down my details on a scrap of paper, not expecting anything to come of it, but the next day a brief arrived from Neal for a client charged with burglary. The day after that came a substantial mortgage fraud. Then an attempted rape. In fact, he sent me everything he had – even an attempted murder and a manslaughter brief. These sorts of serious offences were the province of very senior juniors, and even silks, but I was so full of beans that I did them myself.

The defendant in the manslaughter had punched a neighbour in a row about the volume of his TV; the punch knocked the other man down some stairs, and he died. My client, a man of very low intelligence, was certain to be convicted, but I wanted him to have a trial so that the judge at Winchester Crown Court could see for himself just how vulnerable he was, and how out-of-character the whole sorry affair had been.

He was tried, and duly found guilty, the jury sending a note asking the judge to be lenient. The judge, Mr Justice Turner, *was* lenient: he gave my client probation, then called me into his room.

'Mr Bell,' he said. 'Whenever I have a new barrister in front of me I look him up to see what his call date is.'

'Yes, my Lord,' I said.

'I have to admit that I was rather surprised that yours is 1989.' He raised an eyebrow. 'That makes you... er... one year's call?'

I went from that case to another very serious matter, an attempted murder, in front of another High Court judge. My client was a Heath Robinsonesque inventor who embarked on an eccentric bid to kill his ex-wife. His first attempt involved a home-made rocket, which he attached to a tree she drove past on her way to work. It was activated by a trip wire which he pulled when he saw her coming. She duly drove into the ambush zone, but by the time the rocket was launched her car was at least a hundred yards up the road. Unfortunately, the would-be assassin's own car was parked directly in the line of fire, and he was sitting in it. The rocket exploded through his window and set fire to his beard and hair.

His next gambit was to drill a hole in a light bulb and then to insert petrol into the bulb by means of a hypodermic needle. The idea, showcased in the Burt Reynolds film *The Longest Yard*, was that his wife would switch on the light and be incinerated. It might have worked, but he used too much petrol and it failed to ignite.

The police found the syringe and a video of *The Longest Yard* lying on a workbench in his garage, along with a much larger rocket for another go at plan A. But he wanted a trial, so I gave him one. I'd like to be able to report that my brilliant advocacy saved the day, but he was convicted inside five minutes.

The work continued to flood in, and I was given a locker to store all my briefs. Unfortunately, the locker had been taken from a junior tenant. In a way, this made sense – he didn't have much work coming in – but it started a chain of resentment. I was oblivious to this; I rarely went into chambers, except to collect my briefs.

It all came to a head when the clerks directed me to 'The Big Room' for a conference with a client. I had a look around and found a room which was indeed big. A very senior but largely irrelevant member of chambers, who survived on low-grade prosecution work provided to him by the clerks, was sitting at the desk.

'Excuse me,' I asked, with some trepidation, 'is this the big room?'

'Why?' he snorted. In his previous life he had been an officer in the Rhodesian police force, and had the manner and personality to match.

'I've got a conference for my trial tomorrow,' I replied, 'and the clerks told me to have it in the big room.'

'You what?' he bellowed with rage, slamming down his shoplifting trial. 'You come into the room of a tenant in these chambers and demand that *I* leave for *you*, a pupil? Of all the bloody nerve!'

'I'm sorry,' I said. 'I didn't know it was your room.'

'Well, it is my bloody room, so you can bugger off. Why does a pupil need a conference anyway? Cons are for serious matters. What's the defendant charged with?'

'Armed robbery,' I replied.

'What?' he shrieked, jumping from his seat. 'What is a pupil doing with an armed robbery trial when I'm prosecuting a bloody shoplifter? Has the world gone mad?'

'I'm just doing what I'm told,' I tried to reason with him. 'I don't want any trouble.'

'Well, trouble is what you've got,' he hissed, pushing his face close to mine. 'I'm not having some snot-nosed pupil coming in here and trying to throw me out.'

Spittle flew out of his enraged mouth and landed on my face. I knew the intelligent thing would be to take the bollocking and remain obsequious, but…

'This has gone too far to resolve with words, hasn't it?' I said.

'What do you mean?' he said.

'I mean, why don't we step outside into the car park?' I said, grabbing him by the lapels and pushing him against the wall. 'Then you can repeat the bit about me being a snot-nosed pupil.'

'Are you threatening me?' he said, aghast.

'You said you wanted trouble,' I said. 'I'm happy to oblige.'

It turned out that he didn't want any trouble, and after that incident nobody else in chambers gave me any.

They didn't give me a tenancy, either. My pupil master took me to one side a few weeks later. 'I've heard some very good things about you from the clerks,' he said. 'You're very busy, the solicitors like you, and you generate most of your own work. They rate you very highly.'

I was glowing with pleasure.

'But we're a happy family here, and you don't fit in. You're just not clubbable.'

The next chambers to which I applied again offered me a 'pupillage with a view'.

'No,' I said. 'I'm not interested in a pupillage, with or without a view, I want a straight tenancy.'

'But a tenancy is guaranteed if we like you,' said one of my interviewers.

'That's the trouble,' I said. 'You won't like me.'

* * *

SALVATION FINALLY ARRIVED in the shape of a new set called Bell Yard Chambers. They had a vacancy for a junior tenant and I was invited for interview.

'We can offer you a pupillage with a view,' they said.

'No,' I said. 'I've already had one of those, and the only view I got was of the door as it slammed in my face.'

'What happened?'

I told them most of the truth, majoring on the fact that I generated most of my own work but wasn't 'clubbable'.

'Well,' the head of the tenancy committee laughed, 'we need someone who can generate his own work, and we definitely don't care whether you're clubbable.'

I was offered a tenancy, my solicitors followed me to my new chambers and I continued to be rushed off my feet.

My first case as a tenant was a plea to an attempted rape at Guildford Crown Court. My client had grabbed a sixty-year-old dog-walker, but a passing farmer in a Land Rover saw them tussling and screeched to a halt.

'Oi!' he called out. 'Leave that woman alone!'

My client pulled a machete from under his coat and flourished it.

'Mind your own fucking business,' he shouted, 'unless you want me to cut you up!'

The farmer scurried back to his Land Rover – but only, to my client's dismay, to retrieve his shotgun.

'It *is* my fucking business,' he said. 'Now, leave her alone, unless you want me to shoot you.'

My client was expecting ten years in prison, but he perhaps had a stroke of luck, thanks to the prosecutor annoying the judge.

'The victim in this case,' he said, in his opening, 'was an elderly lady, of sixty.'

'Elderly?' snapped the judge – who was at least seventy. 'Nonsense! She's in the prime of her life!'

My client got five years in HMP Winchester. 'You were brilliant, Mr

239

Bell,' he enthused, afterwards. 'When I get inside I'll tell everyone to have you as their brief.'

Within weeks, briefs were indeed flooding in from the prison. Unfortunately, my client was on a segregated sex offenders' wing, under what used to be called 'Rule 43', and the only prisoners he met were other sex offenders, either serving sentences or on remand awaiting trial.

For the next six months, I was instructed in a torrent of filth, and I had no choice but to represent everyone, thanks to the Bar's 'cab rank' principle. This is a basic tenet of our legal system – that even the perpetrators of the most disgusting, inhuman crimes must be allowed an advocate to speak on their behalf in court. Barristers are in that sense merely cabs approaching the rank, to pick up the next passenger regardless of his behaviour or antecedents. It is an important protection against the abuse by the State of its awesome power over the individual, but it obviously leads us to represent people whom we would much rather not. The only real get-out is that you are too busy with other cases – a reply that I was able to give, for instance, when recently I was sounded out about defending one of the men charged with the gruesome murder of Drummer Lee Rigby in London.

Like most people, I had little knowledge of the sordid world of sex crime until this point, and I found it stomach-churning. Particularly astounding was just how often the mothers of young girls who had been molested by their step-fathers would side with the men, and blame their own daughters for 'bringing it on themselves'.

Like football managers, barristers are only as good as their last result, and my run with the 'nonces' ended when I represented a man who had raped an eight-year-old. My man was jailed for thirty-eight years (I'd happily have hanged him), and, to my relief, the word went around on 'the Rule' that I wasn't such a good brief, after all.

I no longer represent people charged with sexual offences, though only because the law has moved on greatly and it has become a very specialised area, handled by specialist advocates. Over the years I have represented many men charged with rape, and I never had a client convicted. That is not a record of which I am proud, but neither is it one of which I am ashamed. In English law, a defendant is entitled to be defended by a trained advocate (he will certainly be prosecuted by one, after all), to be presumed innocent until proven guilty, and to be judged by a jury of his peers. In a rape trial, as in any other, the jury hears the evidence and applies it according to the law. If it finds that the prosecution has proved a defendant's guilt, beyond reasonable doubt, it convicts. If it does not, it acquits. It's as simple as that.

We barristers are often asked how we can represent someone whom we 'know' to be guilty. But how do you define 'know'? In many cases, *absolute* knowledge of guilt can *only* come via an admission from the defendant (and even then people sometimes confess to crimes which they have demonstrably not committed). If such an admission *is* made, we must recuse ourselves from the case, but other than in those rare and specific circumstances *we* must *also* presume a defendant to be innocent, and put the matter to a jury. It is simply not for me to make any other judgment, and that is the case even if the evidence appears to be *so* overwhelming that it seems blindingly obvious, as a matter of common sense, that he *must* be guilty.

What's the alternative? That we simply take the word of the police? That would surely be an abhorrent state of affairs. Even the best detectives are human, after all, and it is not unknown for them to make honest mistakes as to the people they arrest. Neither, sadly, is it entirely unknown for them to fabricate evidence in pursuance of the wrong man, on the basis that 'if he didn't do this he did something else', so that a rough form of justice is somehow meted out. It's a common enough practice that it has various names – 'noble cause corruption' is one, 'doing the Lord's work' another – and many readers may be tempted to shrug their shoulders and accept it as a price worth paying to put criminals away. But beware: it could happen to someone you care about. It could even happen to you, one day.

A more interesting question is about mitigation. Take a murderer (say) who is either convicted or pleads guilty. How can we advance pleas-in-mitigation to try and get him the lowest sentence possible? Again, the answer is simple. Mitigation is part of the defence to which everyone is entitled; the appropriate sentence is a matter for the judge. When I mitigated on behalf of the would-be rapist in Guildford, *I* didn't jail him for five years – the judge did. And if the prosecution believes a sentence to be unduly lenient then there exists a process by which they can take it to the Court of Appeal – just as a defendant can appeal against sentence.

Barristers have to leave their own feelings at the door to the court. It isn't always easy. I represented a man who admitted the particularly horrific rape of a fourteen-year-old girl. It was a terrible case, and he was given eleven years in prison – a substantial sentence, bearing in mind his guilty plea. He felt that it was too severe, and instructed me to appeal.

A couple of months later, I found myself in front of Lady Justice Rafferty in the Court of Appeal.

As a barrister, Anne Rafferty QC was a breathtakingly brilliant advocate whom I admired greatly, and sought to emulate. She once led me in a case in which our client pleaded guilty to armed robbery and shooting at two police officers. He had been warned to expect a sentence of at least twenty years, with the possibility of life imprisonment. After Anne's mitigation, the judge gave him ten years – an astounding sentence, in the circumstances.

Now Anne had been elevated to the highest echelons of the judiciary. Insofar as the limits of my wit and eloquence allowed, I had always tried to base my mitigations on hers, which were stylishly and brilliantly argued, but on that day it wasn't going too well. (It was almost as though she'd heard it all before.)

'This was a terrible crime, Mr Bell,' she snarled. 'How can you claim that the sentence is manifestly excessive?'

I wanted to tear off my wig and gown in frustration and shout out, 'Do you know what *I'd* do to him if it was up to *me*?' (It would have involved detaching the defendant's bollocks from his body with a blunt knife.) But decorum precluded me from so doing.

Suffice to say the appeal against sentence was not successful.

Because of all of this, it is difficult (miscarriages of justice aside) to criticise English criminal justice. It is said that you can judge how civilised is a society by the way it treats its prisoners; if so, ours is a very civilised society indeed. The two men charged with Lee Rigby's murder made no attempt to deny killing him, but claimed that it was a legitimate act of war since they were soldiers of the Taliban. Ironically, under the Taliban, they might well have had their heads summarily lopped off, but in England they received a fair trial, represented by skilled barristers (including my old friend, David Gottlieb, who valiantly fought the case on behalf of his client in the finest traditions of the Bar). They were able to put their side of the affair to the jury, and the members of that jury had the opportunity to accept it if they so wished.

At the end of it all, the men were convicted and will probably die in prison. But no-one can say that they were not treated fairly: justice was done all round, as the eyes of the world looked on.

* * *

SOME TIME AFTER my run of sex crime, I received a blow. My main solicitor, Neal, was convicted of mortgage fraud and struck off, so his work disappeared overnight. Although I still had work coming in from Paul Selby, my old Asda colleague from Nottingham, things were certainly patchier.

For instance, one Monday I started a two-week armed robbery trial at Guildford. My client was part of an armed raid on a jewellery warehouse, and the evidence against him seemed utterly overwhelming. It consisted of another (uncaptured) robber addressing him by name, a positive identification by a lorry driver, and a footprint in the warehouse which matched not only the design of his trainers but the precise pattern of wear on their soles, and was found at precisely the spot where the alleged gunman had stood. Additionally, my client smashed the police cars out of the way in a stolen lorry with the jewels in a bag; the vehicle was chased half way around Surrey before eventually being stopped with a 'stinger', and armed officers then found my client in the driving seat.

He claimed that he had agreed to be the getaway driver for what he thought was merely the burglary of an unoccupied warehouse, that he had never set foot in the warehouse itself, and that he was terribly shocked when he found out later that guns had been involved. After a hard-fought trial, he was unexpectedly found not guilty by the jury. I was king of the world!

The very next day, my clerks sent me to Sheerness Magistrates' Court to deal with the first appearance of a shoplifter. The case was for a firm of solicitors who were, quite frankly, taking the piss. It was bad enough that they paid a flat fee of only £25 for a magistrates' court appearance – not even enough to cover my petrol – but they were also insistent on two things: the barristers they instructed must be presentable and punctual. Neither of these are my long suits.

On the next occasion they instructed me, I was sent to Ashford Magistrates' Court for a 10am hearing for the usual £25. 'The solicitor is worried about you, Mr Bell,' my clerk said. 'If you're late again they're going to stop briefing you.'

That was the best news I'd had in ages. The next morning, I left for court at 9am, and arrived, hopelessly late, at 11.30am. In my absence, the case was adjourned for a week, and the solicitor was duly furious and never briefed me again. The following week, when the case was re-listed, it went to a member of chambers who lived near me in Shepherds Bush. He called me the night before. 'I've never been to Ashford,' he said. 'What time did you set off last week?'

'I left at 9am,' I said.

He called me again the next day. 'I set off for Ashford at 9am,' he informed me, 'but I didn't get there until 11-bloody-30.'

'Neither did I,' I said.

Other solicitors did still insist on sending me magistrates' court work, which I grudgingly accepted. Around that time, the government of the day was considering restricting the right to jury trial, and I was called in by the BBC to pass comment on the proposals on *Newsnight*.

'This is just a cost-cutting exercise,' I said. 'It would be even cheaper to replace magistrates' court trials with trial by ducking stool. And most of my clients, if offered the choice between the magistrates and the ducking stool, would opt for the ducking stool.'

My tongue was in my cheek, but my comment was based on an unfortunate reality. I'm not saying magistrates *always* convict, but I was often astounded at their decisions. On one occasion, I prosecuted an American aircraft technician in Ipswich for speeding. He bought a technical expert with him and proved beyond a shadow of a doubt that the police measuring system was wildly inaccurate. It was obvious that he was not guilty, but the magistrates spent ages considering their verdict after retiring. Finally, the clerk was sent for and then they all came out of the retiring room together.

'Stand up, please,' said the chairman, addressing the defendant. 'We find the case not proven – you are free to go.'

Later, I asked the clerk about the delay. 'The magistrates wanted to find the defendant not guilty,' he said. 'They just didn't know what form of words to use for a not guilty verdict.'

'Are they newly-qualified?' I said.

'No,' he replied. 'They have thirty years' experience between them.'

On another occasion, I prosecuted a defendant in Great Marlborough Street Magistrates' Court for assault on a female police officer. According to the officer, the defendant had been illegally re-feeding his parking meter. When she told him that this was an offence he told her to fuck off and catch some real criminals. She warned him as to his language and conduct, and he punched her. A passing police van then arrived, by chance, and the defendant was arrested after a violent struggle.

The defendant's case was that he had only just parked his car, and had forgotten to put money in the meter. He had walked back to do so when the officer challenged him, aggressively. He tried to explain what had happened in a polite way, but she cut him short and told him to move his vehicle. He protested, again calmly, that it was legally parked. Then a police van arrived, and a group of officers jumped out and manhandled him into the back of it. At no stage had he physically or verbally assaulted the female officer.

The defence called a witness, an elderly West Indian Baptist Minister who had witnessed the entire incident. His account tallied exactly with that of the defendant, whom he did not know and had never met. The female police officer was obviously lying.

My job was to cross-examine the minister and suggest that he was committing perjury, but the idea disgusted me and I decided against it. There was no motive for him to lie, and he was clearly telling the truth. I said I wouldn't challenge his account. The magistrates *still* found the defendant guilty. I felt thoroughly ashamed of my part in that miscarriage of justice, and still do.

In my view, the problem – certainly when I started practising – lay partly in the make-up of the bench. It's been a long time since I appeared before them, and things have changed a lot, but a working class magistrate was a rare find, certainly in London and the home counties, and I personally never saw a black one. They seemed very out of touch with the lives of those on whom they passed judgment, very ready to find guilt, and harsh in sentencing.

I prosecuted the list at Swindon Magistrates' Court two days before Christmas one year. It was a bitterly cold day with a snow warning, and I was anxious to finish up and set off home to beat the weather. The final case was that of a single mother – with no previous convictions – who had been summonsed for failing to pay her community charge, or 'poll tax'. In spite of numerous court appearances, she still owed the sum of £87.

'Why haven't you paid?' said the chairman of the magistrates, a hoity woman.

'I haven't any money,' said the defendant.

'What about your benefits?' the magistrate scowled. 'I assume you *are* on benefits?'

'They don't last long. I've spent them.'

'What on?'

'Most of it went on rent and bills,' said the girl, tears forming in her eyes. 'The rest went on food for Christmas and presents for my kids.'

'But it wasn't your money to spend!' said the magistrate.

'I know,' said the girl, now crying openly. 'I'm sorry.'

There was a moment's conflab between the three magistrates, and then the chairman spoke again. 'It's too late for sorry, I'm afraid,' she said. 'You've been given plenty of chances to pay this money, and not taken any of them. If you can't pay the debt, you will go to prison for one week.'

The defendant was led, in stunned silence, down to the cells, as the magistrates stood up and left the court – no doubt to get ready for their own family Christmases.

I understand that people need to pay their taxes, or else society collapses, but with two children, and just before Christmas...? I went straight down to the court office and paid her poll tax off, and then went to the cells with the receipt to obtain her immediate release. When I got there, the prison officers were having a whip-round of their own to raise the money themselves. It normally takes a fair bit of time to process the paperwork before release, but the gaolers did it in two minutes' flat, and gave her the whip-round money for good measure.

I don't think that magistrate was a bad woman at heart, I'm sure she was a loving wife and mother; she just could not understand the position in which the defendant found herself.

* * *

PAUL SELBY AND I started a legal advice workshop at a West London community centre run by Sophie's mother, and while I was certainly motivated by a desire to help her foundlings, waifs and strays, it also proved a rich vein of work for us. One client in particular was a prolific offender. I first met him after he had been charged with robbery. I was to make a bail application on his behalf. In preparation, I was noting down a few details. 'What do you do for a living?' I said.

'I'm an apprentice professional footballer at Queens Park Rangers,' he said.

'Are you serious?' I said.

He was, and we came to a deal. If I got him bail, he would play for AC Shepherds Bush that Saturday. I may have found an extra gear that day; I did get him bail, and on the Saturday he scored a hat-trick against the Maltese Cat Reserves.

He was charged on several occasions over the next couple of years, always with robbery, and was always found not guilty, usually on a technicality. Finally, the police made a concerted effort. They put in place a whole team of undercover officers to follow him and see what he got up to. The operation went well: he was followed from his tower block all the way over to Knightsbridge, where he was seen to mug several people. But as the police moved in to arrest him, he fled into Hyde Park, where he outpaced a mounted officer. He was eventually arrested that night as he arrived home. Finally, it looked like he was in trouble.

But the fact that he was at large between the robberies and his arrest was crucial. When the papers arrived, I went through them with a fine-toothed comb. It didn't take long to find the prosecution's weakness. I won't go into all the boring legal detail, but essentially the police had committed an enormous howler by failing to put my client on an identification parade. There was thus no admissible evidence of identification to put before the court – no proof, in other words, that he and the mugger were one and the same man.

On the day of the trial, the prosecution was represented by two senior counsel and supported by about a dozen police witnesses from the team which had followed my client all day. The whole operation had come at a huge cost to the taxpayer. Fifteen minutes later, they were all on their way home. The case was dismissed by the judge after a submission by me.

I knew he'd done it, the police knew he'd done it, even the *judge* knew he'd done it. But law and procedure are there for a reason: to ensure that every defendant has a fair trial, and to protect citizens from the abuse of State power. That lack of identification evidence was something the prosecution should have spotted and rectified before the trial. My job is not to alert them to their errors. Indeed, I am prohibited from so doing: the Barristers' Code of Conduct 'Core Duty 2' requires us to promote fearlessly and by all proper and lawful means the lay client's best interests, and to do so without regard to our own interests. That's what I did in that case, and unfortunately it resulted in a guilty man getting off scot free.

He was very grateful to me afterwards, and offered to turn out for my team the following Saturday, 'as a thank you'.

'That's okay,' I said. 'We haven't got a game this weekend.'

It was a lie, but one I was comfortable with, and I never had him play for us again. I am always friendly towards my clients, but they are not my friends.

That case marked the beginning of an incredible run of victories, often in the face of overwhelming evidence, for Paul and me.

One case involved a West Indian record producer who was stopped at Heathrow airport by customs. In his suitcase were nine sandals – all, oddly, for left feet. The sandals were examined, and two kilos of cocaine were found hermetically sealed in the soles. A further half-kilo was then found in a plastic bag in one of his socks. 'I couldn't fit the half kilo in the sandals,' he explained, as we got ready for his trial, 'so I stuffed it in my sock.'

His defence was duress – unless he carried the drugs into the UK for a St Lucian gangster, he would be shot. Although duress is a defence in law it is rarely used, and neither Paul nor I had ever known it to be successful. We thought it was the biggest load of rubbish we'd ever heard, but the jury didn't agree and, to the fury of the judge, acquitted him.

Our next case was even more troublesome. Our client had been approached by a team of armed robbers to supply vehicles for use in their crimes. He was given clear instructions by the organiser of the robberies. 'If the police come around asking questions,' he told my client, 'tell 'em you don't know nothing about no armed robbery.'

Witnesses had noted the registration number of the getaway car, it had been traced back to my client, and a police officer had been dispatched to ask him about it. Not being the cleverest man who ever drew breath, he did exactly as he was told when the officer knocked on the door, and immediately said, 'I don't know nothing about no armed robbery.'

He was arrested and charged. At the trial, his turn to give evidence arrived.

'You weren't expecting to see a police officer at your door, were you?' said prosecuting counsel.

'No.'

'According to your evidence, you had no idea what he was calling about, did you?'

'No.'

'So why were the first words you uttered, "I don't know nothing about no armed robbery"?'

'Because I didn't,' was my client's disarming reply.

It was good enough for the jury. They found him not guilty, though probably because they felt sorry for him, rather than because of my oratorical brilliance.

CHAPTER SIXTEEN: MR AND MRS BELL

Twenty years to silk

IT SEEMED AS though I couldn't lose at anything, so on the weekend of my thirty-first birthday, two-and-a-half years after we had begun dating, I took Sophie away to Trier, in Germany. Over dinner, I dropped to one knee and asked her to marry me.

Anything I might have achieved in life is as nothing compared with her acceptance of my proposal. I could dream about becoming a barrister, but to have a woman as wonderful as Sophie think me worthy… that was beyond dreams.

We were married on July 18, 1992, at Overton-on-Dee, near Wrexham in North Wales, from where the FitzHugh family hails. The ceremony was at the ancient church of St Mary the Virgin and the reception in a marquee in the garden at the FitzHugh country house. The guests had an equal mix of titles and tattoos, and the Barneses sat in for my family – although my father, who was invited, did turn up, and stayed for over an hour. (This was actually quite a privilege – he hadn't attended Kevin's wedding because he'd been at work.)

I felt as though I was floating during the whole day – not easy for me, even though I had starved myself down from 18st 10lb to 14st 7lb to fit into my suit:

Our honeymoon was in Cuba, a beautiful, but infuriating place. The people lived in grinding poverty, surrounded by crumbling buildings, and watched over by Castro's secret police, on an island whose location and natural bounty should have made them all wealthy. The food – always an issue close to my heart – was disgusting, but at least the cigars and rum were excellent.

We saw as much of the grit of Cuba as possible, but I also found us a pearl, Cayo Largo beach resort, into which I booked us for a few days, and where I had another brush with the old enemy.

Sophie and me on our wedding day: this is thin, by my standards

Sophie had arranged for us to take a day trip to the exotic-sounding Iguana Island, which was a naked lump of volcanic rock populated exclusively by iguanas. We were dropped off in the morning, and collected in the early evening. In between there were no refreshments, no facilities, and the only shade was under the jetty. It was already taken up by hundreds of iguanas, and they weren't going to give it up without a fight.

There was a German couple on the trip, and friendly banter had ensued between me and the male half. There was another island some fifty yards away, but the sea flowed through the intervening channel at an incredible speed. The German had some flippers, and announced that he was going to swim across and claim the adjacent island for Germany. Over his girlfriend's protests, he pulled on his flippers and stepped into the raging torrent. But the current was so strong that he came straight back out.

'No,' he said, shaking his head gravely. 'It's not possible. No-one can swim there. Not even an Englishman!'

Sophie groaned.

CHAPTER SIXTEEN: MR AND MRS BELL

Obviously I made it, or I wouldn't be writing this book, but it was touch-and-go. On the way back, I landed about three hundred yards downstream from where I had set off, and if it had been twenty yards further I'd have been swept out into the open, shark-infested sea. The current tore off my wedding ring, and it now nestles at the bottom of the Caribbean, an eternal monument to my patriotic folly. I've never worn jewellery, and I'd only agreed to wear a wedding ring in return for Sophie's allowing me to have Sky Sports. Now, after only a few days, it was gone. I take some solace from the fact that there is some corner of a foreign sea that will be forever England.

* * *

JUST UNDER A YEAR later, our first child, Harry Arkwright Bell, was born, and named after Harry Flashman, George MacDonald Fraser's anti-hero, and Sophie's ancestor, Sir Richard Arkwright. Harry and Gary sound very similar, but socially there is a vast gulf between them – 'One small step in the alphabet,' as Neil Armstrong might have put it, 'but one giant leap for social class.'

I was a hands-on father, nappy-wise. Partly, this was because Sophie had no experience of babies, while I had changed Dawn's children hundreds of times, and partly it was because I had more experience of having testicles. Sophie approached wiping Harry in much the same way as she approached scrubbing a dirty pan. It made me wince to watch. And neither of us was prepared for how tiring it was. When a baby wants to cry, he cries; when he wants to eat, he cries until you feed him; the same goes for all the bodily functions. But, exhausting as it was, it brought joy that I never previously knew existed. I loved Sophie with a burning passion, as I do to this day, but before my son was born I didn't know what unconditional love was.

During those early years, money was extremely tight. I was fat, having quickly piled back on my lost weight, but I was no fat cat, and while we weren't as poor as my family had been in Cotgrave we certainly lived hand-to-mouth at times. Barristers are self-employed, and our fees are paid irregularly, with VAT bills arriving at inopportune moments. New babies bring new expenses and, at the same time, we had lost a paying lodger to make room for Harry. More than once I had to borrow the cash to put petrol in my car.

I was then invoicing around £40,000 a year, when the average wage was perhaps £15,000. It sounds reasonable – perhaps more than reasonable, to some – but it's a misleading figure. A barrister's income is analogous to a company's turnover, rather than to a normal salary. Out of that £40,000, I had to pay VAT, chambers expenses of twenty per cent, for my indemnity insurance, my practising certificate, and an ever-expanding library of law books, and for my court dress. I was working all round the country, wherever the briefs took me, which meant forking out for train fares and taxis, or petrol and parking. I paid into a small pension, too.

My net pre-tax income was lower than £10,000 a year, and to earn that I often worked a sixty- or seventy-hour week: up at 5am to go through a brief, then a day in court, then working after supper on more papers until long into the small hours. And because barristers are self-employed, you cannot claim those train fares and mileage expenses back from any employer. If you have a day off with the flu, there is no sick pay. Any holiday you take is time when you aren't earning – not that we could really afford holidays in those days. I'd paid for the Cuban honeymoon by maxing out every credit card I could get my hands on, and we tended to rely on the kindness of friends of Sophie's family on other occasions; more than once Chris Huhne's parents generously allowed us the use of their villa in France, for instance.

I'm not complaining. I had my dream job, and it was fascinating, thrilling and challenging every day. I felt – and feel – privileged to call myself a barrister. I'm just pointing out that we are not all as highly-paid as our public image might suggest, and certainly not in the early- to middle-stages of our careers.

This has got more acute in recent years, as successive governments have seen criminal justice as an easy target for cuts. I'm well aware that little public sympathy exists for the two groups of people involved, barristers and alleged criminals, but legal aid fees have been steadily reduced until there is no more fat to trim, or flesh, and we're well into the bone. Barristers can often find themselves travelling hundreds of miles to court and back and earning, effectively, less than the minimum wage – or nothing at all, once expenses are taken into account. In 2013/14, according to the Ministry of Justice's own figures, more than a quarter of barristers received less than £20,000 in public fees. In those circumstances, it's not surprising that many have gone bankrupt, or given up the Bar, or worse.

At the same time, more and more people, attracted by the undoubted glamour of the profession, are knocking on the door to get in. Bar Schools have opened up all over the country, despite the fact that there are not the pupillages, let alone the tenancies, for most of the students to succeed to. Each year, hundreds of Bar School graduates are thus left high and dry and thoroughly disappointed – and many are then snapped up by firms of solicitors and employed as higher court advocates, or HCAs. (It used to be that only members of the Bar could appear in the crown courts and higher, but rights of audience were extended to solicitors some years ago.)

And here there is a tremendous conflict of interest. As the solicitor is the first point of contact for the client, usually at the police station, he or she is in pole position to persuade the client to agree to be represented by a lowly-paid, often inexperienced, and ill-qualified in-house HCA, rather than an experienced barrister from the independent Bar. Why would a solicitor do this? Because where a defendant is represented by an independent barrister, the independent barrister earns the fee. If he or she is represented by an in-house HCA, the fee goes to the firm of solicitors.

Paradoxically, it is less-experienced, more malleable defendants who allow themselves to be so persuaded, and they certainly leave themselves more open to conviction as a result; hardened criminals know the system and demand barristers, thus securing the best representation.

I can't say I really blame the solicitors, either. Just like us, their incomes have been savaged by swingeing legal aid cuts, all designed to make criminal justice cheaper. The politicians have half succeeded, too. It *is* now cheaper, but in many respects it's no longer justice.

For my own part, I tried to earn extra money by doing other things. I wrote articles for a number of magazines and for *The Mail on Sunday*. I appeared on television and radio as a legal pundit, and had my own hour-long show on Radio 4. I even tried writing books. My first was a crime thriller set in Los Angeles; acting on the advice of Nick Hornby, I sent it off to a leading literary agent.

To my surprise and delight, he signed it up. I thought I'd be the next Frederick Forsyth, and immediately took out a subscription to *Country Life* to find the mansion I would buy with my royalties. But the agent couldn't sell it to a publisher.

It was a bitter blow.

* * *

I SOLDIERED ON at the Bar, and gradually built up my roster of friendly solicitors.

But I was not to everyone's taste. I was briefed in a riot in Norwich, with the same solicitor acting for all five defendants. Four colleagues from chambers represented the other alleged rioters, and we were fighting on a united front until a difficulty arose. My client had a previous conviction, for causing death by dangerous driving. Jury members are not allowed to know about such matters unless the prosecution makes an application to put it in front of them, and the prosecution was not intending to make such an application. However, the other defendants – who had no convictions – had all decided to ask the judge for a 'good character direction', meaning that he would tell the jury that they had clean records. The idea was to create a more favourable impression of them, but since my client would conspicuously enjoy no such reference it was obvious that the jury would infer that he *did* have previous convictions.

I tried to persuade my colleagues not to go down that road, which I did not consider to be a united front. But I failed, so I changed tack. I cross-examined the witnesses on the basis that my client was a peacemaker, with the other four causing the trouble. After a six-week trial, the jury returned – not guilty for my client, guilty for everyone else.

I was pleased with my efforts, but my clerk was waiting for me at chambers. 'I've had the Norwich solicitor on,' she said.

'What did he say?'

'He said you had dirty shoes, wild hair, and were often late,' she said, 'and that he won't be using you again.'

'What about the other four?'

'He was happy with their shoes, their hair, and their timekeeping.'

My old friends from Cotgrave, many of whom often trod a fine line in respect of the law, also started to send me dribs and drabs of work. I found this very stressful, as their expectations of me were high. One miner found himself charged with an offence under Section 18 of the Offences Against the Person Act 1871, otherwise known as assault occasioning grievous bodily harm (or, colloquially, GBH). If convicted, he might be looking at five years in prison, but the prosecution offered a deal – if my client pleaded guilty to a much less serious Section 20 offence, unlawful wounding, they would drop the GBH. I advised the client to take it, because I thought there was a real risk he would be convicted if he stood trial. I knew the judge. He was a very heavy sentencer, but I was sure that, once he had heard my mitigation, he would not send my client to prison.

The prosecution alleged that the victim had come to my client's house and, finding the client's son alone in the house with a friend, had stolen my client's wallet. He had then gone on a spending spree before being caught that night, charged and released on bail. The following morning, my client was told that the thief had been spotted in the woods behind the village, and went looking for him with a pickaxe handle. He found him, and had fractured the man's skull.

My mitigation filled in the blanks. The prosecution had neglected to mention that my client's son was sixteen and had special needs, as did his friend. To prepare him for adult life, my client had been advised to start giving his son a little independence… just leaving him to fend for himself for the odd half-an-hour here and there. When the thief struck, he had been out walking his dog for just that purpose.

The following morning, he was again walking his dog when he saw the thief in the woods. He was unaware of the previous evening's arrest – as far as he knew, the perpetrator still had his wallet. He had called out a challenge, and the youth fled. Far from attacking the thief, my client had merely picked up a stick, a flimsy piece of willow, and had thrown it after the youth. It practically fluttered through the air and landed between the youth's legs, causing him to trip. He must have bumped his head on a rock when he fell.

That last bit was a rubbish explanation by my client – not least because of the pickaxe handle-shaped indentation in the thief's skull.

'Where is the victim now?' said the judge.

'He's down in the cells waiting to give evidence,' said the prosecutor.

'Down in the cells? But I thought he'd been granted bail on the theft charge?'

'He was,' said the prosecutor, 'but he's been charged with committing several more burglaries since then, and has been remanded in custody for those offences.'

The judge paused for the briefest of moments, and then addressed my client. 'Stand up, please,' he said. 'This court does not condone vigilantism. If I thought for one moment that you had gone looking for this youth and bashed his head in with a pickaxe handle, I would send you to prison for a very long time. But it is quite obvious that this was little more than an unfortunate accident caused by the willow twig fluttering through the air, tripping the poor victim, and causing him to bump his head. The sentence of this court is a conditional discharge. You are free to go.'

I was in a rich vein of form at the time, and thought I'd never lose a case, but I was brought back down to earth with a bump with my next trial – an armed robbery, heard at the Old Bailey. I had represented the defendant's brother on a charge of possession of cannabis with intent to supply, and he had been found not guilty. As a result, the alleged armed robber had insisted that I defend him.

The crime was farcical, and the evidence was strong.

The gang had lain in wait for a cash delivery van, which always dropped off at the target branch of a bank at the same time on a Monday. It was almost perfect. The only problem was that the day they had selected was a bank holiday – New Year's Day, to be precise. They should probably have postponed the operation for a week, but instead they drove to a nearby pub and burst in.

'Nobody move!' screamed out my masked client. 'Everyone get down on the floor!'

The manager was on the phone at the time: she calmly told the person on the other end of the line to call the police, and then replaced the receiver.

Five minutes later, armed police arrived.

My client made a break for it. A police officer grabbed him and wrestled him to the ground, but my client struggled free, leaving his coat behind, with his mask in the pocket. It was a bitterly cold day, and my client was soon caught running away through the snow, wearing nothing but jeans and a t-shirt. He claimed that he had been out jogging – a poor explanation, upon which further doubt was cast by the discovery that the mask contained his DNA and the coat had his name sewn into it.

After a titanic struggle, the jury found him guilty.

Like buses, defeats all seem to come at once.

My next trial was that of a man accused of murder. An old client, he was anxious for me to take the case, and he insisted that he was not guilty. I could sense trouble immediately – not least because the police had found him with his teeth clamped around the throat of the dead man. There had been a fight between the two of them over which of them would cede ground on a narrow pavement (it's amazing how many murders are committed over utterly trivial matters). My client had won the resultant fight, and had bitten his opponent to death, literally tearing his throat out with his teeth.

He claimed that he had acted in self defence, but the jury was not impressed.

I followed that defeat with the strange case of the arsonist firefighters.

The matter concerned two firemen who had heard that the social club attached to their fire station was going to close, and bought it to run it themselves. They soon realised *why* it had been closing – week after week, they found they were making horrendous losses.

Then, one night, a 999 call came in to report a huge wildfire in a wood at the extreme edge of their patch. All of the engines raced to the scene.

But when they arrived they discovered that it had been a hoax call – there was no fire. No sooner had *that* happened than they received a further call, this time to tell them that the firemen's social club attached to their *own* station was ablaze!

Witnesses reported the fire engines racing back to the scene, blue lights flashing and sirens blaring, at speeds of up to 8mph or even 9mph.

Sadly, by the time they got to the social club it was in smouldering ruins. Thank goodness it was fully insured!

The prosecution believed that it was a put-up job, with the two firemen who owned the club conspiring to burn it down. So, unfortunately, did the jury.

CHAPTER SIXTEEN: MR AND MRS BELL

* * *

AS A SMALL boy, Harry once asked me what I did for a job.

'When the police catch naughty men who have done bad things and put them in prison,' I explained, 'my job is to get them out again.'

'That doesn't sound like a very good job,' he said, doubtfully.

And – allowing for the over-simplification of my explanation – sometimes it's not. But, as I've said, that cab rank rule means we have to take on unpalatable cases. I was briefed in the magistrates' court to defend four Chelsea football hooligans charged with a public order offence. They had been walking drunkenly towards Stamford Bridge when they had passed a house with an Anti-Nazi League poster displayed in the window. They knocked on the door, and it was answered by a young woman of left-wing persuasion.

'You know that Anti-Nazi League poster in your window?' one of them said.

'What of it?' the woman replied, feistily.

'We're Nazis,' said the Chelsea hooligan, 'and we find it offensive. If it's still there after the match we're going to burn your fucking house down.'

She called the police, the four men were arrested within minutes, and charged. But it was a stupid charge – that their actions had caused the young woman fear of immediate violence. I submitted that there was no case to answer because their threats were to burn the house down *if the poster was still there after the match*. It *was* a threat of violence, but not, as was required by the Act, of *immediate* violence. The magistrates had no choice but to find the men not guilty, and as I left court I was berated by a group of ANL protestors. There was no explaining to them at the time, but the law is the law: you may enjoy bending it to secure a conviction against a group of vile thugs, but what about when it gets bent against you? First they came for the Chelsea Nazis, and I did not speak out because I was not a Chelsea Nazi – to adapt Martin Niemöller, slightly inappropriately.

I hoped that the case would be my only foray into the murky world of extremist right-wing politics but, a couple of months later, Paul Selby rang to tell me that he had a young man charged with violence at a British National Party rally in Woolwich.

'Not again,' I groaned. 'I'll be known as the fascists' barrister of choice.'

'Don't worry,' he laughed. 'It's not like it seems.'

I turned up for the trial, running another gauntlet of protestors waiting outside. In the robing room I bumped into a friend of mine, Iggy Hughes, now a QC in Bristol. 'Here he is,' he announced, to the dozens of barristers present, 'Gary Bell, standing counsel to the BNP!'

Four BNP supporters had been walking home after the rally when they heard a noise behind them, and turned to see some two hundred Anti-Nazi League members charging up the road with evil intent. The ANL bunch were led by a young black man who was racing ahead in his eagerness to get at the right-wingers. The BNP group turned and steeled themselves for the fight, and seconds later they were indeed attacked by the young black man. Unfortunately for him, his friends had declined to assist and were now disappearing into the far distance. He took a fearful beating, and was only saved from serious harm by the arrival of a mounted police officer, who chased the BNP men into a housing estate.

Three of them were soon located hiding in a garden shed, and my client was picked up as he stood on a nearby doorstep.

All four were arrested and charged with GBH. The officer on horseback positively identified them, and it looked bleak. The trial started, and the officer on horseback was called and confirmed that the four men arrested were the men involved in the assault. I suggested that, as far as my client was concerned, he was mistaken, but he remained adamant. But I backed up my client's case with evidence: he had been at work that morning, not attending a BNP rally, and had gone straight from work to the house where he was arrested.

It was his sister's house, and she and her husband had been expecting him to talk about his role as a Godfather at her new baby's forthcoming Christening. Rather surprisingly, I added, for an alleged BNP member, the sister's husband was black, and my client's soon-to-be Godson was, therefore, of mixed race.

'What made you think that my client was a racist extremist?' I asked.

'He was wearing boots and had a skinhead haircut,' the officer replied.

'Would it surprise you to learn that, as a builder, he wears boots to work?' I said.

'What about the skinhead?' he spat back.

'Were you aware that my client was recently diagnosed with cancer,' I said, 'and has undergone chemotherapy, which caused all his hair to fall out?'

'No,' the officer admitted, the wind disappearing from his sails.

A co-defendant's barrister thought he could piggyback on my successful cross-examination. 'What made you think that *my* client was a racist extremist?' he said.

'The swastika tattooed on his hand,' the officer replied.

His client was promptly convicted, as was one of the others (the fourth man had fallen ill during the trial, and the jury had been discharged as against him). But my client was found not guilty – which, given his utter innocence, seemed fair enough.

Again, there was a large mob of ANL types outside court: I'm confident that they would have torn my cancer-stricken builder to pieces before the hearing, had they had chance. But that case demonstrated that police officers are not infallible, and that the proper forum for deciding guilt is not a police station, or a lynching on the court steps, but in the court itself.

The fourth defendant was to be tried on his own a few weeks later. I soon received a telephone call from his solicitor. 'My client was very impressed with you during the trial,' he explained, 'and wants you to represent him.'

'I'm sorry,' I said, 'but, having already represented one defendant in the case, I can't. However, I can recommend a brilliant chap called Iggy Hughes…'

Step forward, new standing counsel to the BNP.

* * *

HAVING SUCCESSFULLY THROWN off the yoke of representing right-wing extremists, my next foray was into the opposite camp, representing a hard-left demonstrator who had been involved in the 'Kill the Bill' demonstration in Hyde Park in October 1994.

What had started ostensibly as a protest against the perceived draconian measures contained in the new Criminal Justice Bill – it sought to abolish the right to silence, and criminalised ravers and Swampy-type protestors – had turned into a pitched battle between members of various anarchist or leftist groups and the Metropolitan Police. The 'Kill the Bill' chant was ambiguous, at best, referring either to stopping the Criminal Justice Bill or doing harm to the coppers, and my client had been captured on video throwing a dart at a police horse. He had remained at large until he was identified by officers at another demonstration, this time against the export of veal calves to France, at Brightlingsea in Essex. He was charged with a public order offence, and, given the quality of the video, he pleaded guilty. During my mitigation, the judge asked a question which, I must admit, had occurred to me.

'What I don't understand,' the judge said, 'is how a man who demonstrates against cruelty to animals can throw a dart at a horse?'

'It was a police horse,' said the defendant.

He escaped a prison sentence, probably because of the judge's view of his intelligence, and as a result he passed the word around. For some time after that, I seemed to represent every extreme left-winger going.

Again, Paul Selby and I embarked on a string of fantastic results, and I went for years without losing a trial. Much of the work was for an Irish family from Bermondsey. I won eight straight trials for various members, but then a case arrived that appeared unwinnable. The youngest boy was charged with ram-raiding after being caught, with three of his friends, near the scene of the crime. They all denied it, and my client, who was caught furthest away from the scene, had the best defence, on paper. But in the week before the trial, at the Inner London Crown Court, disaster struck. We were served with a notice of additional evidence, revealing that DNA put my client in the stolen car used in the ram-raid. I anticipated advising him to plead guilty, but upon arrival at court I was pleasantly surprised by the prosecution line.

'There doesn't seem to be much evidence against your client,' he said, clearly not having seen the notice of additional evidence. 'If the other three plead guilty, I'll drop the case against you.'

I rushed off to find the other three barristers who were representing the co-defendants – one of them a glamorous young blonde called Sarah.

'What are you doing?' she said. 'This DNA evidence not only puts you (barristers usually refer to themselves in place of their clients when discussing cases) in the car – as we're your known associates, it's pretty damning for us, too. I've advised my client to plead guilty.'

The other two barristers had arrived at a similar position. I said nothing – though I may, inadvertently, have given the impression that I would be taking the same line. I hurried off in search of the prosecutor and gave him the good news. Ten minutes later we were in court.

Sarah addressed the judge. 'Could the indictment be put again to my client?' she said.

It was, and her client pleaded guilty. The other two defendants followed suit. Sarah looked over at me, expecting a similar application, but, to her surprise, the prosecutor stood up and addressed the judge.

'Those three guilty pleas are sufficient for the prosecution,' he said. 'I offer no evidence against the fourth defendant.'

The other defendants, and their barristers, were furious. As my client was released from the dock, his co-defendants grabbed and berated him, sure they had been tricked. But their rage was as nothing to Sarah's. She attacked me physically as I left counsel's row, calling me a duplicitous bastard.

I could see her point, a bit.

Later, she tracked me down – I thought either to give me another beating, or an apology. But she had other things on her mind.

'Who's that gorgeous man you were with earlier?' she said.

'My solicitor, Paul Selby.'

'Is he married?'

'No.'

'He will be soon,' she said. 'To me.'

CHAPTER SEVENTEEN: THE RETURNING HERO

Sixteen years to silk

TWO YEARS AFTER Harry's birth, our second son, Toby, arrived, and we decided to move out of London. I found new chambers in Nottingham, and Sophie took a job in Northampton as the manager of a housing association.

In October 1996 we bought a house in a lovely village a few miles south of the town. Sophie had soon become a governor at the school, I was elected onto the parish council, and life was idyllic – except for at work. I'd been hoping to return to Nottingham and clean up, as some sort of homecoming hero... The local lad from humble beginnings, made reasonably good.

It did not work out quite like that. Being keen to show my face, I took on everything that came my way, including a lot of magistrates' court cases that were really beneath a barrister of my experience. Once I became known for taking on this more trivial work, a lot of solicitors simply assumed that that was my level, and didn't brief me on proper crime.

But beyond that strategic error, the Nottingham Bar was a close-knit place, and one or two of the judges were keener than I was to see trials 'crack'. This effectively involves barristers persuading their clients to plead guilty in exchange for securing a lesser sentence, and some of my colleagues certainly felt under pressure from the bench to do this. I did not. Of course, I would always advise the defendant frankly about the strength of the evidence against him, the prospects of success, and the discount available on the sentence for a guilty plea, but if – after all of that – he still wanted a trial then I would give him a trial, no matter what the evidence. I must admit that this did not always endear me to the bench.

I found the local appeals system hard to fathom, too. On a given Friday, around twenty appeals against conviction would be listed in front of a judge, Keith Matthewman, sitting with two lay magistrates. Done properly, a list of this kind could easily take days to plough through, but Matthewman had found a way of clearing the decks much more quickly. He would call the barristers and the appellants into court and inform them that, if any of the appeals were dismissed, sentence would be 'at large'. In other words, if he and the magistrates found against them, the sentences dished out would exceed those which they had earlier received.

Given that most people were appealing against magistrates' court convictions, and small fines or community orders, this was, in effect, warning them that an unsuccessful appeal might lead to jail time. In those circumstances, it wasn't altogether unsurprising that many appellants, even those with very strong cases, decided not to chance their arms.

For instance, I ran an appeal for a client convicted of dangerous driving on the evidence of a policeman. The policeman was having an affair with the appellant's wife, which seemed to me to be at least worthy of consideration, and I had a defence witness – another police officer – whose account completely contradicted that of the prosecution.

The case was listed for the whole day, and I was confident of victory.

Judge Matthewman gave us his sentence-at-large speech, the appeal started, and the prosecution called their star witness.

When the time came for me to start my cross-examination, Matthewman fixed me with a steely eye.

'Mr Bell,' he said. 'We warned your client that, if this appeal was dismissed, sentence would be at large. Now that we have heard the prosecution evidence, I should warn you that, if you continue with this appeal and if it *is* dismissed, we intend to impose the maximum sentence of six months' imprisonment on your client. Does he want to continue or not?'

My client decided that he did not.

This bizarre appeals system, and the judicial pressure for prosecutors to accept guilty pleas to lesser offences to avoid effective trials, obviously led to much speedier resolutions, but was it justice? I can't say that I'm sure that it was.

Happily things have now changed, and the recently-retired Resident Judge at Nottingham, the excellent and widely-respected Michael Stokes QC, made his views on the practice perfectly clear when he was called upon to sentence a defendant originally charged with grievous bodily harm with intent, but whose charge had been reduced to unlawful wounding through acting recklessly (the difference in maximum sentences being life imprisonment for the former and five years for the latter) on condition that he pleaded guilty.

'It should have been a matter for a jury to decide whether the defendant in this case was acting with intent or recklessly,' Judge Stokes castigated the prosecuting team, 'and in future I expect such decisions to be left to the jury. The days of grubby compromise are over.'

Not in my day they weren't.

I continued to buck the system by fighting my cases – though, in truth, there were very few of them to fight – and I was seen as a troublemaker.

Things were not panning out well, at all.

My earnings plummeted, and we were heading for serious financial trouble.

Then, out of nowhere, came one of those life-changing events that do seem to happen to me. I was asked to give the best man's speech at Paul Selby's wedding – to Sarah, the barrister from the Inner London Crown Court, who had been as good as her word.

I had just sat down when I was approached by an Indian chap.

'Great speech,' he said.

'Thanks,' I said.

'Can I introduce myself? My name is Tarsem Salhan. I'm a solicitor in Birmingham. Paul tells me you're not happy in Nottingham?'

'That's right.'

'Why not try chambers in Birmingham?'

'I don't really know much about Birmingham.'

'If you move there,' he said, 'I'll get you high quality work. Trust me.'

I'm not a quitter and I wanted to make things work in Nottingham. On the other hand, I was really struggling. I desperately needed some decent briefs. But how could I be sure Tarsem would be able to keep his promise?

Two days later, I got my answer, via my clerk.

'A big gangland protection racketeering case has come in from some solicitor in Birmingham,' he said, looking a little puzzled. 'It's for trial next week.'

I looked at the brief: twelve defendants, and my client alleged to have been one of the ringleaders.

Good old Tarz!

* * *

I SPENT THE rest of the week in some minor thing in Nottingham Crown Court and working on the brief in the evenings.

A group of men from a rough Birmingham council estate had allegedly been running a protection racket, collecting money from local businesses on pain of smashing them up, both the premises and the owners, if they refused to pay. The prosecution claimed that my client was in the thick of it, and, if convicted, he faced a long prison sentence.

At Birmingham the following Monday, I found the court surrounded by armed police, and a gaggle of terrified witnesses who had only been persuaded to give evidence on the basis of three prosecution promises. These were that they could give evidence under false names, that they could do so from behind screens, and that all of the main players would be remanded in custody –

especially the principal defendant, a dangerous, 6ft 6in psychopath who had allegedly killed ten people with his weapon of choice, a machete.

On the first day of the trial, the prosecution made an application that this principal defendant be tried in handcuffs, because information had been received that an escape bid was planned. This sort of thing doesn't aid the defence – a nun would look guilty in cuffs – so it's not something a judge allows lightly.

'What is the information?' he said.

'I don't know,' admitted the prosecution barrister.

'Well,' snapped the judge. 'I can't order someone to be tried in handcuffs unless I know why. All the defendants can go downstairs to the cells whilst you find out exactly what this intelligence is.'

As he stood up to leave court, a barrister called him back. 'Er, my client is on bail, Your Honour.'

'Those defendants who are on bail can have bail renewed,' said the judge. 'The rest can go down to the cells.'

Two defendants were on bail – both bit-part actors, at the bottom of the indictment. One was represented by the barrister who had spoken up, and the other had in fact failed to turn up for the trial. As the judge left and people started gathering up their papers, the intelligence officer came up from the cells and began to explain to the prosecuting barrister, through the locked door of the dock, exactly how the principal defendant intended to escape.

Meanwhile, the gaoler in charge of taking the prisoners back to the cells consulted his list. 'Right,' he said. 'Which two are on bail?'

'Me,' said the man already identified by his barrister.

There was a brief silence, and then the principal defendant stood up. 'Er… I'm on bail as well,' he said.

'Right, you two can go,' said the gaoler, unlocking the door. 'The rest of you, down to the cells.'

The intelligence officer broke off his detailed explanation of the fiendish plan by which this dangerous psychopath intended to escape, and stood back to allow him to lumber out on to the streets of Birmingham.

A few minutes later, I was approached by the prosecuting barrister. 'Gary,' he said, 'can we just agree these edits to your client's interview?'

'That's not really your biggest problem at the moment,' I said.

'What is, then?' he said.

'The fact that the principal defendant just walked out of the front door of the court.'

He thought I was joking, but after making enquiries he returned, ashen-faced. 'Why didn't you stop him?' he said.

'You must be kidding,' I replied. 'I don't get danger money. Would you have?'

He considered the question for a moment. 'Probably not,' he conceded.

The principal defendant couldn't be traced, and it was decided that the trial would proceed in his absence.

After a few applications, all of which the prosecution lost, the first witness for the prosecution was called to give evidence. But just before he took the stand – behind screens, and under the pseudonym of Michael Mouse – he was given some unfortunate news by the prosecution barrister.

'There are three small changes,' the prosecutor told the already-nervous man. 'The first is that we've had to give the defendants your real name. The second is that the judge won't allow you to be screened from the defendants. The third is that the principal defendant has escaped.'

Throughout his evidence, the witness was terrified. He only knew my client by his nickname, 'Tubby', and told lurid tales of acts allegedly committed by him. My client was known as Tubby ironically, because he had the proportions of a stick insect, but in his fearful state the witness was finding it hard to concentrate.

'The man known as Tubby,' the prosecuting barrister asked him. 'Why was he known as that?'

'I don't know,' the distracted witness replied. 'Because he was fat, I suppose.'

He was cross-examined by the other barristers and given a torrid time by all. Then it came to my turn.

'You said the man known as Tubby was called that because he was fat,' I smiled.

'That's right,' the witness replied.

'Some people have been known to describe me as fat,' I said.

Everyone laughed, including the witness, and the judge leaned forward. 'That's very unkind of them,' he said.

'I hope the fat man you've described wasn't thinner than me,' I said.

Mine were the first sympathetic words the witness had heard all day, and he relaxed, and seemed eager to please. 'Oh, no, definitely not,' he said, with enthusiasm. 'He was much fatter than you. Much fatter.'

A few days into the trial came some interesting news. The story was that the escaped principle defendant would never be found: he had fled to America, or Australia. He had links in Ireland, and access to a safe house in Northern Cyprus. He was an international man of mystery, who had vanished without trace.

As it was, he was arrested one morning at his mum's house a couple of miles away.

This stopped the trial in its tracks, and the only solution was to start it again.

'That's not fair to my client, Your Honour,' I said, addressing the judge. 'The case against him is fatally flawed, particularly in relation to identification.'

The judge agreed, and dismissed the charges against my client. Everyone else was convicted and, from that moment on, it seemed that any criminal from my newly-adopted city of Birmingham – and there was no shortage of them – wanted Tarsem and me to represent him.

Within a week, Tarz had sent me an attempted murder trial. My client, a non-English-speaking sixty-five-year-old Bengali man, was accused of trying to murder his wife. He had been represented by a different firm, but wanted to transfer to Salhan & Co., having lost confidence in his previous solicitor.

I made the initial application for the transfer, accompanied by a Sikh solicitor from Salhans called Sukky Johal, and it went well, until, demonstrating an astounding degree of ignorance, I added, 'and, of course, another advantage of transferring legal aid is that my instructing solicitor Mr Johal can speak to the defendant in his own language – thus saving the cost of an interpreter.'

The judge liked the idea of saving expenditure from the public purse, but Sukky seemed to have concerns, and was pulling frantically on the back of my gown. I ignored him, being on a roll, and the judge was finally persuaded.

'Can your solicitor go and talk to the defendant and ask him if he definitely wants to transfer?' he said.

I instructed Sukky to go and ask him, and – with a forlorn look which I couldn't fathom – he trudged towards the dock.

There was a flurry of hushed whispering, and then Sukky could be heard in English almost shouting at the defendant, '*DO YOU WANT TO TRANSFER?!*'

The judge looked at me in consternation, but the defendant said 'yes' so he transferred the case.

Afterwards, Sukky put me straight. 'I speak Punjabi,' he said, 'and the defendant speaks Bengali. Same continent, different language. It would be like me expecting you to speak Danish to a client from Copenhagen.'

How was I to know that there are more than fifteen hundred different languages spoken on the Indian sub-continent?

In the event, the client had to plead guilty. He had gone on a two-week holiday to Bangladesh, but enjoyed himself so much that he stayed for three years, leaving his wife to look after their eighteen children. As he had instructed her to send half of her benefits and family allowance to him every week, she began to find it tough financially, and went to the Citizens' Advice Bureau for help. A Bengali-speaking man was assigned to assist her, and things went well until the defendant finally returned. Upon learning that another man had been in the house, he was left with no choice but to kill his wife. To this end, he attacked her in the kitchen with a *dhati* – a razor-sharp cooking cleaver. As he struck down on her head, she raised a hand to protect herself, and it was cut clean off. Her arm fended off the second blow, and it was severed at the elbow. She fled to the locked door, and opened the Yale lock with her teeth, losing six of them in the exercise, and then dashed into the garden. Her husband caught her there, and was hacking at her with the *dhati*, cursing her in Bengali, when two youths rushed over to stop him. The police were called and the defendant arrested, through chance by a Bengali-speaking policeman.

'Why are you arresting me?' the defendant complained. 'This is a domestic matter – that woman is my wife.'

The judge disagreed. He sent the defendant to prison – though for a mere five years.

* * *

I IMMEDIATELY MOVED chambers to Birmingham, and the work flooded in. Most of the time I was led by a QC, in large-scale drugs conspiracies, or murder and other extreme violence, and some of the cases were terrible.

In one particularly gruesome case, a woman told her partner she was leaving him. He took her to a copse, forced her onto the car roof with a noose around her neck attached to a branch, and said he would drive away and leave her hanging there unless she changed her mind.

She swallowed hard, and gave her answer. 'I'd sooner hang from this tree than be with you.'

He released her, much to her relief, but swore he would get her back another way. The following day, he kidnapped her brother on his way back from school, murdered him and buried his body in an unknown location.

I was led in a terrible trial by Tim Cassell QC, a magnificent silk and a great man. The evidence against the defendant was overwhelming, and he was convicted and received a life sentence with a minimum recommendation of twenty-two years. After I visited him in prison, he gave up the location of the boy's body.

The only case I won that year was even worse. My client had been serving a substantial sentence of imprisonment for an acid attack on a pub bouncer. Towards the end of that sentence, my client's niece had been sexually assaulted by a sixty-five-year-old paedophile who had received a community service order for that crime. My client felt that this sentence was unduly lenient, but rather than apply for an Attorney General's reference he decided to increase it himself on his release from prison. To that end, he bought a gallon of petrol, poured it through the paedophile's letterbox, and threw in a match. The house went up in flames, and the paedophile was forced to jump from the second-floor window, breaking his ankle in the fall. Two young lads came to his aid.

'You haven't got a spare cigarette have you, lads?' he said. 'I've left mine in my bedroom.'

They gave him a cigarette, and he took a few drags. Then he added, 'There might be a young girl in there, as well.'

The young men, rare heroes in a case involving all of life's flotsam and jetsam, made herculean efforts to reach her, but were beaten back by the flames and suffered rather severe burns. The girl was the fourteen-year-old daughter of an alcoholic woman whose garden backed onto the paedophile's. This woman had an arrangement with him whereby, for a bottle of Strongbow and a packet of fags, she would allow her daughter to spend time with him. And so it was that, whilst she drank her cider and smoked her Royals, her young daughter burned to death, tied naked to the vile creature's bed.

Against all odds, my client was found not guilty – perhaps because the jury thought that others were more culpable for the poor girl's death who were not on trial.

The following year I started doing cases on my own, and had another good run of success. A lot of my work was spin-offs from my success in Tubby's gangster trial. It seemed like everyone from Tubby's estate who was charged with a serious offence wanted me to represent them, and it seemed like everyone from Tubby's estate was charged with a serious offence.

One client had been involved in a knife fight outside a local nightclub with members of a rival gang. The police had turned up, but my client was oblivious to this fact. His best friend from childhood ran over and tapped him on the shoulder to inform him of their arrival, but, in the excitement of the moment, my client turned and accidentally stabbed him six times. Leaving his best friend – who, fortunately, did not die – bleeding on the floor, he ran off and tried to hail a taxi. The driver, who had witnessed the stabbing, refused, until my client flourished the knife and warned him that he would be next. My client was later arrested and charged with stabbing his best friend, as well as two members of the opposition gang. He was also charged with kidnap and unlawful imprisonment of the taxi driver.

The trial was a farce.

The police visited the witnesses the day beforehand to warn them to attend court, or face contempt of court proceedings.

Despite this, in the event, none of them – apart from the poor taxi driver – turned up. Witness summonses were issued, and then arrest warrants, but not only did the missing witnesses – including the three alleged victims – still fail to attend, the police couldn't even trace them.

The judge was furious and called me into his room, where he spoke frankly.

'Personally, Mr Bell,' he said, 'I don't give a flying fuck what these people do to each other, but he's going to have to have something for the taxi driver. Do I make myself clear?'

He did. After a brief conference with my client, a guilty plea was entered to the kidnap and unlawful imprisonment of the cabbie.

The prosecution dropped the rest of the case and my client was sentenced to eighteen months' imprisonment. As he had been remanded in custody for nearly ten months, and as prisoners often only have to serve half of the sentence imposed, he was released immediately. He was anxious to take me to the pub for a drink but, remembering what had happened the last time he had gone drinking, I declined.

Occasionally, a case turned up involving someone with no criminal past. Oddly enough, it usually involved murder, which is still overwhelmingly a domestic crime.

One bizarre trial involved a row over five pounds. A Glaswegian called Jimmy (I'll call him Big Jimmy) was living on a rough Birmingham estate.

Next door lived another Glaswegian, a single mum, with her young son.

By coincidence, Big Jimmy and the mum shared the same surname, and her son was also called Jimmy (I'll call him Wee Jimmy).

On Wee Jimmy's birthday, he got a phone call from his aunt in Glasgow asking him if he had received the card containing a five-pound note she had posted to him.

He hadn't, and Wee Jimmy's mother's suspicions as to what might have happened to it were heightened when she saw Big Jimmy from next door walking down the street with a two-litre bottle of cider. It wasn't dole day – how had he got hold of *that* sort of money?!

She checked his dustbin, and there lay the card, opened and discarded, and no five pound note.

Something had to be done, and Wee Jimmy's mum summoned up a group of her female friends for a war council. They immediately came up with a plan, which was to go around to Big Jimmy's flat and beat him (to death, as it transpires) with pots and pans.

My client, a mother-of-five in her mid-thirties with no previous convictions, was alleged to have struck the fatal blow, severing Big Jimmy's carotid artery with a frying pan. She was charged with murder, but her plea to violent disorder was accepted by the prosecution. In the event she was sentenced to a hundred hours' community service.

* * *

IF THERE WAS a problem with my practice, it was the travel. I was instructed nationally, and could end up literally anywhere. One client was charged with swindling bookmakers the length and breadth of the country. He could have been arrested in any of a hundred towns, but the idiot managed to get caught in Middlesbrough.

I set off at 6am on the morning of the trial, bleary-eyed and cursing my luck that he had not been arrested further south. The traffic was horrendous and the journey never-ending, and it looked like I was going to be late. I was running short on petrol and desperately needed a poo, but I am a strict adherent to the unwritten rules of driving for men, to wit: men are not allowed to stop at the first petrol station they see after the reserve warning light comes on, nor can they stop at the first loo after they develop the need to go, however urgent it may be. (Additionally, they may not ask for directions, except in truly exceptional circumstances; if they *are* forced to ask for directions, they may only listen to the first instruction, after which they must switch off mentally.) So I raced boldly on past service station after service station. My petrol lasted okay, but by the time I pulled into the court car park things were looking a little bleak on the other front. I collected my bags and strode purposefully towards the building, but my steps got shorter and shorter until I could only risk fairy steps, so desperate was I.

There were steps up to the court entrance, and I climbed them somewhat laboriously. But as I reached the top I relaxed: I could see a loo just inside the glass door.

Then – to my utter horror – I saw the sign on the door: 'This entrance is locked – please use the entrance at the opposite end of the building.'

The Teeside Crown Court building is roughly Pantheon-sized, and it took me twenty minutes to creep to the other entrance. By the time I got there, disaster had occurred in the underpant department. I was stopped by security and, as is now usual in courts, he came over to search me. But he stopped a few feet short of me, looked at me in disgust, and waved me through unsearched. When I finally reached the loo, to my shame and dismay I found the damage was widespread. I cleaned myself up as best I could and limped into court. There was a terrible stink in the courtroom about which everyone was complaining (myself included, and very vociferously). People checked their shoes to see if they had trodden in something, and I knew it was only a matter of time before they traced it back to source. By sheer good fortune, the main prosecution witness was ill and could not attend, so the case was adjourned. I was back in the car within five minutes and racing home, windows down, to get cleaned up. Four hundred yards later, as I turned onto the elevated dual carriageway, I ran out of petrol.

Do these things happen to other people, or is it just me?

In my next case, I was briefed to represent an armed robber in Winchester, a fellow I'll call Jones.

Jones was an interesting chap. As soon as I heard him speak, I recognised a Canadian twang.

'You sound like you're from Toronto,' I said. 'Lovely city, isn't it?'

'I don't really remember,' he said.

It turned out that Jones was English, and had flown to Toronto fifteen years earlier. On the very day he had arrived, he had committed an armed robbery. He had been arrested immediately and had spent the following decade and a half in a local prison – hence the accent he had acquired – before being deported back to the UK.

The case in which he was now involved demonstrated incompetence of a similar order. The prosecution alleged that he and three chums had conceived a plan to rob a bank.

Cleverly, they had arranged a getaway car in which they would drive to their actual car, which had earlier been parked up half a mile away. This change of vehicle would throw off the scent any police officers rushing to the scene.

Not cleverly, their actual car was a Volvo estate of an unusual and very noticeable orange hue, and they had parked it up in a quiet cul-de-sac which was home to an old people's complex and assorted bungalows full of retired people with time on their hands and an inquisitive nature.

As a result, there were around forty pairs of nosey eyes hiding behind twitching net curtains when the gang roared back into the close, jumped out of the getaway car and piled into the DayGlo Volvo. Within moments, numerous calls were made to the police giving the new car's registration and descriptions of the four men, including my client.

I was a little worried because I'd been told that some last minute additional papers were being sent to the court for me to collect, but the trial wasn't due to start until 2pm. As long as I arrived by 9am, I would have time to read them and be ready to go.

I got to Winchester in plenty of time – so much so that I decided to nip into a shop to buy a birthday present for my nephew, Dawn's son Daniel. It was a new-fangled gadget called a Nintendo Gameboy, and it looked absolutely fascinating. I got changed for court, collected my papers, read through them, and then popped to the loo. I took the Gameboy into a cubicle with me to help pass the time, and started playing Super Mario Land.

It was harder than it looked but, as I've said, I'm not a quitter, and I battled, with gritted teeth, up through the levels.

I was still grappling with one of Tatanga's many minions when my reverie was interrupted by an announcement on the Tannoy: 'All parties in the two o'clock trial, please report to Court 1.'

That's a bit early, I thought to myself, checking my watch.

It was five to two!

I'd been playing the Gameboy on the loo for nearly five hours.

I jumped up and immediately fell over. All the sensation had gone from my legs. Finally, and with great difficulty, I managed to stumble out of the cubicle and up into the court, where the jury was sworn in and the case began.

In the event, my client was eventually found not guilty as a result of an inexplicable prosecution cock-up.

On the day of his arrest, Jones had been roughly as fat as I was on my arrival back in the UK following my triumphant debating tour of the United States. Indeed, the eyewitnesses made great play of his parlous physical state, and reported him waddling, puffing and panting, to the orange Volvo. Jones was not as daft as he looked, and during his time on remand he had joined a hunger strike. Everyone else involved was doing it to complain about the fact that prisoners on the sex offenders' wing were getting first dibs on videos sent in to the prison, but Jones had an ulterior motive. His time on remand enabled him to shed his excess flab, so that by the time he stood in the dock he resembled a stick insect, and nothing like the man described by the witnesses. Inexplicably, the prosecution had failed to introduce into evidence the arrest photographs, and so the jury acquitted him.

In fact, everyone seemed to be found not guilty in that period.

An alleged bank robber found still wearing his mask and holding the money he had stolen – not guilty.

A bouncer who had bitten off someone's ear and was running self-defence – not guilty.

A man who had hit another man on the head with a hammer and then stabbed a third chap and was claiming both acts were accidental – not guilty.

I was even asked by the escaped defendant from Tubby's trial to appeal against his conviction, for which he was serving a sentence of ten years. I took it to the Court of Appeal, which overturned his conviction, substituted a verdict of not guilty, and ordered his immediate release.

'I could murder a pint, Mr Bell,' he said, so I took him to the Seven Stars opposite the Royal Courts of Justice, and bought him one. I'd only ever seen him in custody, and he had always appeared a gentle, thoughtful man. Indeed, in the cells that very morning, when I'd been down to see him before the appeal, he had been as nice as pie.

Two pints later, that all changed. His eyes, his manner, and his gait became those of a machete-wielding maniac, so I made my excuses and left before he started chopping people up.

* * *

I WAS OFFERED more and more work, and my cases got not only more serious but more strange.

I was instructed in a drugs conspiracy in Leeds where the principal defendant had been jailed for fifteen years for heroin dealing, but had continued running his empire from behind bars using a prison phone. Since every conversation was recorded, he was careful to speak in code. One day he was talking to a new courier who had been recruited to replace a fellow who had been arrested, and was giving him his coded instructions.

'Go to Heathrow and meet Imran off the plane,' he told the courier, who – for reasons which will become apparent – came to be known as 'The Little Idiot'. 'Pick up a car from him and deliver it to Saghir.'

'But Saghir just bought a new car,' said The Little Idiot. 'It's a bloody great Mercedes. Why does he need another one?'

'Look,' the drug baron repeated, in a steely voice, 'meet Imran at Heathrow, *pick up the car* and *deliver it to Saghir!*'

'How do I get to Heathrow?' said The Little Idiot.

'Drive!' said the baron. It was clear from the tape that he was losing patience.

'But if I drive to Heathrow in *my* car to pick up a car for Saghir, then I'll have *two* cars,' wailed The Little Idiot. 'How am I supposed to get them both back?'

'Listen, you little idiot,' said the baron, pushed beyond endurance. 'These phone calls are recorded, so we speak in code. A "car" is the code word for a fucking kilo of heroin. Didn't anybody tell you that?'

'Ah, yes,' said The Little Idiot. 'I remember now. Soz.'

The Little Idiot was arrested the following day on the M1 with a kilo of heroin in his boot, and eventually twenty-four people were charged in connection with selling £26 million-worth of the drug. My client was number three on the indictment, just behind the drugs baron and the unfortunate Saghir. The trial lasted three months and I was able to argue that the evidence against my client – the result of his private telephone being tapped – should be excluded. It was a crucial blow against the prosecution case, and the net result was that the jury found my client not guilty and potted everyone else.

As a result of that victory, I was instructed to represent one of the client's twin brothers on a murder charge in Sheffield.

Although only sixteen, and of Pakistani origin, such was their reputation that they were known locally as 'Ronnie' and 'Reggie'.

They had annoyed the local drug overlord, a huge West Indian in his forties, by failing to show him sufficient respect. He was not really a man to annoy, and indeed he expressed his annoyance by kidnapping Reggie and bundling him at gunpoint into his car. He then drove him to a local beauty spot, intending to shoot him in the head, thereby teaching him to respect his elders and betters.

But as they walked through the park, Reggie's phone rang.

'Answer it,' ordered the drug overlord, 'but don't tell anyone where you are.'

Reggie answered the call and had a brief conversation – in Mirpuri.

'Who was it?' asked the drug overlord.

'It was my mum asking when I'd be home for tea,' said Reggie. 'I said I'd be late.'

'You're right,' the drug overlord replied, with a vicious smirk. 'You're going to be very late!'

Five minutes later, a surprised drug overlord looked up to see a huge crowd of Pakistanis racing towards him, waving knives and cudgels. He managed to get off three shots before they were on him, and by the time they had finished he had more perforations than a Tetley teabag.

As many of the group as the police could identify were charged with murder – Ronnie being one of them.

I considered his options. Self-defence was unlikely, given the number of stab wounds, so I offered the prosecution a plea to violent disorder. The drug overlord had a large string of convictions, including several for assaulting police officers, which surely went in my client's favour?

It did: the prosecution agreed to drop the murder charge if Ronnie pleaded guilty to violent disorder, and he was sentenced to a hundred and twenty hours' community service.

A barrister's lot can feel like that of the millkeeper's daughter in the fairy tale, *Rumpelstiltskin*. The girl is locked in a tower by the king and ordered to spin a pile of straw into gold. If she succeeds, she lives, but she is rewarded with an even bigger pile of straw. If she fails, the king will have her head chopped off.

Barristers who fail aren't decapitated – at least, I hope they aren't – but their work does dry up, which is the next worst thing. My sojourn in Yorkshire came to an end over a baby's dirty nappy. My client was taking the soiled nappy to the dustbin in his yard, but as it was raining and he was only wearing socks he merely threw it towards the bin from the back door. It missed, hit the fence between his house and his neighbour's, and burst open, spilling its contents onto next door's yard.

The woman who lived there came out and started berating my client, who told her to fuck off (he was himself not as pure as the driven snow). The woman reported the incident to her son, who knocked on my client's door and smashed him across the face with a baseball bat, breaking his nose.

When my client returned from hospital that night, he in turn knocked on the neighbour's door. The son opened the door, and my client shot him in the face. Luckily, the son didn't die – the bullet missed his brain which, given the size of the organ involved, was perhaps not surprising. But when the police arrived my client was still there, and still holding the gun, and he had no choice but to plead guilty to grievous bodily harm, offered by me to the prosecution as an alternative to attempted murder.

He received a sentence of ten years, which I thought a rather good outcome, all things considered, but this was a view with which the criminal fraternity of Sheffield and its environs disagreed. As a consequence, they began to look elsewhere for their advocacy needs for a while.

Actually, this was a relief, as the travel was killing me. On my first visit to Sheffield I had booked into the Holiday Inn. After court, a group of itinerant barristers had gathered together in the bar. We all got ourselves a pint and sat down. Half an hour later, after thirty minutes of everyone talking absolute shit, I declined a second drink, checked out, and drove home. By 6.30pm I was playing football in my back garden with Harry and Toby. I have rarely stayed in a hotel for work since.

* * *

THE HARDWORKING CROOKS of Birmingham soon stepped into the breach. My next case concerned a BMW with a dodgy gearbox which had been purchased by a man of Pakistani origin from a local garage which was run and staffed by men also of Pakistani origin. As he drove it home, it became apparent to the buyer that the gearbox was on its last legs. He took it back and demanded a refund.

'Buyer beware,' said the vendor, loftily. As the disgruntled customer moved menacingly towards him, two garage staff brandished wrenches. The purchaser retreated and drove home to round up reinforcements, to return and plead his case more effectively. He had married an Irish girl whose brother lived locally, so he decided to request his assistance.

'I've been sold a duff car and I'm getting a posse together to go round and get my money back,' he told the Irishman. 'Are you in?'

'To be sure,' the brother-in-law replied.

'It might get a bit tasty, though,' said the Pakistani chap, 'so come tooled-up.'

Half-an-hour later they were back at the garage. The purchaser repeated his demand for a refund, this time with seven friends standing behind him. The two garage hands picked up their monkey wrenches, and, by way of an answer, the customer and his pals produced their own array of weaponry, which ranged from cricket bats to hockey sticks.

At least, that's what seven of them did.

According to the prosecution case, the eighth, the Irish brother-in-law, whipped out a gun, stepped forwards, and knee-capped the garage hands.

Everyone was a little startled at this turn of events, considering it to be something of an over-reaction to a relatively trifling matter of consumer satisfaction, and the posse fled.

But the Irishman was soon picked up, and I represented him at trial. I was assisted by the fact that neither of the garage staff had got much of a look at him, their attention having perhaps been distracted somewhat by the pistol in his hand. They described a bearded man of Pakistani origin, whereas my client was a very pale, clean-shaven, ginger-haired Irishman covered in freckles. The result was inevitable. My client was found not guilty, while everyone else was convicted and sentenced to ten years.

Most of my cases now involved allegations of murder, and most of my clients were acquitted. One bizarre exception involved a man who came home to find his girlfriend in bed with his best friend. He grabbed a knife from the kitchen drawer and stabbed his friend in the leg.

But he was immediately overcome by remorse and dialled 999 to summon an ambulance, and the police. He was driven off to the police station to be interviewed about an offence of GBH, while his friend was taken to Mid-Staffordshire Hospital. It would have taken a doctor about five minutes to treat his wound and send him on his way, but, in a rare instance of Mid-Staffs NHS incompetence, no doctor was called and he was left on a stretcher in a corridor all night.

As a consequence of that, he slowly bled to death.

Unfortunately for my client, the law of murder requires death to have been caused by the perpetrator, and in this case it certainly was. The cause of death was loss of blood – but due to a stab wound, not NHS incompetence. That didn't help my client one jot, and he was duly convicted of murder. Legally, the conviction couldn't be criticised; morally, one might argue differently.

After that, I got back on track in a particularly difficult case. Two market traders who specialised in selling counterfeit clothing were at a house complaining that a new stall had been set up on the market stealing their business. According to the prosecution, they resolved to go to the new trader's house that night, and to kill him.

Also present at the house was a registered police informant, and he later told the police about the conversation.

That night, the market trader's house was indeed broken into and he was clubbed to death with a baseball bat, rolled up in one of his own carpets, and taken to a nearby lake where his naked body was dumped.

The wheels almost came off what had seemed to be a perfectly planned murder when, five minutes after setting out on their journey, a police car put on its blue light and pulled them over.

Two policemen got out of the car and made a beeline for the carpet sticking out of the boot in which the murder victim's body was rolled up.

'You should tie a coloured rag to that carpet,' said one of the officers. 'So that other drivers see it.'

'Thank you,' stammered my client. 'I will.'

At which, the policemen got back into their car and drove away.

Once they realised their error, the police searched my client's house, where they found partially-burned fibres from the carpet in his fireplace. The victim's clothes were then discovered buried in my client's back garden, and my client was captured on CCTV selling the victim's jewellery at a pawnbroker's the morning after the murder.

I was asked to submit in the magistrates' court that there was insufficient evidence to commit the matter for trial to the crown court. With little hope of success, I did as I was asked – barristers must follow their clients' wishes, we can only advise. My only hope lay in the fact that, at that time, the body had not been recovered.

The magistrates came back after deliberating for an hour or so. 'We find no case against your client for murder,' said the chairman of the bench. 'He's free to go.'

It was something of a surprise, even for me. (When the body eventually turned up, my client was committed for trial; I represented him and the prosecution dropped the case after some shenanigans involving the police informant came to light.)

Sophie and I had settled well in Northamptonshire, with two wonderful sons, and both our jobs going well. Only one thing was missing: Sophie was desperate for a little girl. Putting that matter right was not a task to which I was averse and, in 1999, my daughter Emily was born. My family was complete.

I often felt guilty at my good fortune, as I still do – especially when I compare myself to my brother, Kevin. I've already mentioned his struggle with his height, and the death of his first child, Rebecca, in infancy. He and his wife had gone on to have a second daughter, Emma, and their son, Richard, had become Kevin's pride and joy.

Richard grew to be a fit six-footer, and followed his father into the Army. He was due to be posted overseas, and the night before his departure he went to the pub for a drink with some other soldiers. Before taking a sip of his pint, he dropped down dead. The post mortem revealed no cause – it was down to sudden adult death syndrome.

A terrible, unfair tragedy. Why is it that so many bad things happen to some people, while others live gilded lives? I'm not sure I know the answer. But when I think about the life I've led to date, I feel bemused and blessed in equal measure.

Incidentally, Kevin – who was brighter than me and, not having to contend with Jack Fairlie, always came top in his yearly school exams – careered off the rails a bit in the mid-seventies. It happened after he went on a sponsored walk with Jimmy Savile as part of his Duke of Edinburgh Award, though I'm not sure the two matters were related. On his return he announced emphatically that Savile was a paedophile. He'd arrived at this conclusion after observing the TV presenter's conduct with young girls for an afternoon.

How sad and extraordinary that it took another thirty-six years for everyone else to realise it!

CHAPTER EIGHTEEN: FRAUD

Thirteen years to silk

A DECADE OR SO into my career, my practice included every type of serious crime imaginable, except for the most complex (and lucrative) – fraud.

Large fraud cases tend to be dealt with by boutique firms of specialist solicitors, one of the biggest and most respected of which, Nelsons, was based in Nottingham. It had been set up by Richard Nelson, and I had been desperate to work with him during my miserable sojourn in chambers in the city. But I never even got to meet him.

Sophie and I had taken to spending our family summer holidays on the Flete Estate, a beautiful sprawl of pretty cottages with a private beach, set in the South Hams below Dartmoor. We usually rented a small cottage in a row of three. They tended to be booked up by the same people, summer after summer, but one year we found we had new neighbours – a family of four. I bumped into the father one evening as he was coming back from fishing in the estuary.

It soon became clear that I had wandered into another of my life's fortuitous and preposterous coincidences: he was, of course, Richard Nelson.

We chatted for a while, and I discovered that he lived in Wollaton, a posh part of Nottingham five minutes from where I had been born. He'd started his professional career as a general criminal solicitor at Freeth, Cartwright & Sketchley in Nottingham, and in his early days had represented a lot of football hooligans – most of whom, it transpired, I knew.

'I was charged with football hooliganism in 1978,' I said. 'Chesterfield Magistrates. My solicitor was from Freeth Cartwrights, as it happens.'

Unless I'm amusing myself by pretending to be an Old Etonian, I'm always frank about my past.

'Was that the riot in The Painted Wagon?' he said.

'How did you know that?' I said, puzzled.

'Because it was me who represented you.'

From his extensive experience as a criminal solicitor, he knew the culture of Cotgrave intimately; not only did he know that I came from the wrong side of the tracks, he actually knew the precise tracks involved.

You might think a ferociously successful man like Richard would be a serious-minded type, but not a bit of it. His great loves in life are red wine, rugby and fishing, and he was excellent company. We got on extremely well, and bonded further through working late into the night (we really do take our work on holiday), and then having a glass of red and a chat in the small hours of the morning. Nothing came of it professionally – I was happy enough to have made a new friend – but the following year we found ourselves in Devon again, and Richard came around as soon as we arrived.

'I've just picked up a big case in Bristol, Gary,' he said. 'I wonder if you might be interested?'

'I'm sure I would be,' I said.

'It's a fraud,' he said. 'There are so many papers that the prosecution can't count them, but they've been weighed and they amount to seventeen tonnes.'

This paperwork had all been seized from the defendants. It was vetted initially by independent counsel in order that confidential material unrelated to the case could be weeded out. But the rest – thousands upon thousands of letters, bills and bank statements – still had to be read through carefully and understood, which perhaps indicates why this strand of the criminal law is so specialist and, relatively-speaking, well-rewarded.

It was a dream introduction to the area of work I'd craved: a systematic fraud, on a gargantuan scale, featuring some twenty-eight solicitors who had supposedly been ripping off the legal aid fund for countless millions of pounds over decades, by billing for giving advice to clients to whom they hadn't given advice. I was acting for the first defendant, the owner of the business, and was led by David Etherington, a QC from London, one of the wittiest and most wonderful men I've ever met, and an utterly brilliant advocate.

That trial lasted for over a year. As a barrister, you get used to ridiculous defences. If your client's instructions are mad, you should advise him of the consequences but ultimately you must run them. One of the defendants in this case took the absolute biscuit. The prosecution had analysed his billing records and had noticed that he had claimed on one day to have been working for thirty hours. This seemed *prima facie* unlikely, but he produced a home-made cardboard mask contraption, which he attached to his face by means of an elastic band. The front of the mask featured an extended piece of card which separated his eyes. He claimed to have the ability, when wearing the mask, to read two sets of papers simultaneously, one with each eye.

My man was found guilty, and got six years.

From then on, most of my work has been fraud – though not all.

Big, multi-handed cases require exhaustive preparation, can take two years to come to trial, and the trials themselves often last for several months. In court there are often long periods, sometimes weeks on end, when the evidence has no relevance to your client, and it can be a little like being the cymbal player in Tchaikovsky's *1812 Overture*: you wait and wait, and suddenly it's your turn. I remember one particular case, which was actually a rare exception to my growing fraud practice. My client was alleged to have been involved in a conspiracy to supply thirty million pounds-worth of heroin. Originally one conspiracy, it had been divided at a late stage into two separate conspiracies which were to be tried, one after the other. One defendant was involved in both of them, as a kind of link man, but my client had no involvement whatsoever in the first one.

Despite this, I had been engaged to be in court, and so in court I would be.

It is practically impossible for any human being to remain laser-focused, week after week, on a case which is unfolding with incredible tediousness in ways which have nothing whatsoever to do with their client. Still, it happens – more often than one might wish – and, barristers being creative people, they will often look to use such time in counsel's row productively. The more conscientious members of the profession might seize the opportunity to address the paperwork for another forthcoming trial, or to polish up a written advice; others might doze off, or do the crossword, or perhaps write a book.

Anyway, I confess that my focus had waned in one way or another when… disaster!

'Mr Bell?'

Somewhere, subconsciously, I heard my name being called.

'Mr *Bell!*'

I looked up in panic. The judge was addressing me.

'Are you prepared to make the admissions that the prosecuting barrister has invited everybody to make?' he said.

What was I going to do? I had no idea what admissions he was talking about. I knew they must be irrelevant to my client – his case hadn't even begun – but that wasn't really the point.

I swallowed hard and looked imploringly for help at a barrister to my right, Courtenay Griffiths QC. He gave me an imperceptible but re-assuring nod.

'Yes,' I said, with great relief.

'And are you prepared to make those admissions in a *limited* sense,' the judge continued, to my great dismay, 'or in the *wider* sense invited by the prosecution?'

'I think I've taken the fine old barristerial art of bluff as far as I can,' I said, 'and at this stage I'm going to have to ask, what admissions is Your Honour talking about?'

Everyone laughed, assuming I was joking, but Courtenay passed me a note, reading, 'Admissions fine in extended sense.'

I breathed a sigh of relief. 'Of course, I'm prepared to make them in the extended sense, Your Honour,' I said.

As I sat down, Courtenay passed me another note: 'Tricked you!'

I never did find out what the admissions were, extended or otherwise, but perhaps Courtenay should not have made them. His client got twenty years – a rare defeat for the great man – and mine was found not guilty.

After the trial was concluded, and having a gap before the next one began, I decided to finish off a book I'd been writing. Undeterred by the failure of my LA crime thriller, I had begun work on a comedy romance, which was loosely based on a fat barrister of my close acquaintance and was imaginatively entitled *Fat Barrister*. My brother-in-law, Andrew/Wilf, kindly showed the manuscript to an agent friend of his who *begged* me to allow her to represent me and *Fat Barrister*. I met her for lunch and was delighted to find that not only was she a beautiful blonde, but that her last effort had won the Booker Prize. I played hard to get, for about five seconds, and then agreed to let her be my agent.

A few weeks later, she called with the news that a publisher had agreed to take it on. Excited doesn't cover it – I even renewed my subscription to *Country Life*.

But just as she was negotiating my advance, there came a rare setback in the life of G. Bell… the publisher was taken over by an American company, and they withdrew from the fiction market.

My dreams of being a successful writer were dashed again, and it was back to the day job.

* * *

IF THERE IS a problem with fraud cases it's that they can be excruciatingly boring, especially for the jury. As often as possible, I introduce humour into the proceedings and it has proved a very successful tactic.

It all came to a head in Ipswich, when I was involved in an extraordinarily dull trial which was dragging on for several months. The case involved my client allegedly running a 'boiler room' – selling worthless shares in fanciful companies to hapless investors. They bought millions of pounds worth of shares in companies who would auction sporting memorabilia online or a mining plant which claimed it could turn rock into gold. In my speech, I suggested that, if the investors who had bought shares in these ludicrous companies were so careless with their money, they only had themselves to blame.

'Perhaps you might like to invest in myself and Mr Lobbenberg,' I said, 'because we're launching ourselves as a pair of exotic dancers to rival the Chippendales, and we need funding for a couple of diamond-studded thongs.'

Nick Lobbenberg QC, the prosecution silk, was, if anything, fatter than me. It got the jury laughing. And they carried on laughing, as did the judge, all the way through my speech. They were still laughing when they found my client not guilty, but then put on more serious faces as they convicted everyone else.

'That's quite a gift, Gary,' Nick said to me in the robing room. 'You literally had the case against you laughed out of court.'

His words came back to me a few weeks later whilst I was out with friends watching a comedy show at Jongleurs. Harry Hill was headlining, and he was brilliant, but some of the other acts were distinctly average. We were discussing one of them in a pub after the show when one of my friends turned to me. 'You could do better yourself, Gary,' he said.

I demurred, but the more I thought about it, the more I thought, *Why not? If that bloke can do it, why can't I?*

Of course, it's not quite as simple as that. I'd always been regarded as mildly amusing, if I say so myself, but making people laugh around the dinner table, or in court, is very different from doing so on stage in front of a hostile audience. I found the very idea terrifying. But I believe that a man's reach should always exceed his grasp, so I entered a national comedy competition and set to writing an act.

Hundreds of jobbing comedians entered, and heats were held all over the country. Mine was in Leicester, where I was one of forty acts. I turned up on my own, and parked outside the venue, where I sat, hyperventilating, for the next ten minutes. What had I *done*? But eventually, screwing up my courage, I skulked inside. It was already well underway, so I bought myself a soft drink and stood at the bar, watching people go through their three minutes of material. To my relief, while some of the other comics were very good, some were merely okay and most were awful. My confidence grew a little. Other competitors milled around, chatting: they all clearly knew each other from the circuit, and it amused me to watch them pretending to chat amiably, while obviously sizing each other up. I was much older than most of them, and they ignored me, which suited me fine.

I was the last act on, and eventually it was time. I stood nervously on the bare stage for several seconds: I was armed only with a half-remembered act and my wits, and was facing a by-now drunk and bolshy crowd. I wasn't sure whether to begin or dive for the exit.

'I've got a confession to make,' I said, finally. 'I'm not really a stand-up comedian – I'm just a fat barrister going through a mid-life crisis.'

It raised a laugh, which relaxed me totally and I had them whooping by the end. I was sure I'd won – a feeling confirmed by the sullen looks I drew from the other competitors as the judges retired. They were all experienced comics, and I was a total civilian; it was as though I'd picked their pockets, which, in a manner of speaking, I had. I was duly named the winner.

The compère, a chap called 'Spiky Mike', ran his own clubs in the East Midlands, and offered me a few gigs. That was fortunate; it enabled me to hone my limited skills before my semi-final, the first of six, at a venue in Wimbledon. I put the word out to my friends, and more than eighty people turned up to support me. Buoyed on, I stormed into the finals – and immediately realised that I had a significant advantage over any other winning semi-finalists. The tickets for the final were on sale, but I was the only act thus far who had definitely made it through. Within days, friends from all over the country were booking seats.

In between the semi-final and the final, I attended Susanna Gross's wedding and she introduced me to two other male guests with the words, 'This is Gary, he's a stand-up comedian.'

'Do you enjoy it?' one of the men asked.

'It's very exhilarating,' I replied, 'but it's also terrifying. It's just you standing on a bare stage, facing a hostile crowd, armed only with your wits. It's hard to convey what it's like.'

'Oh, I think I can imagine,' said both men, in unison.

It was at that point that we all had moments of realisation. I realised that the two men were Harry Enfield and Griff Rhys-Jones, while they realised that I was an idiot.

The final of the competition was a bit like a private party, and I was a little embarrassed; 135 out of a crowd of 150 were friends of mine, and the only others were reserved by the tournament organisers for their guests. But long before I started my act, I realised that I was never going to win.

The organisers of the contest worked closely with one of the judges in offering expensive comedy courses, and three of the finalists were named on their website as examples of what these courses could do for you. To make matters worse, the main judge was a not-very funny comedian whom I'd beaten in another one-night competition in London, and he didn't much care for me.

I was drawn last. The compère switched off the microphone as he handed it over, and it took me a minute or so to get going. With the crowd well on my side I still gave a good account of myself, but it was never going to be enough. The announcement that I hadn't won caused a near riot, led by James Barnes' father, David, but I consoled myself in the knowledge that Bill Hicks himself could have come back from the dead and it wouldn't have made much difference that night.

After a brief appearance at the Edinburgh Fringe Festival, courtesy of another Spiky Mike competition, where I was deservedly trounced in the semi-final, I put myself in for 'Midlands Comedian of the Year 2006.'

I progressed to the semi-final, held at Coventry. I was up against Henning Vehn, an excellent German comedian whom I highly recommend. He started well. 'This is the first time I've been to Coventry and I have to say it is a very ugly city,' he said. 'It looks like a bomb has hit it!'

When my turn came, I pointed out that Coventry was, in fact, an historic Roman City.

'Who were the Romans?' he heckled me. 'I've never heard of them.'

'They built an empire,' I said, 'which lasted a bit longer than yours.'

I won again and went into the final in Derby. I drove up on my own, knowing not a soul in the audience apart from a Scotsman whom I'd defeated at Leicester. He was with his wife, a very pretty Dutch girl, and he was drunk as usual. As soon as I took to the stage, he yelled out, 'Get off the stage, you fat bastard!'

'What are you doing here?' I said. 'I thought we'd chased you out of Derby with Bonny Prince Charlie.'

'I'll tell you what I'm doing here,' he slurred. 'I'm shagging your women!'

The audience laughed, and I waited for it to subside before responding. 'So where is the woman in question?' I said.

'She's here,' he said.

'And where are you from, madam?' I said.

'Amsterdam,' she said.

'I thought you were shagging *our* women,' I said, 'not Dutch ones. And here's a word of advice... you're supposed to rent them out for the hour, not bring them home.'

It was not particularly gallant of me, but it silenced him, and I carried on my way.

The winner was decided, democratically, by audience cheers at the end of the evening; my failure to pack the audience with ringers concerned me, but I need not have worried. I got by far the loudest cheer and was duly crowned Midlands Comedian of the Year 2006.

There was a first prize of £100. A hundred quid isn't a lot, but there were times when I hadn't seen that much cash in a month or more. I handed it back to Spiky Mike to dish out to someone who needed it more than I did, had a drink, and drove home with my trophy on the passenger seat. That was the end of my career in comedy.

* * *

ENJOYABLE AS IT WAS, it had not cured my mid-life crisis. I needed a new distraction and one arrived courtesy of my brother-in-law, Andrew. Married to my sister Samantha, Andrew runs his own business, something to do with computers, and is an excellent husband and father to their four children. But he has two weaknesses. He's a world champion procrastinator – except for when he's *not* procrastinating, when he is driven entirely by the impulse of the moment. For instance, I visited Samantha's house for Sunday lunch a couple of years ago.

'Andrew's just popped out,' she said. 'He's gone to pick up a surprise he's bought off eBay for my birthday.'

He turned up half-an-hour later, driving a fire engine. My sister has now banned him from eBay.

It was better than the Christmas gift she had received that year. He'd left it late, as is his wont, and had dashed into Asda just before closing time on Christmas Eve. Like myself, my sister is on the large side, but, even so, she was less than happy with the size 24 nightdress Andrew had purchased. To make matters worse, he'd left in the price tag: reduced from fifteen pounds to a fiver.

He was determined to push the boat out the following year. 'I'm learning to fly,' he confided one day, over a pint. 'I'm going to surprise Sam on her birthday by flying her to Le Touquet.'

He enthused about his secret flying lessons, and I had to admit that it sounded fun. The following weekend, I took myself off to Wellesbourne Airfield near Stratford-upon-Avon and met my flying instructor, the indomitable Ken Masters. After one test flight in his single-engine Piper Cherokee, I was hooked. Like Andrew, I kept my lessons a secret while planning a surprise birthday flight for Sophie, but unlike Andrew I actually stuck at it and, after a few lessons, Ken said I was ready to fly solo.

Bubbling with excitement, I did all the static pre-flight checks on the Cherokee, and then taxied over to refuel it. Light aircraft tend to have a fuel tank in each wing, for the purposes of 'trim' (balance), so I carefully filled them both and then taxied over towards the runway, doing the rest of my pre-flight checks on the way. As I arrived at the runway, I radioed the air traffic controller.

'Golf Papa India, ready for take-off.'

'Roger, Golf Papa India,' he replied. 'Runway clear for take-off.'

I was about to pull back on the throttle when I glanced down at my port wing. It was lucky I did. My fuel cap lay loose on the leading edge. Organisation has never been my strong point.

'Er… Golf Papa India not *quite* ready for take-off,' I radioed, before jumping out of the cockpit and hastily screwing the cap into place.

Two minutes later, I received clearance again, released the brakes, put on the power, and raced down the runway. At sixty-five knots, I pulled back on the yoke and rose gracefully into the air. I maintained the angle of take-off, so as to avoid stalling, until, at 1,000ft, I straightened up and turned out of the circuit.

I have always been astonished that a heavy, misshapen lump of metal can fly, and that astonishment was magnified a hundredfold now that I was the one flying it. I headed out over rural Warwickshire, climbed to 4,000ft, and pottered around for a glorious half hour. I flew over my own house before heading back to the airfield for the most terrifying experience of my life – landing.

I joined the circuit at 2,000ft and descended slowly, nervously approaching the runway on my base leg at 1,000ft. I reduced power to slow to a landing speed of sixty-five knots, and progressively put in three stages of flap to lose more height. The runway loomed ahead, I glided gracefully onward, and, at about fifty feet, the asphalt appeared underneath me; I killed the power and drifted down, keeping the nose up – but not too much, we don't want her to balloon. I hit the runway with a thud, applied the brakes and taxied into my parking bay.

Amazing!

I continued my lessons with the excellent Ken, learning emergency landings, 360-degree turns, getting out of a free-fall spin and other terrifying aerobatic manoeuvres. I also passed all of the various exams, did my solo qualifying cross-country flight via Cambridge and Leicester, and gained my pilot's licence.

I never did take Sophie on that birthday flight, though. When she found out about my secret lessons she was furious, and refused ever to set foot in an aircraft of which I had control. I've never flown since, but I remain ridiculously proud of my now-expired licence.

* * *

MEANWHILE, BACK AT the Bar, I found myself involved in another massive fraud at Southwark Crown Court.

My client was a director of a private mailing company, set up after the end of Royal Mail's monopoly on delivering the post. The business was remarkably successful, mainly because it was able substantially to undercut the Royal Mail's prices. One reason they might have been able to offer such low prices was hinted at in the prosecution papers.

As soon as the various letters, parcels and packets were delivered to my client's business premises – it was alleged – they were promptly thrown into skips and then taken to a landfill site in Essex and dumped, in their millions. My client was on trial with her co-director and eight members of staff for conspiring to defraud those who had paid to have their mail delivered.

There was a further allegation against her and her co-director – that *before* they started dumping mail they had been fraudulently under-declaring the weight and class of the post which the Royal Mail had sub-contracted to deliver for them, thus costing the Royal Mail hundreds of thousands of pounds.

I immediately had the case set down for dismissal proceedings, on the basis that there was no evidence to support the prosecution's contentions. That is, there *was* evidence – on the face of it, a *lot* of evidence – but, at the time the defendants had been charged and committed to the crown court from the magistrates' court for trial, the prosecution didn't have all of their evidence in place. I argued that the dismissal application should be based on the state of the evidence at the time of the defendants' committal, and not on the state of the evidence at the time of my application. It sounds a legal technicality, but it's important that a defendant has certainty at all points in any proceedings; he or she cannot mount a defence if only half of the prosecution story is told.

The judge, much to everybody's surprise, found my arguments persuasive and dismissed the charge against my client.

'Right,' he said. 'What's next?'

'Next?' said the ashen-faced prosecutor. 'There is no "next". It applies to *all* of the defendants. You've just dismissed the case against everyone.'

The judge, realising the enormity of his judgment, looked visibly stunned, as did all the defence barristers present. Silence reigned in the court for what seemed like an age, before I got to my feet.

'Not quite *every* defendant,' I said. 'There are still money-laundering counts faced by the company accountant.'

The company accountant was represented by a barrister whom I will call Pillsbury who was shell-shocked at finding that his client was the only defendant left, and was waiting to make his own application to have those charges dismissed too.

'Mr Pillsbury's application has no relevance to anybody else,' I continued, 'so might all of the other defendants and their barristers be allowed to leave?'

'Of course, everyone can go if they wish,' said the still-stunned judge. 'Unless anybody wants to stay and listen to Mr Pillsbury's submissions?'

'Well, I've heard him before,' I replied, 'so I, for one, shall be leaving.'

For some reason it broke the ice, and everyone – apart from Pillsbury – started laughing uproariously, including the judge and the prosecution barrister. After quite some time, everyone calmed down and Mr Pillsbury stood up to address the judge. No sooner had he started to speak than the judge started giggling again, quickly followed by everyone else in court. After a herculean effort, the judge managed to get himself under control and turned, grim-faced to Mr Pillsbury.

'I'm sorry, Mr Pillsbury,' he said. 'What were you going to say?'

'Your Honour,' Pillsbury began, but the judge immediately dissolved into laughter again, as did everyone else.

And this time there was no stopping him. Eventually he announced, through tears of mirth – if you've heard the Brian Johnson/Jonathan Agnew Test Match Special 'legover' recording you'll get the idea – that he was going to have to adjourn, and stomped off out of court. The rest of us left, leaving a sad and sombre Pillsbury to make his application in peace.

I heard the next day that Mr Pillsbury had been sacked by his client; I couldn't help feeling partly responsible.

The case was eventually resurrected by the prosecution, who had to go to a High Court judge to get what is called a voluntary bill of indictment, but it was doomed. Eventually, I offered a plea on my client's behalf to under-declaring the weight of postage to the Royal Mail, as long as the prosecution dropped the allegation that any of the defendants had been guilty of dumping even a single letter, parcel or small packet. A battered and bruised prosecution barrister almost snatched my hand off. The case was dropped against all other defendants except the co-director, and he and my client received short prison sentences.

The police were furious – naturally enough, they don't like seeing people they perceive as being guilty of crimes walk free. In my view, they should chalk these things up to experience and learn from their mistakes, and many do. But others, in their determination to secure a conviction, will occasionally tiptoe over the line into illegality themselves. Although it's rare to encounter a 'bent copper', it's not unheard of, and during that period of my career I was involved in four big cases where I caught police officers lying in court.

In one, a policeman had alleged that my client had tried to kill him with two ninja swords whilst he was arresting another man; unfortunately for and unbeknown to the policeman, a newspaper photographer had captured the whole incident. Much of the officer's evidence – which, had it been believed, would have resulted in my client going to prison for a very long time – was completely untrue. He said my client had been wearing traditional Indian dress, a flowing white robe, an orange turban, and had a long, bushy, grey beard and was carrying two swords.

The photographs, of which there many, showed him to be clean-shaven, wearing jeans and a sweatshirt, and slightly balding. There was not a trace of a single sword, let alone two.

I first asked the officer to repeat his evidence and confirm that he had only attempted to arrest one man on the day in question. I then showed him the photographs.

'Can you point out the flowing white robes?' I said.

The police officer looked at the photographs for an age, before replying, 'I can see what you're saying.'

'Can you point out the orange turban?'

'I can see what you're saying.'

'Can you point out the long, bushy, grey beard?'

'I can see what you're saying.'

'Can you point out the two ninja swords?'

'I can see what you're saying.'

At this point the judge could take no more. 'We can all see what Mr Bell is saying,' he interrupted, 'but what we can't see are the swords!'

'Well, well...' stammered the officer, and his eyes rolled up into his head and he collapsed in the witness box. He had to be taken to hospital, and was admitted from there to a psychiatric unit.

In another case, the police were surveilling a social club car park, having intelligence that a major drug deal was due to take place. My client turned up on a bicycle, carrying a large haversack. There were two vans in the car park, and he got into the back of one with the bag, before getting out empty-handed and cycling away. A minute later, another man exited the back of the van, carrying the bag, and climbed into the second van. The police then pounced and arrested everyone. The bag contained a substantial quantity of cannabis.

Rather astonishingly, the police made no attempt to stop the first van, into which my client had originally taken the bag, and it was allowed to drive away unhindered.

I took the view that it was a crucial weakness that the police had failed to stop the first van so, before the trial-proper, I had the case listed to argue that the failure to make any enquiries about the van amounted to an abuse of the court's process.

The police officer in charge of the investigation gave evidence at that hearing.

'Why didn't you stop the van driving away?' I asked him.

'It was not the focus of our investigation,' he said.

'Have you made any enquiries at all in relation to the van?'

'None whatsoever.'

In the event, the judge ruled that not stopping, and failing to make any enquiries about, the missing van was not an abuse of process but a jury point, and the case was set down for trial.

During the trial the police officer in charge of the investigation was called to give evidence again.

'Why didn't you stop the van driving away?' I asked him.

'We tried,' he said, 'but in the confusion it managed to get away.'

'Have you made any enquiries at all in relation to the van?'

'I put out an all-cars alert to try and stop it, but it was never seen again,' he told the jury. 'I made enquiries with the DVLA to find out the registered address and attended the address, but the householder said he had never heard of the van. I then sat outside the address all night keeping watch, but there was no sign of it.'

I then took him through the evidence he had given at the earlier hearing, highlighting the differences from what he was now saying. When I had finished, the judge said she had a matter she wished to raise in the absence of the jury.

'Mr Bell,' she said after they had left court, 'you intimated that the officer was lying but you didn't put it in clear terms – you appreciate there are implications for calling a policeman a liar?'

I did appreciate it. If you call a policeman a liar – or any witness, for that matter – you put your client's own character in issue. That allows his previous convictions, if any, to be put before the jury.

'I thought I'd made it perfectly clear, Your Honour,' I said.

'I wasn't sure if you were saying he was lying,' said the judge, 'or that he was simply mistaken.'

'Let's get the officer back, then,' I said, 'and we can clear matters up.'

Five minutes later the officer was back in front of the jury.

'There is some confusion,' I said, 'about whether I was suggesting that you were merely mistaken in your evidence earlier, or that you were lying.'

'I see,' he replied.

'So let me make it clear in front of the jury. I am accusing you of being an absolute and total liar. I am alleging that you are so crooked that you can't lie straight in bed, and that you are such a liar-liar that your pants are on fire. Does that make things any clearer, Your Honour?'

Her angry stare told me that it did; she was clearly annoyed that I had the temerity to accuse a police officer of lying, which I found rather astonishing as he had clearly done so.

So, it appeared, did the jury. They found all of the defendants not guilty.

A similar thing happened in a case involving a group of travellers who had set up camp on a children's playing field in a rough part of Birmingham. They had driven around the area clearing rubbish from gardens and houses for a small fee; then, having collected truckloads of junk, they had unceremoniously dumped it next to their campsite.

My client – I'll call him Smith, which is not his real name – was one of a group of locals who went to confront them, and the police were called. According to the evidence of two officers, when they arrived my client was running amok with a hammer and, as soon as they got out of their car, he attacked them, causing them to flee for their lives.

Mr Smith was later arrested and charged with violent disorder, a serious public order offence. He was in trouble. It was his word that nothing untoward had happened against statements made by two honest and courageous police officers.

Fortunately, however, an amateur ornithologist – wholly unconnected with either side – was in the area hoping to film some rare bird which had apparently been spotted nearby. The bird was nowhere to seen, but he had filmed the confrontation on the field instead and the video found its way into the hands of my instructing solicitor.

I took the view that, given its contents, I would play it to the prosecution barrister and the Crown Prosecution Service lawyer before the trial, instead of surprising the officers with it in court.

I did, and they gasped: it showed Mr Smith – calm, collected, and entirely hammerless – talking jovially to the police officers who alleged that he had attacked them.

The prosecution immediately dropped the case. My client sued the police for malicious prosecution and they agreed to pay him twenty thousand pounds in damages.

The last trial I'll deal with in this section was particularly bizarre. It involved a client – this time I'll call him Bloggs – whom the police were so desperate to 'get' that they placed two undercover officers onto his estate, living as man and wife.

At the end of a six-month investigation, they arrested and charged thirty people, mostly with drugs offences. They all either pleaded guilty, or were found guilty – apart, that is, from my client, on whom the jury couldn't agree a verdict.

The prosecution decided to re-try him on the same charges, which they can and usually do in the case of a hung jury. The second trial was a hard-fought affair, in front of an extremely hostile judge. In fact, hostility was that particular judge's default mode, and, as the case progressed, he became more and more obdurate. To be honest, it was partly my fault for winding him up. At one point, an undercover police officer was giving evidence about trying to obtain heroin from a man who, the prosecution alleged, was himself supplied by my client.

'He told me that he couldn't get any heroin because his supplier was on holiday,' the policeman told the jury, 'and we did checks and found that Mr Bloggs was on holiday at the time.'

'Oh, really,' said the judge. 'Where did he go?'

'I think it was the Bahamas,' I told the judge, trying to assist him – or so he thought.

'The Bahamas?' The judge looked over at the jury and raised his eyebrows in mock surprise. 'It's alright for some, isn't it?'

'No, it was actually Butlin's in Skegness,' said the police officer.

The jury started to laugh, and the judge fixed me with a withering glare. The gloves were off.

The turning point came during the defence case, when I tried to call an important witness to give evidence that my client's frequent trips to Nottingham were to buy clothes, and not drugs. The witness had not turned up to court, and I applied to the judge for a witness summons. This was duly granted and served. But he still didn't turn up, and I applied to the increasingly irritable judge for an arrest warrant.

'Mr Bell,' he said, frowning. 'My job is not to tell you how to do yours, but in all my thirty-five years as a barrister, and then a judge, I have never heard of an application by a defence barrister to have one of his own witnesses brought to court in handcuffs. I advise you to re-consider your application.'

'Thank you for your advice,' I said. 'Now, can I have my arrest warrant?'

He had no choice but to comply. The following morning, my star witness was brought to court in handcuffs. He duly gave evidence exactly in accordance with his statement, which enormously assisted my client's defence.

'I have a few questions for you myself,' announced the judge, addressing the man when I had finished. 'You knew that you were supposed to be at this court on Monday morning, didn't you?'

'Yes,' said the witness.

'Yet you refused to come, even when a witness summons was served upon you, isn't that right?'

'Yes.'

'In fact, you had to be arrested and brought to court this morning in handcuffs, didn't you?'

'Yes.'

'So can you explain to the jury why, if you were simply coming to court to tell the truth, you were so reluctant to do so?'

'Because the police came to see me last Friday to ask me to be a prosecution witness,' said the man. 'But I told them I was already a defence witness. They said that if I knew what was good for me I wouldn't come to court.'

CHAPTER EIGHTEEN: FRAUD

The judge looked stunned. The police had acted entirely improperly, failing even to inform me that they had seen the witness.

I rose to my feet. 'I'm sorry,' I said. 'I wasn't listening… could you repeat what you just said for my benefit – slowly?'

He repeated his evidence, and I let it sink in for several seconds before continuing. 'I'm going to sit down now,' I said. 'If prosecuting counsel thinks that you are lying, he will have to get to his feet and accuse you of it. If, on the other hand, he accepts that what you said is true, he will remain in his seat.'

I sat down and stared at my opponent. He twitched and half-rose to his feet, before flopping back down with the look of a defeated man. I got back to my feet. 'Thank you for your evidence,' I said. 'You're free to go. That is' – I turned to the judge, trying to keep the smile off my face – 'unless Your Honour has any more helpful questions?'

He didn't, and after speeches and summing up, the jury retired to consider their verdict.

Outside court, one of the investigating officers, a man of senior rank, clearly had something he wished to get off his chest. 'I don't know how you can sleep at night,' he spat at me, 'representing scum like him!'

'I just do my job to the best of my ability,' I replied. 'As long as I've done my best, I don't care whether the defendant is convicted or acquitted. If you took the same approach, you might win a few more cases.'

The jury were back shortly afterwards and the verdict – a foregone conclusion, really – was not guilty.

As I walked out of court, the investigating detective sergeant glared at me. 'Well done,' he snapped. 'I hope you're proud of yourself!'

'I was just doing…' I began.

Before I could finish my sentence, the senior officer lunged towards me.

'If you say you were just doing your fucking job,' he screamed, 'I'll smack you in the mouth!'

The prosecution junior rushed to pull him away, and I made my way to the robing room.

The next day the detective sergeant came to talk to me in my chambers.

'It's about yesterday,' he said. 'The boss was under a lot of pressure to win this case. I'm afraid the pressure got to him and he's been booked into a psychiatric hospital as a result of the acquittal of your client. I was hoping you weren't going to make a complaint.'

I wasn't. I didn't think it would be good for my image to admit I'd been beaten up by a middle-aged policeman.

CHAPTER NINETEEN: ANIMAL, QC

Silk

THE HIGHEST ACCOLADE for any barrister is to be appointed Queen's Counsel. Appointments are made by Her Majesty on the advice of the Lord Chancellor, after a rigorous selection process that involves the applicant producing evidence of his or her having worked on a number of very high level cases, providing suitable references from judges and lawyers, including existing silks, and undergoing a challenging interview.

As a rule of thumb, you need to be at least twenty years' call, and you must also be able to demonstrate excellence in a number of different competencies – oral and written advocacy, legal knowledge, teamwork, case preparation, and ethics and diversity. It's an expensive process to apply, costing several thousands of pounds, and not something to be undertaken lightly.

But it is every barrister's ambition, and ambition is not something I have lacked – at least, not since I decided to go back and do some O levels.

In 2008, as I approached the magical twenty years, I thought I was ready. I obtained a form and filled it in with uncharacteristic fastidiousness.

I was required to list ten substantial and serious cases in which I had been involved during the previous two years. There was no difficulty with that.

I was then required to list six barrister references, not from my chambers, and six instructing solicitors who had been involved in those cases with me. No difficulty with that, either.

Finally, I was required to list a number of judges in front of whom I had appeared. That was slightly more problematic. In most major cases, I had been led by a QC, and only two of the judges had seen me doing anything important. And – call me paranoid – I doubted they would have a particularly favourable opinion of me.

The first judge was in charge of a huge fraud case in which I was involved. One afternoon I raised a technical legal point which – if ruled in my favour – would result in my client being found not guilty. The prosecution were fighting tooth and nail to defeat it, and the judge ordered us to lodge written skeleton arguments the following morning.

A skeleton argument is a document, provided in advance of a hearing, which summarises the issues you will be addressing and the authorities – previous court cases – upon which you will be relying. It gives the judge a heads-up as to your legal argument, and should be brief (though some people can't help themselves: the Court of Appeal has complained recently about skeletons of more than a hundred pages, with dozens and dozens of footnotes).

I duly drafted my argument overnight, and printed out three copies, one each for the judge, the prosecution, and for myself. But as I was driving to court, disaster struck; a nasty road accident blocked my way and caused a major traffic jam. I managed to get off the motorway before I became completely enmeshed, and picked my way across country, but it still took forever. Anxious glances at the dashboard clock told me it was touch-and-go as to whether I'd be late. As I was planning to put this judge forward as a reference for silk, I couldn't afford that.

I was also running low on petrol, and needed a wee, but I hadn't a second to spare so I pushed on – hoping that both my petrol tank and my bladder would hold out.

I roared into the court car park with five minutes to spare, but by now I was in real trouble. I was absolutely *desperate* for a wee.

Panicking, and with nothing else for it, I opened the rear door, unzipped my laptop bag and pretended to be checking through some papers whilst I surreptitiously unbuttoned my fly and peed on the ground. Then I put the bag on the back seat, dashed off to get a ticket, dashed back, and snatched up the bag. But, in my haste, I had forgotten to re-zip it – and now, to my utter horror, my papers tumbled out into the steaming puddle of urine at my feet.

In some dismay, I picked up the sopping wet mass and rushed over to court, where I arrived just as the judge entered.

'I'll see your skeleton arguments now,' he said.

I selected the least-wet copy, and handed it to him. He took it by the corner of the page, using one finger and his thumb, and dropped it, with a disgusted look, into a nearby bin.

Luckily, I still won my legal argument, and my client was acquitted, but I didn't think that particular judge would give me a glowing reference.

The second had presided over a massive international 'long firm' fraud trial. Long firm fraud involves setting up a company and ordering goods which are then sold on to customers, while never actually intending to pay the suppliers for those goods. In this case, my client had ripped off his suppliers to the tune of hundreds of thousands of pounds.

The money he made was all traced or accounted for, with the exception of a £20,000 VAT rebate, which he had withdrawn in cash from the bank under the very nose of the liquidator.

The defendant claimed not to remember what had happened to it, even though I explained to him that, unless he could account for the money, he would be ordered to pay it back or go to prison. I had no choice but to call him to give evidence at his confiscation proceedings, and to tell the judge that he didn't remember what had happened to it.

But when he got into the witness box he suddenly experienced what Arnold Schwarzenegger might call Total Recall.

'Actually,' he said, 'I remember now that I gave it to a nightclub bouncer to settle a debt.'

'And are we going to hear from this nightclub bouncer?' said the judge.

'He's dead,' said the defendant.

'So how is it that you are only telling us about this now?' said the judge. 'Why didn't you mention it in your confiscation statement?'

'Ah,' said the defendant. 'It's like this. My mum was having a séance last night, and the bouncer's ghost turned up and reminded me that I had given the VAT rebate to him.'

The judge was not impressed, either with the defendant's explanation or with his barrister.

I probably didn't help myself when appearing in a different case in front of the same judge. This time it was a big international fraud trial where my client had pleaded guilty, on an extremely limited basis, and had received a very short prison sentence. The prosecution then set about trying desperately to locate the several million pounds which had gone missing, in order that some of it could be sold off to settle outstanding debts. They focused their financial investigation on my client.

But all he had in his name was a rusty Ford Escort. He was asked to provide a value for it and stated that it was worth £100. In fact, it wasn't even worth that, as I pointed out.

'This is a car that is on bricks, with no wheels, in my client's back yard,' I said. 'It has chickens living in it, and has absolutely no value.'

The truth was that the car had not even been driveable in the recent past, which I knew to be the case since the client had turned up to a conference at chambers a few weeks before in a different, perfectly roadworthy vehicle. He'd been on edge and fidgeting throughout, and regularly looking at the clock, and had abruptly ended matters after only an hour or so. When I asked why he had to leave before we'd finished, he said that his neighbour was a taxi driver who worked nights, he'd pinched the car from the man's drive, and he needed to return it before he woke up.

'Well,' said the prosecutor, 'the defendant said the Ford Escort was worth a hundred pounds. If it's worth less than that, it's his own fault.'

'That seems fair enough,' said the judge, to me. 'If I make a confiscation order for a hundred pounds and the car is worth less than that, it will be your client's own fault.'

'Are these proceedings being recorded?' I said.

'Yes,' said the judge. 'Why?'

'Because if you make an order for a confiscation order in the sum of a hundred pounds, let me tell you what will happen,' I said. 'The defendant will try to sell the car which, as a matter of common sense, he will not be able to do, as it is worthless. That will lead to an inadequacy of a hundred pounds, so the defendant will have to apply to the High Court for a Certificate of Inadequacy. As the non-payment of the hundred pounds will activate a prison sentence in default, probably for one day, the defendant will have the right to legal aid for his High Court application. When, at a cost to the taxpayer of several thousand pounds, I stand up in front of a High Court judge to make the frankly irresistible application for a Certificate of Inadequacy, and he asks me who is responsible for the ludicrous waste of court time and public money involved, I simply want to be able to reply that it is not me.'

The judge and the prosecutor backed down, and no order was made.

But when one speaks frankly to judges, one must accept that it is unlikely to persuade them to offer fulsome support to one's application for silk.

I was rejected.

* * *

BUT I WASN'T too dismayed. How could I be? Most applicants for silk are rejected – even those who *do* succeed seldom do so at the first attempt – and I was extremely content as a junior barrister.

In any event, any disappointment had been put firmly in context by the recent and terrible but not wholly-unexpected news of the death of my legendary father-in-law, William FitzHugh. William had never followed the recipe for a long life. He liked a smoke, he liked a drink, and his definition of exercise was a brisk walk to the pub. It had all caught up with him in February 2007, just short of his sixty-fifth birthday, when he had suffered a massive heart attack, and died instantly.

It was a sad time, and it obviously hit Sophie, Gillie and Rafela hard, though I always knew Gillie would find someone else, as William would have wished. It took a few years, but I was right, and when she told me she had a new chap I was very happy for her. I was even happier when I found out he was a Labour MP from Stoke! I'd spent enough time as the token working class member of the FitzHughs – now, at last, I was being reinforced by someone from my own *milieu*, a gritty, northern socialist, who wasn't afraid of getting his hands dirty.

When I met him, Mark Fisher was not what I had expected. William had been very tall, very slim, with a full head of hair. Mark was very short, very fat, and very bald.

'So you're from Stoke?' I said.

'Yes,' he replied – and I couldn't help noticing his accent wasn't the purest Potteries.

'Did you... er... go to school in Stoke?' I said, suspiciously.

'No,' he said. 'Eton.'

(I'm glad to say that he has since stepped down from the House of Commons in order that his seat in Stoke could be taken by a real man of the people – Labour's The Honourable Tristram Julian William Hunt, son of Baron Hunt of Chesterton, University College School, Hampstead, and Cambridge.)

After a whirlwind romance, Mark and Gillie were married and we welcomed him into our family with open arms – not that we could actually get our arms around him. Among his many excellent qualities, Mark is a fantastic cook – hence his shape. Gillie was concerned about the size of his tummy, and vowed to narrow the vast gulf between their respective weights. She has been very successful. Mark's weight is now much closer to Gillie's, though he still weighs exactly the same as he did when they met.

At home, our children were growing up, and having a very different childhood to my own, my goal being to behave in a way that was diametrically opposite to that in which my father had behaved. The most obvious way in which this manifested itself was in their education. Although there are some very good State schools, I experienced a bad one (though Toot Hill is now much improved, and was attended by both of Dawn's children and all four of Samantha's). As a result, my children all go or went to private schools, and while it has been cripplingly expensive it was the best money we've ever spent.

One thing that all parents can give, free of charge, is their love and time. Although Harry boarded at Stowe, we saw him very regularly. Most Saturdays I would travel down to watch him play hockey or cricket for the school, or I'd take him to see Nottingham Forest play. I was assiduous in ensuring his allegiance, and he is a Forest fanatic – in fact, here he is at his very first game:

He also follows Nottinghamshire County Cricket Club, studied politics at Nottingham University, and sees himself, in spite of never living there until he was eighteen, as a native of Nottingham. He's currently in Belgium, doing a Masters in European Politics at the University of Leuven, though his course did not start well. On his first night, he attended an International Students' drinks reception, particularly looking forward to sampling the Belgian beer. He must have sampled a lot because he called me at 1am to explain, slurringly, that he was in hospital as he had 'stumbled and hurt his foot'. He thought it was a sprained ankle, but the following morning further tests revealed that he had broken both of his legs. His mother had to drive over and collect him, and the first few weeks of his Masters were done by correspondence from his wheelchair at home.

Toby is much happier playing sport than watching it, and he particularly excels at cricket and football. I always thought that watching Forest win the European Cup against Hamburg in the Santiago Bernabéu Stadium in 1980 was the pinnacle of sporting spectacles, but I was wrong. Seeing an eleven-year-old Toby win his debut school cricket match, with a six onto the school roof in an unbeaten 54 not out, was far, far better. I called Sophie to tell her about the game as the teams walked off, but I couldn't speak because I was so overcome with emotion. He is now reading politics and economics at Exeter.

Emily, as Toby was, is at Rugby. She is bright, but lazy – though if her school subjects were clothes, boys, Facebook and texting she'd be an A* student. Like her brothers, she is very good at sport, particularly tennis. A few years ago, I rashly bet her that she would never beat me over three sets. She was a little girl and I was pretty good, if I say so myself. A few years later, I was older and slower and she was in the Rugby School team. Worse, we played our grudge match in Turkey in 110°F heat, after I'd had a very boozy lunch. Within half an hour, I was 6-2 and 4-1 down, and staring at the humiliation of losing to my little girl. To my relief, just then the club professional told us our time was up, and I limped gratefully away. After a night's sleep, a massage, and a booze-free lunch, I reeled in my nervous daughter to win 2-6, 6-4, 6-2. She called it 'cheating'.

Whatever it was, it was one of the rare occasions on which I have managed to get one over on her, the boot usually being firmly on the other foot. A few years ago, Sophie was taking our sons off to Holland for the weekend to stay with an old university friend who had boys the same age. Emily had to stay at home with me, and was none too happy about it.

'Don't worry,' I said. 'Let's have a daddy-and-daughter weekend? We can do whatever you want!'

She took me literally. When I got home from work the following day, she was waiting to ambush me with her two best friends, Emma and Hannah Wakeford, who lived in our village. Not long before, their mother Belinda had suddenly collapsed and died from a very fast-growing brain tumour, and we were all still coming to terms with that.

'I've been speaking to Emma and Hannah about the daddy-daughter weekend,' said Emily. 'You said we could do whatever I wanted, didn't you?'

'Absolutely,' I said.

'Well, I'd like to go to Disneyland Paris,' she said, 'and I'd like Hannah and Emma to come with us.'

How could I refuse? In the circumstances, it was game, set and match.

I must admit that I wasn't all that keen on the rides – you get seriously bruised on lunatic devices like Space Mountain or The Rocking Roller Coaster at my age – and since Hannah found them scary, she tended to sit with me. These things go upside down and round and round at tremendous speeds, so they always strap you in tightly with a large bar across your stomach; the trouble was that when it was tight against *my* stomach it was a good two feet away from Hannah's. I had to keep a good grip on her to stop her falling out. Still, we had a great time, and we've been every year since.

The death of Hannah and Emma's mum at such a young age was a terrible thing. By coincidence, Sophie and I had been at university with Belinda, though we'd lost touch after graduating. When we moved to Badby we bumped into Belinda and her husband Mark in the village church and found that they lived practically next door. We soon became great friends, the more so when our daughters were born so close together. When Belinda died, Mark was running a major construction company, and his girls ended up being at our house more often than not. Most nights I ended up walking them home, and I'd often sit up with him after the kids had gone to bed, chatting and putting the world to rights over a glass of wine – which turned into a bottle or two, and then a wine-tasting course. I would turn up with bottles of Cabernet Sauvignon, Shiraz, Merlot and Pinot Noir and, using the pointers in our kit, we would try to guess which was which. Even allowing for fifty/fifty questions, we ended up some way off being wine masters, with me getting fifty-two per cent right and Mark forty-eight.

Belinda's loss made me reflect all the more on how lucky I was. We are a very close family. I know some parents can favour one of their children – my own father preferred Samantha – but I can never understand this. I love all three of them equally, and unconditionally. I know that they love me in return, and I hope that they are proud of me, even though I know they find me a little embarrassing at times. The older I get the less I understand how my own father could abandon his family. Perhaps because of his behaviour, I do spoil mine. They have more gadgets and clothes than they really need, and they do take advantage of me. Perhaps the most astonishing thing about my children, given their ancestry, is that they have grown upwards rather than outwards. Harry stands at 6ft 4in, Toby is 6ft 6in and still growing, and Emily, aged sixteen, is fast approaching 6ft and will soon overtake me. Here are my sons on one of the very few occasions that they have met their grandfather:

* * *

My upbringing has meant that Sophie and I have also made sure we go away as a family as often as we can, though work has meant that I've often joined family trips late, and sometimes missed them altogether (Sophie's mum is my stand-in). When I was a boy, the abortive trip to the caravan in Skegness aside, our family went on *one* holiday – a week in Cornwall – and it was a disaster. Kevin and I had to sleep in a very flimsy tent, which was ripped away by the wind on the first night. Thereafter, we slept in the car. There's nothing intrinsically wrong with a camping week in the West Country, and it's true that my father earned far less money than I do. But then, he spent every night at the pub; if he had saved the money he smoked and drank away we could have gone wherever the Co-op travel agents of the 1970s could send you. If I had remained a fork lift truck driver at Pedigree Wholesale – and I easily could have – then my children would still have fared better than I did.

Skegness, Cornwall, and a single day trip to London aside, my mum never left the East Midlands during her short life. Luckily – and driven by the guilt I still feel at being mean with my mother over that pair of jeans all those years ago – I've been able to make sure that Dawn and Rowland's family have seen more of the world. Early in my career, it was all I could afford to send them to Butlin's; as I became more secure, I've been able to help them go further afield. They've now been to more American states than I have, but their finances have often been tight, and I've been glad to help.

I've made some important connections on holiday, too. I mentioned my chance meeting with the solicitor Richard Nelson on the Flete Estate near Dartmoor; it was in Turkey, at the Hillside Beach Club in Fethiye, that I met another great friend, Nick Freeman. Nick, arguably the finest solicitor of his generation, is known to many newspaper readers as 'Mr Loophole' for his work in extricating celebrity clients from seemingly impossible jams. We bonded over a few drinks and a shared love of puerile humour, but a week after we got back to the UK I got the astonishing news that Nick had been arrested, in a blaze of publicity (rather suspiciously, the press knew it was happening before he did), and accused of perverting the course of justice.

It was a huge coup for the police and for the establishment generally; Nick had been a thorn in their side for many years, because of the uncanny way in which he was able to take advantage of their incompetence to win pretty much every case he fought – mostly for high-profile people like Alex Ferguson, David Beckham, Ronnie O'Sullivan, and Jeremy Clarkson.

At the time I had only known Nick for a week; he was and remains a well-connected man who could have had any lawyer in the country to represent him.

To my immense pride he chose me.

I spent hundreds of hours poring over every aspect of the case, though two things were immediately apparent. The first was that

Nick was entirely innocent. The second was that the police were desperate to get him.

To be fair, the prosecution case was not mindlessly vindictive, but was based upon an honest and frankly stupid mistake.

Some of Nick's clients appeared to have lied to the authorities, and the detectives thought that this had happened after he had attended those clients and encouraged them to do so. Their evidence for this was a series of 'attendance notes' in various files.

But the whole thing was based upon a fundamental misunderstanding of what an attendance note is. The police assumed that it meant Nick himself must have met the client, when this was not the case at all. They were so certain of this 'fact' that they didn't even bother to ask the clients about it. There was also an incriminating document on a file which they assumed had Nick's writing on it. Again, for reasons which ought to astound me but sadly do not, they didn't think to check this out.

The case required a very careful line to be drawn. I decided that the best way forward was for Nick not to answer open-ended questions in interview, but to provide statements setting out answers to every query the prosecution raised. After substantial conferences with him, I drafted three set statements which explained everything. The only person unhappy with them was Nick's clerk, whom I named as the author of the writing on the incriminating document (and who was ultimately charged).

The prosecution then spent an inordinate amount of time trying desperately to find *any* evidence with which to charge him, and eventually approached the clients – who confirmed, to the officers' chagrin, that they had neither laid eyes on nor spoken to Nick Freeman. The case against him was dropped, and our friendship was cemented through the amount of time we had spent together working on it.

If it sounds as though I am gloating at the police, I'm not – I just wish they would not waste their time and our tax money building ridiculous cases featuring not a shred of evidence against men who are clearly honest and wholly innocent.

* * *

ALTHOUGH MY CAREER was going very well, I needed a new project to feed my seemingly eternal mid-life crisis. I had always liked the idea of becoming a television personality, but actually doing so is another thing altogether. How do you set about breaking into such a closed world? I was pondering the dilemma one day when I received a telephone call from a fellow who announced himself as 'Phil Roberts'.

'I'm calling from Fulcrum Productions,' he announced, in an unmistakably Old Etonian accent, 'and we're looking to cast a practising barrister to star in a new show we're making for BBC1.'

'That sounds interesting,' I enthused. 'Tell me more.'

'It's called *The Legalizer*,' he explained, 'and we need a barrister in the title role. He'll meet people who have allegedly been ripped off and then advise and guide them through the small claims process until they obtain judgment.'

'And what would my role be?'

'We want you to be The Legalizer.'

'That sounds fantastic,' I said. 'But why me?'

'Partly because of your national reputation as a fantastic lawyer,' he replied, 'partly because of your international reputation as a witty raconteur, partly to provide some eye candy for female viewers, and partly because I'm your son Harry's Godfather.'

We began filming almost straight away, and by the middle of my first day one thing was crystal clear – there is absolutely nothing glamorous about filming a television show. The director, Jamie, love him and hate him as I do, was a perfectionist. I spent hours and hours walking down streets whilst he filmed my feet. I pressed doorbells thousands of times whilst he filmed my finger to get the perfect shot. And there was take after take after take of conversations with the victims.

CHAPTER NINETEEN: ANIMAL, QC

Slowly, very slowly, it came together. We were commissioned to make five programmes, with two cases featured in each.

One young girl's pony had been loaned out to a third party and had ended up in an abattoir. A disabled lady had been ripped off for her mobility scooter by an unscrupulous dealer. A woman had been thrown out of an unbuilt marina after paying her rent. Rent deposits had been stolen, kitchens and camper van conversions left unfinished or bodged up, people had been sold unroadworthy and dangerous cars... All of the cases involved relatively small sums of money, but they were all of great importance to the victims.

For example, the lady with the mobility scooter, Zahida Altaf, suffers from cerebral palsy, and can only walk a few yards at a time. Her husband is registered blind and doesn't speak much English. They have four children, the youngest of whom is five. Zahida took her scooter in for a very simple repair, and was told it was going to cost a fiendish amount of money. She was then subjected to weeks of high pressure sales patter, with the chap involved turning up at her house unsolicited and unannounced with a shiny new scooter in his van. Eventually, even though the family were as poor as church mice, they relented and traded in the old scooter for a new one, taking out a substantial loan to do so. The first time she used her shiny new scooter it broke down a hundred yards from her home, in the middle of a busy road.

The shop owner, a charlatan called Peter Brown, was called and turned up in his van to collect the scooter and take it off to repair. She never saw it again, nor any of her money, but I was able to guide her through the small claims process until she obtained judgment for every penny she'd spent.

I specialise in major fraud cases, with the amount of money involved often running to over a billion pounds. The trials usually involve multiple defendants, have over a hundred thousand pages of evidence, take years to come to court, and then last for several months in front of a jury. I can't remember a case that was as satisfying to me as helping Zahida Altaf obtain justice.

Small claims cases are supposed to finish within three months, but many of them lasted for over a year. Even filling in the claim form on occasion required the intellect of a rocket scientist, but eventually all of the cases were finished, and the victims had obtained some sort of redress.

That wasn't the end of it. I spent hours in edit suites and voiceover booths, and days filming pieces-to-camera, as well as more hours walking around aimlessly as Jamie filmed my feet. Finally, the finished tapes were delivered to the BBC, and the show was eventually broadcast in November 2013.

I was invited to appear on a BBC current affairs programme, where they asked me a little about *The Legalizer* and a bit about my past life. I watched it back later, and one thing struck me – I looked the same size as Jabba the Hutt. Despite that, it was a success – we pulled in more than thirty per cent of the audience across all channels, even defeating Jeremy Kyle on four of the five days it was shown.

The BBC feedback was very positive, and I was tasked by the BBC to do it all over again, with a slightly different and racier format. Watch this space!

With all this going on, I did find a small window to continue my day job, and decided it was time to make another application for silk.

* * *

I HAD APPEARED in plenty of substantial cases during the intervening three years, and, of the ten cases on my application, I'd been led by a QC in only one matter. This had allowed plenty of judges to get a good look at me on my feet, which was necessary if I were to succeed.

One client was a teenager who had been drinking with friends at an all-night club when he was approached by a bouncer.

'Could you put that cigarette out, please?' the bouncer said.

My client viewed this mode of address as being insufficiently respectful, and declined to do so. The bouncer was left with little alternative but to throw him out bodily; five minutes later – said the prosecution – the client returned carrying a German World War II-issue Luger, and shot the insubordinate bouncer five times.

His defence told an entirely different story. Far from returning to the club with murder in his heart, he had done so only because he had realised the error of his ways, and wanted to apologise to the bouncer. As he walked into the club, he saw something glinting on the floor and picked it up. To his surprise, it turned out to be a Luger. As he looked at it in disbelief, the bouncer saw him, put two and two together and made five. The bouncer dived on my client. During the resultant struggle, as my client tried frantically to explain to him that he was making a mistake, he accidentally shot the bouncer in the hip, chest, shoulder, neck, and face.

To my client's amazement, the jury didn't believe him.

Of the remaining cases on my application, two were settled by negotiated pleas of guilty. One was a multi-million pound fraud where my client escaped a prison sentence, and the other was part of a rogue car-clamping gang who also escaped prison. Two more fraud cases were won by me on legal submissions, and three were won after jury trials. One of these was an extraordinary case that started out as a dispute over a dog.

My client was a lovely fellow whose only hobby in life was a little innocent dog-fighting. To further that perfectly harmless interest, he had purchased a Japanese fighting dog from a group of Irish travellers. The dog, for which he paid a thousand pounds, was the envy of his friends, but it had a dark secret. Its mother had briefly escaped from the travellers' camp and had been covered by a giant poodle. Tough as the resultant offspring appeared, it quite refused to fight.

Luckily, one of the envious friends offered my client £1,500 for the dog, which offer he eagerly accepted.

Before he had chance to spend his windfall, the RSPCA busted the whole gang. One of them owned a kitchen showroom and, after dark, it was often turned into a dog-fighting pit; it was there that the investigators caught them all in the act one night. A search of their homes was made, and my client's extensive collection of dog-fighting videos and associated equipment was discovered, along with a few Rottweiler puppies who were in the process of being trained up. The lot of them were taken to court, where most were given short prison sentences. Their dogs were all destroyed.

'And the RSPCA claim to be animal lovers,' my mystified client later complained to me.

I was not involved in the dog-fighting trial myself, and I was lucky that I wasn't, for as will become clear, these were not men with whom one should trifle.

The chap to whom my client had sold his half-Japanese fighting dog/half-poodle demanded the return of his money, but my client was having none of it.

Whereas you or I might have tried the small claims court, the disgruntled friend was made of different stuff.

Recruiting a local Pakistan-born enforcer to assist him, he attacked my client in the street with a baseball bat.

As my client recovered in hospital, his brother went to the enforcer's house and torched his car.

The enforcer retaliated, attending my client's brother's house and torching *his* shiny new BMW convertible.

The problem was, my client's brother didn't *have* a shiny new BMW convertible.

But the West Indian drug overlord who lived next door to him did. He was also not a man for the small claims court; his preferred method of registering his displeasure at this turn of events was to drive past the Pakistani enforcer's house and fire a machine gun through his front window. This he accompanied with a threat that he would return if his car wasn't paid for.

330

Something had to give, and it was the Pakistani enforcer's nerve. He paid up. The argument over a £1,500 poodle ended up costing more than £60,000 in burned-out cars, and the front of a house had been destroyed.

It was too much for some members of the community. A local councillor went to see the parties concerned, and persuaded them to attend a peace and reconciliation commission meeting at an establishment called Uncle Charlie's chip shop.

My client and his brother attended, as did the man he had sold the dog to, and his Pakistani enforcer friend. They went up to a room above the chip shop and stood facing each other, bristling with rage, until the local councillor read them the riot act.

'You are all from the same community,' he said. 'You must stop this madness now. Shake hands, and let's put an end to this.'

He stood to one side to allow the two sides to kiss and make up, and it was fortunate for him that he did. All four men allegedly drew guns and started shooting at each other.

My client was hit in the back, shattering his spinal cord, and will never walk again, and all four were tried for the attempted murders of each other.

The trial went well for my client – I was able to have the charges dismissed against him at the half-way point – but the other three were convicted and given long prison sentences. In spite of winning his trial, I doubt anyone would feel that my client's experience proved that crime *does* pay.

* * *

OF COURSE, I ALSO required new references for my application. Those from solicitors and fellow barristers were easy enough, but once again that left the thorny issue of the judges.

It works like this: you are permitted to nominate one judge as a referee; the secretariat panel then approaches a further three from a list of possibles that you provide.

My nominated judge was a lovely man called Robert Juckes QC, who had not only seen me conduct two cases in front of him but had prosecuted me and co-defended with me several times when he was a barrister, including in an extraordinary murder trial at the Old Bailey. According to the police, our defendant, along with two others, had shot the victim and then stabbed him multiple times, before cutting his body into small parts with a chainsaw, and driving him to a landfill site in Essex to feed him to the rats. They would have probably got away with it, too, had they not amused themselves on the way by using the victim's severed arm to make hand signals out of their car window.

The QC secretariat panel don't tell you which judges they have approached, though the information has a way of leaking out in the small world that is the Bar. One took the trouble to obtain my mobile phone number and called me to discuss his reference. Another turned out to be a High Court judge in front of whom I'd conducted a very tricky case. I had no idea as to the identity of the fourth until, as I walked through Birmingham one day, a car pulled up alongside me. The passenger window descended and a voice boomed out from the driver's seat. 'Hey, you fat bastard… don't you think I've got enough work to do without having to waste my time writing a QC reference for you?'

I had done two cases in front of that particular judge.

The first was that of a drugs courier stopped with a million pounds-worth of heroin in his car boot. He had pleaded guilty and, although the tariff sentence for such a large amount of heroin is around fifteen years, I managed to get him a sentence of three-and-a-half. The prosecution were furious and appealed the sentence, which appeal they promptly lost. Then they gunned for the defendant in the confiscation proceedings, asking for a confiscation order of over a million pounds. I argued that it should be capped to £200, which was the amount the defendant had been paid for couriering it. My argument succeeded, and a confiscation order was made in the sum of £200. The prosecution were again furious, and again they appealed, unsuccessfully.

The second case was doomed from its very outset. My client had been in the back of a van which was stopped by police. Under my client's coat a gun was found, a Walther PPK of James Bond fame; sitting opposite him was another man holding an AK47, of Osama bin Laden fame. The Walther was forensically examined and found to have been used to commit an armed robbery in Birmingham the previous year, in which two police officers had been fired on. My client's mobile phone was also examined, and cell site analysis was done which showed that, on the day of that robbery, the mobile had left my client's house in Coventry, travelled to the exact scene of the robbery at the precise time of it, and then travelled back to Coventry. To make matters worse, that offence had been committed only a week after my client had been released from prison after serving a ten-year sentence – for armed robbery.

My client's defence was alibi: he claimed to have made the trip to Birmingham to see a girl who lived near the scene of the armed robbery – which, of course, had nothing to do with him. He called the girl as an alibi witness.

'Do you know the defendant in this case?' I asked, stating his name.

'Who?' she replied.

'The man in the dock at the back of court,' I said, pointing out the defendant and repeating his name.

'Oh,' she smiled, 'you mean The Bullet. Yes, I know him.'

It was an unfortunate nickname for an alleged armed robber. He was found guilty, on an 11-1 majority verdict. I wanted to ask which idiot thought he wasn't guilty, and could I have him/her on all my juries?

* * *

MANY APPLICATIONS FOR silk are submitted each year, and the first round involves sifting out those which are doomed from the start, and which candidates are worth inviting for interview. An age after I put in the application, I received a letter telling me I had made it through to interview.

I had been expecting the third degree, but in the event I experienced a very gentle, half-hour grilling on the various competencies, and then a thanks and goodbye. I'd either had an easy ride because my application was strong and the interview was a rubber-stamping exercise, or because it was hopelessly irretrievable. I had no idea which.

It was several months before the decisions were announced, and I tried to put it from my mind – successfully, at first. But, as the day drew closer, I began marking off the time, often hourly, until the precise moment that I had been told that I would be contacted by e-mail to learn my fate.

Finally, just as I thought that time would stand still completely, the fateful day dawned. The morning dragged slowly and I found myself checking my watch at thirty-second intervals. The e-mail was expected at noon, and I was sitting at my computer by 11.30am waiting for it to arrive.

It was there at twelve on the dot.

I took a deep breath before clicking on it.

It had taken me thirty-two years of effort to reach this point.

Gary Bell QC? Impossible.

Me? At the heart of the establishment? Ludicrous.

I tried to persuade myself that it didn't matter if I failed. There'd be no shame: many very able practitioners never take silk.

But I wasn't fooling anybody, certainly not myself. I wanted to be a QC, desperately.

Steeling myself, I opened the e-mail.

CHAPTER NINETEEN: ANIMAL, QC

The Queen has approved the Lord Chancellor's recommendation that you should be appointed one of Her Majesty's Counsel.

I am not ashamed to say that I burst into tears.

EPILOGUE

IN *BLADE RUNNER*, Rutger Hauer's android says, as he is dying, 'I've seen things you people wouldn't believe.'

I know what he means. Here I sit: fifty-five years old, a QC and pillar of my local community, with a beautiful wife and family, and a Cavalier King Charles Spaniel called Rosie at my feet. It's been a preposterous life; I can scarcely believe it myself.

My journey can be broken down into two halves – the descent into football hooliganism, crime, and homelessness, and then my steady climb, with the help of many very kind people, through education, into marriage and fatherhood, and a successful career at the Bar.

It's all been marked by an extraordinarily eclectic mix of characters, most of whom I'm still in touch with. Not long ago, I took my son Harry to Loftus Road to see Forest play Queens Park Rangers. Sadly, we were on the wrong end of a 5-2 thumping, but it gave me chance to catch up with a few of my hooligan mates from the old days. As we walked disconsolately out of the stadium, I began telling Harry of my first visit there, in 1977 – as Animal of The Mad Squad. I had hitch-hiked to London on the Friday night, planning to doss down on a Circle Line tube train, but my plans were scuppered when I discovered that the Underground closed at midnight. Instead, I slept rough outside the ground. I was pointing out the very spot to Harry, when a pair of QPR supporters loomed up in front of us.

'Hi Gary,' said one of them. 'Where are you off to?'

It was Michael Gove, my Oxford debating rival of yesteryear, and a friend to this day.

'Back up north to lick our wounds,' I said.

'Why don't you hang around and come to supper?' he said.

So we did.

It must have felt surreal for Harry – a third year politics student, and Labour Party member – to find himself discussing affairs of state around the dinner table with a Tory cabinet minister. But it was even more surreal for me.

In his song *Both Sides Now*, Glenn Campbell sang that 'something's lost and something's gained, in living every day'. How right he was. Most objective observers would surely say I've gained a great deal, but there's a slightly bittersweet feel to it; every time I go back to Cotgrave I see what I've lost. The community there marches on. Everyone belongs, and most have no interest in setting sail onto stormy seas.

But my message to anyone out there who does wish to experience all that life has to offer is simple. The biggest thing holding you back is yourself. There are always others who've had more opportunities and encouragement, but success, to a degree, is within the grasp of anyone. If you really want something, it's up to you to seize the day!

Fighting at football matches, stealing from fruit machines, sleeping rough: these things have all faded far into my past. Yet they are all things which have been the making of me. When I look back on my life so far, and consider whatever it is that I have achieved, it's my wife and children who take centre stage. Next I would rank personal honours – being best man at the weddings of Tony Ryland, Paul Selby and David Gottlieb, being selected to be Godfather to the children of numerous friends… these are not ambitions which you can set out to achieve, but are a reflection of what people think of you as a person.

As I have got older my priorities in life have changed, along with my capabilities. Football gives way to golf, lager gives way to wine, a thirty-inch waist gives way to a thirty-eight-inch waist, which gives way to… I don't like to say.

But life remains fulfilling.

Of course, I yearn occasionally for my salad days. Last year I went to Amsterdam on a stag weekend, and found myself standing outside a nightclub with another fifty-odd-year-old QC, Craig Howell-Williams. We noticed a couple of stunning Dutch girls giggling at us.

'Hey, Gary!' said Craig. 'We've still got it!'

We stood up tall, sucked in our tummies, and smiled seductively at the pair of them.

They dissolved into raucous laughter. 'Hello, old men!' they called out, in unison.

They would have been about eighteen – a time when I could get up and down a football pitch, or sink a dozen pints of lager on a big night out, or think nothing of setting out to hitch-hike my way to somewhere new and exciting. And yet, were I by some miracle to be offered the chance to be eighteen again, I wouldn't consider it for a second. I have rich memories behind me, a happy present, and, I hope, an exciting future ahead.

Of course, I have regrets. The biggest is that my mother did not live to see her grandchildren, nor to see what I have achieved. She might not have believed it, but she'd have been very proud.

As for my father, I have only seen him on a handful of occasions over the last four decades. The last time, I was driving through his town and I saw him heading the other way. I pulled a quick u-turn and followed him, parking next to him when he stopped.

It had been ten years or so since we'd last met.

When he saw me, he simply said, 'Hey up, Gary.'

'Hey up, dad,' I said.

'How are you?'

'Fine. How are you?'

'Not good, son,' he said, with a grimace. 'I've got terrible arthritis in my joints. I'm in constant agony. I've been to the doctor and he told me it's to do with my diet. I eat nothing but oranges, but he's told me to cut them out. It's the vitamin C that does it. He reckons that'll cure it.'

'So why are you still in so much pain?' I said.

'Because I still eat loads of oranges. No doctor's going to tell me what to do.'

I'll finish with a chance meeting I had with an old friend. I was walking through Nottingham a few weeks ago on my way to a Forest match, when I bumped into Chalkie White, of Pork Farms days. He was selling Forest programmes outside The City Ground.

'Alright, Chalkie!' I said, warmly.

'Alright, mate,' he said. The quizzical look on his face said he clearly had no idea who I was.

'Come on, Chalkie,' I said. 'Don't say you've forgotten me. Gary Bell? You remember. We worked at Pork Farms together, on the production line. It was thirty-seven years ago, mind.'

'Oh, bloody hell,' he said, a light of recognition entering his eyes. 'Yes, I remember you. Gary Bell. You were the bugger who went for a pint at lunchtime and never came back!'

'That's right,' I said, 'but do you blame me? I can't believe that job. It was soul-destroying. Standing around all day putting trays of pork pies onto a rack? It was the worst job I've ever done.'

'Bloody terrible job,' he said, nodding. 'But don't worry. I won't be there much longer!'

ACKNOWLEDGMENTS

THERE IS A GREAT temptation when compiling a memoir to mention by name all of those people who have been important figures in one's journey.

In the first draft of this book I indeed did a great deal of that.

My editor mercilessly excised many such names, leaving in only those which, in his view, added something to the narrative or drove my story forwards in some significant way.

I would like to take the opportunity here to thank all of the many people who are *not* mentioned in these pages but who have greatly contributed to my preposterous life.

You all know who you are, and how you fit into my strange jigsaw. Thank you.

Gary Bell, July 2015